**NOTES FOR PROFESSIONAL LIBRARIANS
AND LIBRARY USERS**

This is an original book title published by The Haworth Press, Inc. Unless otherwise noted in specific chapters with attribution, materials in this book have not been previously published elsewhere in any format or language.

CONSERVATION AND PRESERVATION NOTES

All books published by The Haworth Press, Inc. and its imprints are printed on certified ph neutral, acid free book grade paper. This paper meets the minimum requirements of American National Standard for Information Sciences–Permanence of Paper for Printed Material, ANSI Z39.48-1984.

Contemporary
Sales Force Management

HAWORTH Marketing Resources
Innovations in Practice & Professional Services
William J. Winston, Senior Editor

New, Recent, and Forthcoming Titles:

Managed Service Restructuring in Health Care: A Strategic Approach in a Competitive Environment by Robert L. Goldman and Sanjib K. Mukherjee

A Marketing Approach to Physician Recruitment by James Hacker, Don C. Dodson, and M. Thane Forthman

Marketing for CPAs, Accountants, and Tax Professionals edited by William J. Winston

Strategic Planning for Not-for-Profit Organizations by R. Henry Migliore, Robert E. Stevens, and David L. Loudon

Marketing Planning in a Total Quality Environment by Robert E. Linneman and John L. Stanton, Jr.

Managing Sales Professionals: The Reality of Profitability by Joseph P. Vaccaro

Squeezing a New Service into a Crowded Market by Dennis J. Cahill

Publicity for Mental Health Clinicians: Using TV, Radio, and Print Media to Enhance Your Public Image by Douglas H. Ruben

Managing a Public Relations Firm for Growth and Profit by A. C. Croft

Utilizing the Strategic Marketing Organization: The Modernization of the Marketing Mindset by Joseph P. Stanco

Internal Marketing: Your Company's Next Stage of Growth by Dennis J. Cahill

The Clinician's Guide to Managed Behavioral Care by Norman Winegar

Marketing Health Care into the Twenty-First Century: The Changing Dynamic by Alan K. Vitberg

Fundamentals of Strategic Planning for Health-Care Organizations edited by Stan Williamson, Robert Stevens, David Loudon, and R. Henry Migliore

Risky Business: Managing Violence in the Workplace by Lynne Falkin McClure

Predicting Successful Hospital Mergers and Acquisitions: A Financial and Marketing Analytical Tool by David P. Angrisani and Robert L. Goldman

Marketing Research That Pays Off: Case Histories of Marketing Research Leading to Success in the Marketplace edited by Larry Percy

How Consumers Pick a Hotel: Strategic Segmentation and Target Marketing by Dennis Cahill

Applying Telecommunications and Technology from a Global Business Perspective by Jay Zajas and Olive Church

Strategic Planning for Private Higher Education by Carle M. Hunt, Kenneth W. Oosting, Robert Stevens, David Loudon, and R. Henry Migliore

Writing for Money in Mental Health by Douglas H. Ruben

The New Business Values for Success in the Twenty-First Century: Improvement, Innovation, Inclusion, Incentives, Information by John Persico and Patricia Rouner Morris

Marketing Planning Guide, Second Edition by Robert E. Stevens, David L. Loudon, Bruce Wrenn, and William E. Warren

Contemporary Sales Force Management by Tony Carter

4x4 Leadership and the Purpose of the Firm by H. H. Pete Bradshaw

Lessons in Leisure Business Success: The Recreation Professional's Business Transformation Primer by Jonathan T. Scott

Contemporary
Sales Force Management

Tony Carter

The Haworth Press
New York • London

The Haworth Press, Inc., 10 Alice Street, Binghamton, NY 13904-1580

Cover design by Monica L. Seifert.

Library of Congress Cataloging-in-Publication Data

Carter, Tony, 1955-
    Contemporary sales force management / Tony Carter.
        p.   cm.
    Includes bibliographical references and index.
    ISBN 0-7890-0423-2 (alk. paper).
    1. Sales management. I. Title.
HF5438.4.C37   1998
659.8'1–dc21   97-33155
                                                                                      CIP

To Mary, Calvin and Walter,
My parents,
Walter Palin and the family.

ABOUT THE AUTHOR

Tony Carter, JD, MBA, is Professor of Sales and Marketing in the Graduate School of Business at Columbia University and Wagner College. At Columbia, he teaches sales management in the MBA Program and Executive Management Program for Sales Managers. He has also taught in the Executive MBA Program at Columbia. In addition, he is an Assistant Professor at Wagner College, where he teaches in the undergraduate, MBA, and Executive MBA programs. He has been published in the *Harvard Business Review,* the *Columbia Journal of World Business,* the *Journal of Professional Service Marketing,* the *Journal of Global Competitiveness,* and the *Journal of Employment.* Prior to entering academe, he worked as a sales and marketing manager for corporations. His case studies on management and sales and marketing have been adopted and used by various universities and organizations around the world, including the University of Buckingham, the Netherlands Institute, the University of Kent, University College Dublin, ENSPTT France, Erasmus University, Hay Management Consulting Group, Petroconsultants, and Unisys Corporation. Still an active consultant, he works on sales and marketing issues for a variety of companies worldwide.

CONTENTS

Foreword

When Tony Carter came into my office several years ago with a proposal that he teach the Sales Management course to our MBA students, he promised that he would provide them with state of the field thinking in sales management. For several years he has delivered on that promise and now has packaged much of his teaching material into *Contemporary Sales Force Management*.

This book focuses on an important topic and addresses many relevant issues. In recent years, as competition has increased and become global in scope, in order to become more competitive, corporations have focused significant attention on the cost element of the "Profit = Revenues − Costs" equation. Downsizing, rightsizing, reengineering and other fashionable approaches for managing organizations have been implemented with the explicit intention of reducing costs.

Increasingly, senior management is realizing that cost reduction alone is insufficient to propel the firm into the twenty-first century, and as the focus begins to shift to the revenue side of the equation, corporate attention is now being directed to managing the single function whose explicit task is to bring in revenues, the sales force.

Managing the sales force is the focus of this book, but *Contemporary Sales Force Management* is not a conventional sales management text. Rather, Professor Carter has traveled widely and interviewed many senior sales managers to identify those topics he believes are critical to managing the contemporary sales force. He focuses on those topics in this book. Included in the coverage is use of technology in the sales force, total quality management, team-building diversity, customer advisory boards, and crisis management.

Each of the twelve chapters is packed full of up-to-date examples and contains several small cases to force students to grapple with the very real contemporary issues faced by sales managers. In addition, the book as a whole is peppered with results from Professor Carter's personally conducted survey of sales managers.

Students who are fortunate enough to read this book will find much that does not make its way into conventional sales management texts, presented by a former sales manager who "has been there," and who has a passion both for understanding the very real challenges faced by today's sales managers and for passing that knowledge on to his students in both the Columbia MBA and Sales Management Executive Program and to the readers of this book.

Noel Capon
Professor of Business/
Director of the Sales Management Program
Graduate School of Business
Columbia University

Preface

Sales force managers experience rapid changes due to constant developments in the marketplace. Managers and business professionals with customer dealings must know the relevant issues that drive and impact revenue in their firms and they need to have "cutting edge" perspectives to be most effective. The goal of this book is to provide a current look at sales force management. For over two years I have worked on developing a book that reflects what companies are doing to be successful in sales force management. I understand that students, professors, and businesspeople look for rules and concepts of effective sales management and they are a necessary ingredient of any acceptable book. This book has extensive content in the form of theoretical principles, but is accompanied by modern, practical examples of how the theory works in the various subject matter areas covered in actual sales force management.

Contemporary Sales Force Management examines topical areas such as sales force technology, globalization and its impact on sales management, reengineering, crisis management, selling skills and negotiation, TQM, time management, mentorships, planning and forecasting, gender and diversity in sales force management, and customer relationship building. Section I deals with the role of the sales force manager in organizations; Section II examines sales force technology; Section III looks at the strategic issues for an international sales effort; Section IV discusses effective sales force management in a volatile business environment; and Section V deals with current selling skills, strategies, and tools. Each chapter ends with the use of questions and case studies to demonstrate and reinforce the principles discussed in that chapter. The emphasis of case analysis is meant to help:

1. Define the issues or problems stated or implied in the case narrative.
2. Develop analytical thought.

3. Develop solutions, recommendations, and plans for implementation.
4. Demonstrate and reinforce the principles discussed in that chapter.
5. Encourage thorough preparation and active participation during case discussions and act as a training or teaching guide.

I have used surveys and interviews to examine how various companies are handling issues related to sales force management. Many service and product-based corporations responded to the surveys and interviews to provide me with current, relevant information on how they achieve effective sales performance. I have made *Contemporary Sales Force Management* consistent with the theme of a contemporary look at sales force management by spending considerable time profiling the sales effort at European Union offices in Brussels, Belgium, and with various companies throughout Europe and the People's Republic of China.

Hopefully, business students at the undergraduate, MBA, or Executive Education level, managers, salespeople, entrepreneurs, and consultants will find this book unique and extremely useful.

I will always be grateful for the confidence, trust, and support that Bill Winston and the rest of the editorial staff at The Haworth Press gave me while I wrote this book. I am especially grateful to John Moran, Larry Barton, Ken Preiss, Tony Williams, Harold Theurer, Dudley Coker, Kevin Handerson, and Marta Yagos for their contributions and for being a part of this book. I also wish to convey my sincere appreciation to Don Spiro for establishing and maintaining the highest level of integrity to the ideals of effective management. Last, I would be remiss if I did not give special mention to my "mentors" Walter Rohrs of Wagner College and Noel Capon of Columbia University's Graduate School of Business. They represent academic excellence in its truest sense, and have been proponents of bringing sales management into the full scope of the academic milieu.

SECTION I:
INTRODUCTION TO CONTEMPORARY
SALES FORCE MANAGEMENT

Chapter 1

The Role of the Sales Force Manager in Organizations

CONTEMPORARY SALES FORCE MANAGEMENT

Sales performance levels are interesting concepts for the purposes of managing the sales force. Sales is the lynchpin of capitalism; sales drives activity in today's business world. As such, sales is not just a profession, but also a process that has relevance to anyone in business. It is the essence of business itself.

Sales managers today must develop an integrative management style using adaptive, problem-solving, extensive information, in many cases in an ever-changing marketplace. The overwhelming majority of business environment workers are service providers such as investment bankers, consultants, and information technology specialists. Sales managers in the current business environment must have the ability to add value, which certainly means functional expertise in sales and marketing along with knowledge of the industry. However, managers must also have the skills to lead, communicate, use changing technologies, build teams, motivate salespeople, form strategic alliances with customers, and build teams within the sales force. Sales managers need access to a flow of reliable information to initiate sound decision making that turns on a dime. As a necessary precondition to high levels of sales force performance, empowerment, and control of their own work process, sales managers should also have a system of sharing information with the sales force.[1]

These are times of drastic corporate downsizing in which sales organizations are expected to do more with less. Sales managers must also be more knowledgeable and possess a myriad of demanding new business skills. Many internal and external changes among

3

organizations have dictated the need to conduct business differently. The external business environment has experienced changing technology, globalization, catastrophic business crisis, a more frantic competitive climate, and more demanding, sophisticated customers. Internal changes have included reengineering, accompanied by structural realignments and downsizing, greater emphasis on quality levels in product and service output, faster communication channels, and a more educated, skilled employee base with higher expectations from management.[2]

Sales as a profession has had a negative connotation in our society. It implies that salespeople are pushy, talkative, lacking in technical knowledge, and unprofessional. Many organizations, in order to circumvent the negative stigma that sales evokes with customers, will give salespeople a job title such as "relationship managers," "account executives," "customer development managers," or "marketing representative." The reputation of salespeople as "sleazy" business peddlers concerned solely with closing a sale has often led to an adversarial relationship between buyer and seller before and after a sale. Several studies have found that college students generally have a negative perception of the sales profession and feel the profession lacks a variety of desired job characteristics. While the sales profession may not be felt to make a contribution to society or have any status or security, this is based on limited information. The sales role has many dynamic positive characteristics. These entail "front line" marketplace knowledge, opportunity for rapid advancement, freedom to make decisions, attractive compensation, and challenges from client dealings that provide learning situations and the opportunity to reach one's professional goals. Sales organizations will continue to need sharp, focused, well-skilled sales professionals who can contribute in a highly competitive marketplace.[3] Currently, sales is a complex process and a sophisticated profession that requires a variety of demanding business skills. Today's sales manager must possess these skills to effectively lead a sales force to successful results (see Table 1.1).

Salespeople, depending on their level of experience, can earn a lucrative salary in today's sales profession. For example, in 1996 the median total cash compensation for senior salespeople was $63,700, for intermediate salespeople it was $46,000, and for

TABLE 1.1. Top Qualifications of the "Ideal" Salesperson Profile

The top qualifications of the "ideal" salesperson profile	
➤ Good listener	➤ Negotiation skills
➤ Strong communication skills, oral and written	➤ Strong industry knowledge
➤ Risk takers	➤ Financially astute
➤ Patient, but at the same time persistent	➤ Analytical
➤ Technical knowledge	➤ Effective time management skills
➤ High energy level	➤ Integrity
➤ College graduate	➤ Self-confidence
➤ Sales experience in a quota-driven environment	➤ Intelligence
➤ Leadership skills	➤ Problem-solving abilities
➤ Professonalism	➤ Good relationship-building skills
➤ Team experience	➤ Strong selling skills
➤ Loyalty	➤ Highly motivated
➤ Broad business background	➤ Competitive

Source: *Carter Sales Force Survey* (1996).

entry-level salespeople, $36,000. Accordingly, the corresponding sales revenue that is generated on average per salesperson has increased 22 percent in recent years to about $1,400,000 per year. This reflects both the heightened earning opportunities and performance demands that now exist in the sales profession. Currently, the average age of a salesperson is thirty-seven. Women now comprise 24 percent of all salespeople and currently 65 percent of all salespeople, male or female, have a college degree. On average, salespeople remain with their companies about seven and one-half years which has been fairly consistent in recent years.[4]

The relationship between salespeople and customers is changing faster than sales orders can be processed (see Table 1.2 and Figure 1.1). Most remarkable is the fact that it is the customers who are driving the change. They are asking for, if not demanding, better service from their vendors. The shift has radically changed the way selling is done. Companies are building relationships, improving technologies, processes, and systems along the way. Almost 90 percent of 222 sales units surveyed by Hewitt Associates reported the selling job is now more complex.[5]

TABLE 1.2. The New Sales Force Process

Business Issues	Lowering mutual costs and building long-term customer relationships
Strategic Intent	Create partnerships with customers
Key Drivers	Continuous improvement, shared values
Structure	Reengineered work processes, customer teams
People	Team leaders, organizationally aware, tenacious
Compensation	Competency-based salary bands; incentives for improvement
Culture	Boundaryless organizations: "I work for the customer"

FIGURE 1.1. Today's Sales Force

DIFFICULTY IN SALES

The prospect of facing rejection in customer dealings poses the greatest difficulty in sales. Rejection for people involved in customer development means that they have to confront the reality that customers may refuse to do business with them. However, this is also one of the great challenges to be overcome and is why it is important to keep salespeople motivated and functioning at high morale levels.

Customers may reject requests for their business either because they are not interested or they do not like something about the product, service, or company. They may also not be able to afford the product or just will not respond favorably to inadequate sales ability. Whatever the reason, it is necessary to stay upbeat, focused, and at the same time realize that rejection is actually a normal part of a successful sales effort.

The key to managing rejection is not to allow it to impede the customer development effort. Sales managers should use the fact that salespeople face rejection to get the salespeople to:

- improve their sales skills and prevent complacency;
- use this feedback to develop more effective strategies, and
- realize that this challenge is the reason the job can pay well and lead to success.

Salespeople can mentally accept the reality of rejection by developing "mental toughness." Sales managers and salespeople should use "mental toughness" as a tool to:

- avoid making excuses for reaching a goal;
- find ways to ask for business despite being afraid that the customer will say no; and
- rehearse new sales techniques and give one more client presentation, even when exhausted.

So, in a customer development effort it should be accepted that rejection is really a necessary ingredient that can remind the sales force that success in sales is a journey, not a destination.

MOTIVATION AND MORALE

Most sales managers use motivational techniques to improve the performance levels of the sales force because motivation and morale have particular importance with those involved in the sales effort. *Motivation* is the amount of effort that a person puts into achieving a task. *Morale* involves the mental and emotional response that individuals express about their particular work environment. The consequences of having a poorly motivated sales force with low morale can be devastating. Symptoms include poor performance levels, turnover, and complaints, internally and with customers. Other occurrances include lost opportunity due to ineffective performance, and replacement costs for departing salespeople. Conversely, positive motivation and morale can mean a dedicated effort by the sales force that results in salespeople operating at peak performance levels.

The conditions that can cause problems with motivation and morale entail employee satisfaction, career security, compensation, job enrichment, good work environment, and a general feeling by employees that their efforts are being appreciated. When these components are present, salespeople will feel good about their performance. In fact, when motivated, the sales force may not only perform at expected levels but go beyond and do more than asked. An interesting study was recently done titled "Do You Know What Motivates Your Staff?" In looking at the top five motivational criteria managers ranked the following:

1. Compensation
2. Job security
3. Growth opportunities
4. Good working conditions
5. Interesting work

This contrasted with the employees rankings in order of importance. They listed the following:

1. Interesting work
2. Appreciation by management
3. Being well informed
4. Job security
5. Compensation

This study shows that contrary to managers' opinions, compensation may not be the most important motivating factor to employees.[6]

MANAGEMENT EFFORTS
TO ENSURE GOOD SALES PERFORMANCE

Motivational Theory

Need-driven motivation professes that people will not engage in certain behavior or performance until certain needs have been met. These various needs and their impact on motivation levels were recognized by psychologist Abraham Maslow. He believed that a "hierarchy of needs" starts with meeting physiological needs, such as food, drink, shelter, then progresses toward esteem, self-actualization, knowledge, and beauty (see Figure 1.2). This might apply to a salesperson who has an interesting job and feels motivated to perform because of the sense of prestige and pride that it gives him or her.

Reward-driven motivation deals with identifying a particular reward structure (usually monetary) and building it into some desired action.

Expectancy theory operates on the principle that provides a reward for engaging in a particular behavior or performance. When the reward is valued by the employee, he or she will be motivated to perform. With reward-driven motivation, the things that get rewarded are the things that get done.

By rewarding salespersons in the way they want to be rewarded, such as a salary raise, they may perform better and feel better about what they are doing.[7]

Goal-driven motivation is contingent upon the ability to reach objectives. It involves a process of identifying individual goals that an employee must achieve. This can be done alone or with the assistance of one's manager.

Management by objective (MBO) is a collaborative effort between manager and subordinate to discuss and determine how the subordinate can help reach company objectives. A feedback and monitoring system should be built into this process.

In the case of a salesperson, MBO might draw attention to the treatment of customers that improves the reputation of the company. With goal setting, establishing revenue goals to be reached by the

FIGURE 1.2. Maslow's Hierarchy of Needs

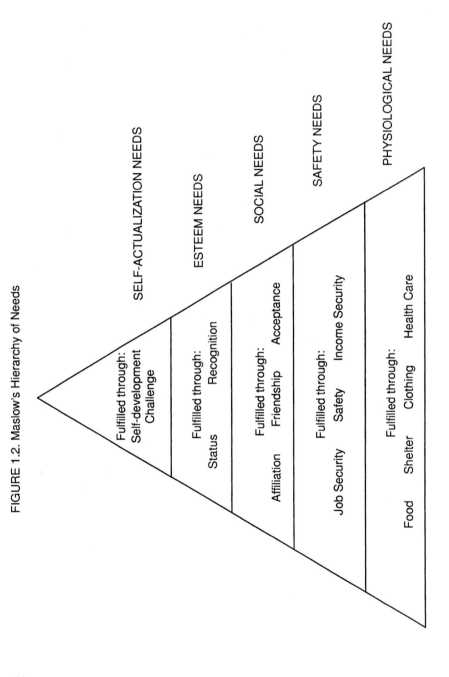

SELF-ACTUALIZATION NEEDS

Fulfilled through:
Self-development
Challenge

ESTEEM NEEDS

Fulfilled through:
Status   Recognition

SOCIAL NEEDS

Fulfilled through:
Affiliation   Friendship   Acceptance

SAFETY NEEDS

Fulfilled through:
Job Security   Safety   Income Security

PHYSIOLOGICAL NEEDS

Fulfilled through:
Food   Shelter   Clothing   Health Care

sales force might be used by sales managers to provide salespeople with clear expectations and direction. In both, accomplishing these goals can provide motivation for the salesperson.[8]

INCENTIVE PLANS AND MOTIVATION

Financial rewards have always been assumed to motivate salespeople and improve performance, but this could be subject to debate (see Figure 1.3). Some research has said that the quality of work declines over time when pay is linked to performance and employees become less interested in what they are doing and more interested in the

FIGURE 1.3. Financial Compensation Methods

The use of nonfinancial compensation methods, such as telling employees they did a good job, sending them to a conference and so on, in various organizations.

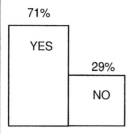

The use of financial compensation methods, such as salary, bonus, and commission, rewarding salespeople in various sales organizations.

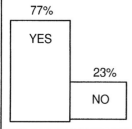

Source: *Carter Sales Force Survey* (1996).

reward.[9] Employees under these reward systems will choose the easiest tasks, avoid risks, and even seem addicted to these rewards. The research shows that the quality of work and creativity improves when rewards are taken away. The following are critical concerns of compensation plans:

- Salespeople may be unwilling to share what they know if this helps make others in the sales force or company successful. In fact, they may promote an attitude of "my success must come at your expense."
- Sales managers are resorting to an easy solution that gives temporary compliance instead of exploring the long-term factors that individually may motivate each salesperson.
- Salespeople believe that in some way this compensation system is not fair and they become resentful.
- These are in effect just manipulative strategies to control how people perform.[10]

LEADERSHIP

Leadership is the use of influence over the behavior of others to encourage them to achieve certain objectives. True leadership deals with ideas about what to do, providing a sense of vision and optimism. Leaders have a commitment to see their objectives through to conclusion. Many possess charisma—the intangible ability to evoke strong positive emotion in others. Two types of leaders are commonly seen: transformational and transactional. Transformational leaders inspire others to strive to do better. They also:

1. identify themselves as charge agents;
2. are courageous;
3. believe in the people that they work with;
4. are value driven and principled;
5. are willing to grow and learn;
6. can deal with complexity and uncertainty; and
7. are risk takers.

Transactional leaders approach people with the philosophy of "If you do this for me, I'll do something for you," similar to a business deal.

To motivate salespeople and maintain good morale levels, sales managers should be leaders who have a meaningful set of values.

Salespeople as Leaders

Sales managers should also encourage the sales force to exhibit leadership qualities. Salespeople who can develop their own sense of vision, i.e., developing creative new ideas in an energetic way, can be more effective on the job. To determine this vision salespeople should ask "Do clients really need our service?"; "What are my values, priorities, and goals?"; or "What role do I want to play in meeting my clients' needs?" Vision is distinguished from goals because, while not as measurable and focused, vision deals with long-term values and efforts that are broader in scope.[11]

EFFECTIVE ORGANIZATIONAL COMMUNICATION

Good interpersonal relationships are no longer a luxury but a bona fide qualification for effective job performance. To be competitive the sales force must have a responsive system for sharing information and getting work done. From the salesperson's standpoint, good channels of communication and positive work relationships provide social support and a sense of identification and participation in the organizational dialogue. From the sales manager's viewpoint, without good communication and positive work relationships, it is tough to accomplish work. Considering that anywhere between 30 percent to 70 percent of sales managers' time is spent communicating with subordinates, it becomes obvious that how this time is handled can have a clear impact on the motivation and morale of the sales force.

Sales managers should get to know their subordinates on the sales force for the following reasons:

1. To overcome any distrust
2. To build loyalty
3. To contribute to a stable work environment
4. To facilitate sales productivity
5. To have the opportunity to go behind the numbers to access the performance and capabilities of the salespeople.

So, sales managers should manage with communication by being open, supportive, keeping the sales force informed, and being an empathetic listener. To build trust they should not reprimand the salespeople in public or "hit them over the head with their power."

INFORMAL NETWORKS

The informal network is important because this is how and where employees communicate and develop how they feel about the company. This network can provide support and informal work groups that can enhance or inhibit motivation and morale. It can consist of an *advice network*, in which prominent players who may even have some technical expertise are sought out to assist with problem solving. Also involved may be a *trust network* in which salespeople might informally discuss politically sensitive information about the company. Last, the *communication network* could be used, which provides an opportunity for employees to talk about work-related issues. This could even take place after work hours. Sales managers should want to tap into this informal information resource to be better informed themselves. By either building up levels of trust with the salespeople or using surveys or focus groups, it is possible to gain access to some useful information.[12]

SALES FEEDBACK AND MONITORING

A good monitoring system can help prevent possible motivation and morale problems and identify these that have occurred. The following methods can provide this:

- Use employee surveys that monitor the level of employee satisfaction within the organization. Companies such as IBM use them with their salespeople to assess the level of satisfaction within the company as well as effectiveness of their sales manager.
- Have a channel of communication for any concerns that the salespeople may have. This may even involve having an outlet for complaints. Although this can be draining on a manager, in the long run it may be worthwhile. It helps identify any pos-

sible or actual motivation and morale problems and the salespeople will appreciate your concern.
- It can be helpful to conduct exit interviews when salespeople
leave to determine why they are leaving and get their impres-
sions of the company
- Make a commitment to be a good listener on an ongoing basis.

OTHER METHODS

To motivate their salespeople, several companies have used "fire
walking," which is the ancient ritual of treading barefoot over a bed of
red hot coals. Metropolitan Life Insurance Company and Digital
Equipment, in particular, are trying this motivational exercise. The
point of the exercise is to get salespeople to realize that "cold calling"
on customers is no comparison to walking over 1,200-degree coals.[13]
Other companies such as DuPont, Digital Equipment, Data General,
and Tandem Computers are using team selling. Salespeople, engineers,
technicians, and production managers are put together on teams to
serve customers and win new accounts. Their rationale is that the
essence of a successful customer development effort entails team
building, teamwork, and cooperation.

PROFILE: Donald Spiro, Chairman, Oppenheimer Management Corporation

"The sales process is extremely dynamic and demanding. This is due to
the changes in the business world which have been incredible, mainly in the
area of technology and customer expectations. Sales managers today must
understand how to use technology effectively and expect the same of their
sales force. However, while technological skills are a key in sales and sales
management today, an appreciation for the "human dimension" of customer
dealings is essential. A winning spirit along with a strong work ethic, persis-
tence, energy, and enthusiasm are important for success in sales."

Source: Donald Spiro (February 19, 1997). Personal Interview. Oppenheimer
Management Corporation, New York.

SUMMARY

The role of the sales manager is necessary to generate business for the firm. This position is demanding due to changes in the business environment, including customers. To keep the sales force focused on the task of generating business from customers, especially in lieu of possible rejection, sales managers must maintain good levels of motivation and morale. This can be done by using motivational theories, noncompensation strategies, and good management skills. The benefits of having a focused sales force with positive morale are loyalty, stability, cooperation, and performance.

Questions

1. Why is managing motivation and morale necessary for the sales force?
2. What are the consequences to the sales force of low morale? High morale?
3. Recommend some ways that a sales manager can identify causes for poor motivation and morale.
4. Give five examples of various sales management action steps that can improve the motivation and morale of the sales force.
5. In trying to provide performance incentives for a poorly motivated sales department, would you use noncompensation methods? Why?
6. What are the characteristics of "today's" sales force?
7. What changes in the business environment do sales managers face?

CASE STUDY: LILLIAN SPIRITS

Lillian Spirits is a wholesale beer distributor of beer in Pennsylvania. It is also in the business of interstate trucking (it picks up beer at breweries in Wisconsin and Michigan and ships groceries and related freight back to those locations). It has twenty-five employees, no turnover, and 63 percent market share. The culture is one of: (1) strong teamwork, (2) total quality management, and (3) excellent service.

Problem

Lillian Spirits does not have a sales manager and senior level management wonders if a sales manager is necessary. No one is currently in charge of sales or marketing. The company seems to network in an effective fashion with no one giving orders. The driver/salesmen who deliver the beer are hired on the basis of their marketing skills and are grouped into four small teams that are self-motivated and seem to be very effective. These people earn an average of $50,000 and many have some college education. Market share grew 4 percent, 3 percent, and 5 percent over the past three years respectively and continues on track this year. There are monthly incentives worth $500 for each person if the objective for that month is achieved. This is the only formal sales management that Lillian Spirits employs. There is regular dialogue between the four team members.

If communication lines are open and full of information, can people, like computers, simply "network" together with no person/ unit "superior" to the others?

They have an "inverted organization chart" with the customer at the top, the driver/salesmen in the middle, and management at the bottom. The managers are facilitators who must find and supply the resources needed by others in the organization chart. The two senior-level and three middle-level managers have assumed the task of: (1) fine tuning the design of a system to review customers to ensure that their needs are being identified and communicated, and (2) developing a mechanism to assure an equitable, timely, efficient, and effective response to these needs. Once in place, they hope these systems will perform and assist the "inverted organization chart" that causes their sales effort to be more reactive than proactive.

Questions

1. Is such a design a model for the future or simply naive?
2. Is a sales manager necessary for Lillian Spirits?

CASE STUDY: TELLCO MANAGEMENT, INC.

Modifying a Sales Compensation Plan

Tellco's headquarters are located in Nashville, Tennessee. They manufacture, service, and sell telecommunications equipment. Their customer markets are global as well as national and their equipment is produced in Massachusetts, Tennessee, and Germany. Customers mainly consist of long-distance suppliers, phone companies, and cellular phone operators. Sales revenue expected for the upcoming year should be about $400 million.

Rick Merritt is the Vice President for Corporate Sales and Marketing and has been asked by senior level management to review Tellco's sales compensation plan. In the past four years their sales revenues have increased from $210 million to about $400 million. The revenue increase, despite a minimal increase in the sales force, can probably be attributed to selling larger telecommunication systems and having an experienced sales force. A few years ago an account manager's territory would generate about $4 to $6 million whereas now it provides $10 to $15 million in sales. The sales compensation plan that was developed a few years ago might now pay an account manager three or four times more. However, there are still some territories that generate the same sales levels as a few years ago, due to the nature of their markets.

A sales incentive plan had been recently proposed by a task force appointed by senior level management. The task force has recommended that the sales incentive plan use a "flat percentage" to calculate commissions. A problem under this plan was that any account managers who had territories with a large sales volume would earn less next year than this year. This created a great deal of dissention between the sales force and the management-appointed task force.

Question

Rick Merritt will try to propose a workable alternative to the management task force proposal. How should he develop a plan that motivates and rewards the sales force but also helps the goals of Tellco Management, Inc.?

CASE STUDY: PALIN ELECTRONICS
AND THE "PAY AT RISK COMPENSATION PROGRAM"

Palin Electronics manufactures, sells, and services a full line of power management and power protection systems. The uninterruptible power systems (ups) manufactured by Palin Electronics are sold domestically and internationally through a variety of channels. This includes end-user direct manufacturers' reps, distributors, national accounts and computer OEM's that are used for financial, industrial, telecommunications, and military applications wherever continuous power is essential to daily operations. Lauren Borelli is the sales and marketing manager for the company. Lauren recently helped Palin Electronics design and implement a "pay at risk" sales compensation program. This is a compensation program where most sales and marketing personnel have the opportunity to earn commissions of up to an additional 50 percent of their salary if annual marketing and sales goals are exceeded. They also have an opportunity to receive a considerable incentive if they exceed goal. However, a portion of their pay is also at risk if marketing goals are not at least met.

Palin Electronics was built using direct manufacturer's reps for all product sales. In the past few years there has been dramatic growth in sales through indirect channels of distribution such as value and added resellers, distributors, and computer OEM's for the lower end of the product family. A sales channel conflict has developed between direct reps who sell high-end products and indirect channels of distribution who sell low-end products. Both are assigned territories and are compensated under the "pay at risk" program. However, the conflict exists because this program places a certain percentage of the sales reps salary "at risk" if the sales goal is not met. Although the traditional direct rep business with higher end, larger units has leveled off, the indirect channels selling to the lower-end market has grown 35 percent in the last two years. The conflict between selling channels is a problem because direct reps feel indirect reps have an easier chance of reaching their goals in the program. Actually Lauren's department, almost to a person, is finding the transition difficult.

It seems that most of the salespeople are focusing on the "at risk" part of the program and do not seem to be motivated by the incentive beyond the goal. This is the first time that the company has placed anyone's pay at risk for not meeting a specific goal. Executive management has stated quite adamantly to Lauren that they want to keep this program in place and not (as they put it) "change horses every time someone grumbles." In fact, they are even considering using this type of incentive compensation program for all employees with goals that are either sales, financial, or customer service oriented. Lauren is becoming concerned not only with the negative feedback from her department over the program, but because she is compensated when reps sell products for commission.

Lauren is also managing the department in the aftermath of a very recent reorganization which resulted in a 30 percent reduction of the sales and marketing department.

Question

Lauren is concerned that all of this will be adverse to the ultimate success of the "pay at risk" program. Are there any solutions that Lauren should try to improve the situation?

SECTION II:
AUTOMATION
AND SALES FORCE MANAGEMENT

Chapter 2

Sales Force Technology

TECHNOLOGY AND THE SALES FORCE

A complex selling environment and greater pressure to respond to customer needs in more detail has forced companies to assess opportunities to automate their sales forces. The need to stay competitive with sales information and technology is important to future sales force effectiveness. Customers are more sophisticated and expect better answers to their problems from the sales organization.[1] Sales managers must be involved in this process.

Sales managers must understand where current and prospective sales opportunities exist in order to fully utilize automation. The ability to develop a dialogue with clients also helps sales managers to understand how to quantify a sales force technology investment and determine return on investment based on augmented sales and enhanced customer service levels. It is helpful to take both an internal and external look to assess sales force technology opportunities. By talking to the sales force, customers, and other employees, and examining technological trends, opportunities for automation can be determined.[2] Actually blueprinting the sales process can define the requirements and framework for a sales force technology system (see Table 2.1).

The average cost to provide a salesperson with sales force technology ranges between $8,000 to $17,000 with an average increase in revenue of 20 percent to 40 percent. The average annual cost to

TABLE 2.1 Sales Force Technology

- DEVELOPMENTS IN SALES FORCE TECHNOLOGY
- USING SALES FORCE TECHNOLOGY
- A LOOK AT SOME DYNAMIC SALES SOFTWARE

maintain a sales force technology system ranges between $2,100 to $2,500 per salesperson. The average time to implement a sales force technology system is between six to eighteen months with an annual payback period of twenty-four months.[3]

Use Technology as a Sales Resource

Texas Instruments has seen its revenue grow from $6.7 billion to $13 billion since 1991. Texas Instrument's growth is due to a worldwide sales force of 2,000 salespeople equipped with technological tools. The company uses a wide area network that links operations located in over thirty countries and high-powered software developed within their information technology department. Texas Instruments spends more than $400 million a year on its technology budget. They spent an additional $120 million on technology recently as part of a companywide reengineering project.[4] The end result is an empowered sales force. However, computers will not replace salespeople because of the need for innovation, consultative abilities, creativity, personality, and intelligence. To think that computers can replace salespeople assumes that salespeople are just order-takers. Top salespeople succeed because they understand customer needs and are good consultants who are more in tune to the customers needs than any computer can be.

Currently, the vice president of sales does not just review the number of calls that salespeople make. He or she has to be knowledgeable in technology to stay competitive. Many competitive sales organizations are making the sales force technology investment. For them it is just the cost of doing business and not a huge undertaking. For sales organizations that do not have sales force technology, it is a question of survival. (See Table 2.2 for percentages of techology use.)

THE VIRTUAL MOBILE SALES FORCE

An estimated 8 million Americans worked in virtual offices in 1995, and that number is expected to increase by 120 percent.[5] Technological advances such as powerful notebook computers, sales applications software, and voice mail have created the virtual office concept which says that work can be done virtually anywhere.[6]

TABLE 2.2

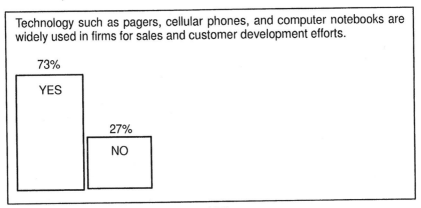

Source: *Carter Sales Force Survey* (1996).

The driving force is how these technological tools will impact the bottom line. Companies have visions of all the overhead costs saved by closing offices and allowing salespeople to work outside of their company offices. Global computer notebook sales have increased 30 percent to 10 million from 8.6 million units in 1994. The driving factor is the transition to faster Pentium processors.[7] Many sales managers are intrigued with the idea that their salespeople, armed with laptops, cellular phones, and beepers, will spend more time on the road, in front of customers.

However, shifting to a virtual office also poses serious new questions and challenges for sales managers. For example, how do sales managers manage and monitor salespeople who they rarely ever see? How do sales managers develop teamwork and build a corporate culture when salespeople are geographically dispersed? A major concern for sales managers is to not have salespeople who are not effectively selling functioning with laptops in virtual offices. To avoid this dilemma, sales managers should be tracking three things. First, are salespeople calling on the right prospects and customers? Next, are they setting up enough customer meetings to generate the amount of business needed to hit their goals? Last, are they closing business?

Over a period of time, the relationship between the amount of time spent using the sales force technology and the number of sales should become very productive. Some sales organizations report a gain of eight hours per week from the use of sales force technology. This time can be used by salespeople to nurture ties and develop consultative relationships with customers.[8]

ELECTRONIC COMMERCE

Forrester Research predicts that by the year 2000, business conducted through electronic commerce will exceed $45 billion.[9] Industries that can deliver their products electronically, execute transactions over the Internet, and build its infrastructure will benefit from the Internet economy. Forrester estimates that running a site on the World Wide Web currently costs anywhere from $300,000 to $3.4 million, depending on the size and complexity of the site. Forrester predicts that number will continue to skyrocket and that costs will increase 50 to 200 percent over the next two years as more customers flock to the Web.

Electronic commerce is connecting buyers and sellers. In fact, 90 percent of sales organizations using electronic commerce have targeted the consumer market. The business-to-business marketplace is also lucrative, since it is worth about $600 billion.

The power of electronic commerce comes from a buyer and seller being able to conduct the full range of a business relationship on-line, from creating the initial impression, to allowing for competitive comparison, to negotiation, to closing the sale, to delivery of the product, and finally, to customer service. The full spectrum of a business transaction can be supported, in many cases, entirely on-line. Electronic commerce occurs as "cashless" transactions conducted over computer networks. The total volume of remote purchasing of any transaction that is not face to face worldwide was $1 trillion for 1995, and about half of that was electronic commerce.

VIRTUAL MOBILE OFFICE

The virtual office will present sales managers with a challenge to perform their jobs. In a virtual office mode in which sales reps carry their "office" in their portable computers, communicate electronically, and make rare office appearances, managers will wrestle with these developments:

- Sales offices can be replaced by alternative arrangements such as the home, or eliminated completely.
- Salespeople will spend most of their time in the field with customers.
- Other information networks play a larger communications role between sales managers and the sales force.

Sales managers will find the virtual office a more demanding environment to work in and a priority will be put on their ability to manage and plan time more effectively.[10]

Technology will basically help the sales manager monitor the performance of sales reps who are not seen as often (see Figure 2.1).

FIGURE 2.1. The Virtual Mobile Sales Force

SALES FORCE TECHNOLOGY SUGGESTIONS

Sales managers should make sure that salespeople are well organized before trying to automate them. It is important to take some time to analyze the sales processes, to determine what the sales force would like automation to do for them, and to pinpoint which tasks are the most difficult to automate.[11]

To minimize any anxiety, sales managers should keep salespeople well informed. This means reassuring them that the new automation may take some getting used to, but will simplify the sales process and increase productivity. Technology-shy salespeople will need time to adjust to the changes. Some basic computer training is a good investment.

Sales force technology can do a lot to shorten a salesperson's cycle time, boost their productivity, and keep them organized, but it will not work miracles. Sales managers must make sure they clearly understand the capabilities, any new technological tools, and how that new automation will affect their performance.

Tips for Implementing Sales Force Technology

Top management has to endorse sales force technology. Sales force technology needs a very visible internal champion who must make it clear to the sales force that management is backing the program 100 percent.

The sales force has to be involved in designing the automation system. That gives the sales force ownership of the project, which will help to guarantee its success. They are likely to provide practical suggestions that will ensure that the project supports the selling process.

Customer involvement will provide practical suggestions regarding support for the customer's buying processes.[12]

Recommended Checklist for Managing Sales Force Technology

1. Provide thorough training.
2. Set clear skill and time frame learning goals for the sales force.
3. Reinforce the purpose of using sales force technology.
4. Apply sales force technology toward better time management.
5. Have the sales force involved in the selection of sales force technology.
6. Make sure these technology tools are "user friendly."
7. Designate a "contact person" for questions.

8. Once in use, generate a dialogue with the sales force for improvements.
9. Build the use of sales force technology into performance results.
10. Management involvement and evaluation will lead to successful technology use.

See Figures 2.2 and 2.3 for information concerning sales force technology.

PRACTICAL APPLICATIONS OF SALES FORCE TECHNOLOGY

OverQuota, a Lotus Notes-based sales force automation product, enables sales professionals to sell more by selling smarter. Over-Quota integrates sales, marketing, and service functions with real-time financial and operations data in one powerful, automated sales information system. OverQuota gives account executives and managers the information they need, when and where they need it, in a single system that is remarkably easy to use. OverQuota lets companies manage their sales process throughout the extended network of distributors, agents, resellers, and partners.

OverQuota is ideally suited to the needs of mobile sales forces. Information is shared throughout the organization, and relevant information is synchronized by a single phone cell with the mobile user's notebook computer, allowing users to work off-line and dial in periodically to send and receive updates to:

- manage the sales process across organizational boundaries;
- establish virtual sales teams;
- leverage knowledge throughout the sales network to sell smarter, and improve quality;
- present a unified message to customers throughout the sales network;
- provide a highly secure environment; and
- make anytime/anyplace work a reality.

In today's business environment, a company's products, markets, customers, and distribution channels are constantly changing and the sales process should evolve with them.

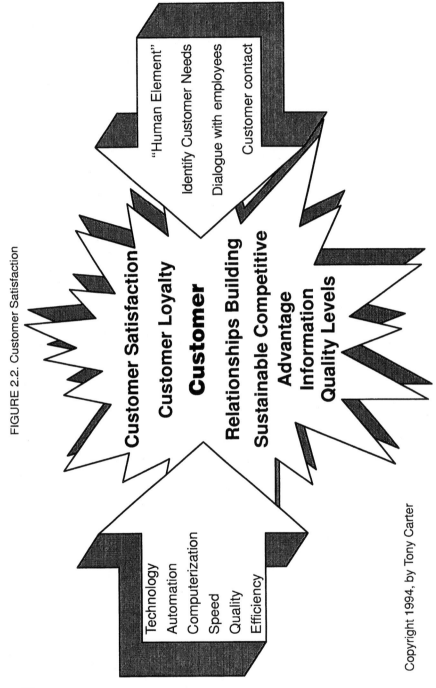

FIGURE 2.2. Customer Satisfaction

Customer Satisfaction
Customer Loyalty
Customer
Relationships Building
Sustainable Competitive
Advantage
Information
Quality Levels

"Human Element"
Identify Customer Needs
Dialogue with employees
Customer contact

Technology
Automation
Computerization
Speed
Quality
Efficiency

Copyright 1994, by Tony Carter

FIGURE 2.3. Facts About Sales Force Technology (SFT)

SFT increases productivity 20 percent - 40 percent	3 out of 4 salespeople use SFT
Growth in SFT sales: 1990 - $ 99 million 1993 - $215 million 1994 - $350 million 2000 - $ 1.3 billion	Industries with high SFT use: * Health care * Manufacturing * Business services
What's available? computers, cellular phones portable PCs, pagers, and palmtop PCs	Trends Tie-ins to on-line services Color screens, smaller notebooks use for customer presentations

Strategic sales automation solutions must effectively address those activities that most directly impact the efficiency of the sales process and organizations must move toward a comprehensive sales automation structure that focuses enterprise resources on the needs of the prospective customer.

Sales force technology focuses on the critical sales cycle steps. These steps transform a lead into a prospect, and finally into a customer. Then the concentration focuses on shortening that cycle and the ability to get effective support materials to the sales force in a timely, cost-effective, and efficient manner (see Figure 2.4).

OmniLink has a powerful intranet application development environment, to tailor or customize solution as sales needs dictate. OmniLink is the only application development environment that provides everything necessary to construct, tailor, and rapidly deploy saleable, cross platform, client/server, workflow automation, and document management applications.

OmniLink is a new Intranet/Internet solution that allows any Web client to participate in Notes applications securely. Bridging the open networking environment of Internet standards and protocols with the powerful application development facilities of Notes, OmniLink provides businesses and organizations with the ability to rapidly develop a broad range of business applications for the internet and intranet.

OmniLink workflow provides powerful, yet easy to use, workflow management tools. Users can graphically create, modify, manage, and implement serial, parallel, or conditional workflow processes. Graphical workflow maps provide immediate status of workflows that are in process. More detailed status information can be obtained from the complete audit trail that captures every event in the process. A complete work package is routed to users including all the information they need to do their job, such as due dates, specific instructions, documents and an area for comments.

FIGURE 2.4

Sales manager distributes laptops and relevant software to the sales force. The salesperson is now spending a disproportionate amount of time with the tools and in front of the computer and not enough time out with customers. What is the solution to this dilemma? How should it be approached by management?

OmniLink Search allows for full text search and retrieval of virtually any type and number of documents over the Intranet. Users connect via Web browsers such as Netscape Navigator, Microsoft Explorer, and NCSA Mosaic to perform text searches on the entire contents of a database of documents.

Sales organizations must support the collaborative efforts of many people across departments, distances, and multiple technologies. With OmniLink, sales managers can boost productivity and eliminate the obstacles to working across diverse distributed networks. Sales managers can also control, structure, and monitor any number of projects, so the Intranet workflow engine streamlines and automates strategic work processes involving any number of documents and contributors. Universal search and viewing engines remove the barriers to information access, allowing sales managers to focus on their work instead of cross-platform mechanics.

Benefits of OmniLink

- Improved communication
- Better control of decentralized processes and working groups
- Lowered installation and maintenance costs for applications because they are deployed on a server and accessed through a cross platform "desktop" (Web browser)
- Increased organizational flexibility by enabling "virtual work groups" to form around topics
- Increased organizational flexibility by using a low-cost global infrastructure to give access to information and manage decentralized processes
- The ability to include workers in work groups regardless of their physical location
- A practical way to bring the power of advanced applications such as workflow, document management, and searching onto everyone's desktop with a minimal impact in terms of training, installation, and maintenance
- A radical expansion of work groups as they collaborate on projects
- Ready access to information in all of its formats, through search and view capabilities increasing the value of work already done
- Centralized control of distributed processes

- Document review and distribution, for example, are tracked; businesses can better assess their efficiency
- Increased flow of information and increased control over business processes allows products to be brought to market faster
- The increased centralized control makes it easier for organizations to comply with government industry regulations

Examples of OmniLink Applications

- Customer service
- Sales automation: lead generation and tracking
- HR benefits program information and sign-up
- Threaded discussions for internal teams or for communities of customers

CONTACT MANAGEMENT

ACT!, a contact management package, was one of the first software applications. ACT! allows salespeople to track their customers daily, remember important phone calls and meetings, and report their activities. ACT! has a very good calendaring program, which enables salespeople to improve their time management. This software can also cover customer orders, shipments, backlogs, communications, and, eventually, competitive information.

Goldmine for Windows by Elan Software Company is a sales automation program available for IBM compatible and Apple Macintosh computers. Goldmine can be used to perform everyday business tasks, reminders such as "tickler files," scheduling meetings, processing leads, and maintaining address files in the program.[13] Then salespeople can use the program to send out follow-up letters and brochures. The functions involve managing customers, telephone and written contacts, scheduling, word processing, organizing outgoing and incoming faxes, and e-mail. Effectively used, sales force technology helps businesses organize and focus their efforts to gain new customers and keep existing ones. Companies are achieving growth by replacing manual paper filing and traditional sales management tools with sales force technology and other related tools such as Goldmine in order to help their firms meet today's growth challenges and those of the future.

A key is to choose technology that is appropriate for the task, considering the hundreds of choices. Criteria to consider are the firm's number of customers, sales cycle, needs, customer-related procedure, and computer proficiency of the sales force. The transition period to get the sales force acclimated may take some time, but sales force technology will help by expediting the user of technology. Some selling features may take time to integrate. A sales management program's fax capabilities can provide the ultimate in desk top automation, dialing up and forwarding low-cost, overnight connections to an electronic phone book full of prospective clients.

MULTIMEDIA PRESENTATION

Multimedia allows salespeople to give outstanding presentations. Using a multimedia or upgraded multimedia-ready laptop computer, or a panel projecting onto a large screen, salespeople can make their presentations come to life using color, animation, video, special effects, sound, and interactivity.

Multimedia is a popular sales force technology. According to a survey of 100 senior managers by OmniTech Consulting Group, 72 percent currently use multimedia for business presentations, 68 percent of it for sales, and 42 percent use it for customer contact. Of those managers who use multimedia, 61 percent plan to increase their use for presentations, 58 percent plan to increase their use for sales, and 66 percent plan to increase their use for customer contact.

Sales and marketing managers must decide how multimedia will benefit their salespeople and customers. Multimedia involves customers in the sales call and allows salespeople to customize presentations in minutes, demonstrate products using video or animation, and bring "live" customer testimonials to any sales call.

Multimedia is interactive and can even allow the viewer to choose the presentation. Consequently, salespeople can "drive" their presentations to address the specific concerns of each customer by instantly repeating information, skipping screens or subjects, or stopping at any point. They can present detailed information on their products without overwhelming their customers because the customer chooses the information he or she is interested in.

Using multimedia should be taken seriously because a great deal of work is involved in developing a presentation and training the salespeople. It takes substantial time and research to find the right multimedia software and the presentation must then be designed and used properly. American Airlines uses computer notebooks loaded with multimedia software for client presentations. This software has helped their sales force of 500 people save more than $150,000 in presentation expenses and the presentations are made with more impact. Tools such as overhead transparencies do not have the same level of visual and audio intensity or state of the art interactivity to reach customers. The advantage of Multimedia software technology is that it allows the sales force to customize dazzling presentations for clients.[14]

A multimedia presentation should not just be a dazzling dog-and-pony show that overshadows the message. It should provide a clear message and leave time for dialogue. Salespeople should be selective about when to use a multimedia presentation. Will it enhance the sales call? Is it appropriate for the client and surroundings? The decision to use it or not varies by salesperson, and depends on the customer and his interests. For some salespeople, being able to take advantage of the multimedia presentation's interactivity can be a real problem solver. To achieve success, interactive salespeople must be trained not only to operate the presentation, but also to sell as a result of using it. Some salespeople are intimidated by the technology until they see the benefits.

DATABASE SALES

The goal of database sales is to allow sales managers to use computer-generated information about customers' buying decisions to pinpoint those people who are most likely to buy a particular product. Database selling also needs to be understood—and controlled if sales managers are to benefit from its potential (see Table 2.3).

ACT!, the customer management software program, helps to build a thorough database that can be searched quickly by categories such as customer segments. These software programs also consolidate efforts to develop leads into sales. This can be used to compile attendance lists from various conventions attended during the year. Usually a standard

TABLE 2.3. Customer Database

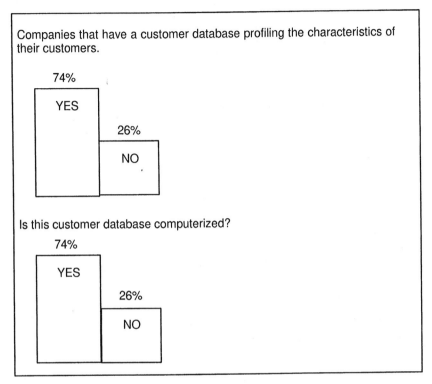

Source: *Carter Sales Force Survey* (1996).

database program such as "Microsoft Access" takes ten to fifteen minutes or a lot less to search out contacts once input in the program. This helps to track follow-up mailings and reports on prospects who respond to mail or phone contacts, thus saving expenses on the cost of promotional mailings and forces salespeople to be original in their sales efforts.

Lotus Notes is another database groupware software program that effectively provides information and communication software that allows users to share data inside and outside the company and the sales organization. The best way to keep customers is to know who they are and what they do; that is the essence of database sales.

In London, Barclays Bank started its own shopping service, open to anyone with a credit card and access to the Internet. In Germany, Deutsche Telekom updated its antiquated computer service and has added 100,000 clients in six months.

Impressive on-line efforts by CompuServe, a joint venture by America Online and Germany's Bertelsmann, and Europe Online, a Luxembourg-based consortium led by publishing giants Burda of Germany, Britain's Pearson, and Matra-Hachette in France, cannot be dismissed easily. CompuServe subscriptions have already significantly expanded since it began marketing its service in Europe. The Internet is a complex business resource providing a forum for companies to repackage information in a friendly, accessible way.[15]

See Tables 2.4 and 2.5 for information regarding customer knowledge databases.

TABLE 2.4. Customer Knowledge Database

Sophisticated, demanding and knowledgeable customers need specialized solutions to be kept satisfied.	The assumption that customers essentially want the same things is no longer true.
Using individualized data about customers and linking it with computer technology in the form of a database provides a foundation to give customers what they want and need.	The database gets maintained and updated.

TABLE 2.5. Customer Knowledge Database (Part II)

By listening to the customer, the database helps build a dialogue with the customer that is being "Market Driven"	Acting on this dialogue develops "Relationship Selling."
"Relationship Selling" improves customer loyalty and increases sales volume and business from referrals.	The customer knowledge database sales process is a tool that helps find the most effective way to reach, maintain, and sell products and services to customers.

THE INTERNET

Much of the current expansion in Internet use, accelerated by the emergence of the World Wide Web, is driven by sales goals to provide products and product information to potential customers.

More than half of the Internet's nearly 7 million host computers are located in the United States, with the remainder spread across 100 other countries.[16]

Small companies offering specialized niche products should be able to find the customers necessary to succeed through the world-wide reach of the Internet. The Internet's low-cost communications permits firms with limited capital to become global marketers at the early stages of their development. U.S. households with access to the Internet number doubled in the past year to about 15 million. This reflects the interest that consumers have for information access from the Internet.[17]

The Internet can connect customers with sellers directly and thereby increase speed and value. The ubiquitous availability of the

Web enables buyers, particularly in emerging markets, to access a broader range of product choices, and even purchase their goods on the world market at lower prices. For example, customers can put out a request for a proposal for equipment over the Internet, secure bids, select a seller, and have the products delivered immediately. Few inventories will be needed in the worldwide distribution system and less working capital will therefore be tied up in inventory (see Tables 2.6 and 2.7).

TABLE 2.6. The Internet in the Selling Cycle

Key: Customer now controls the flow of info and drives the selling process

Sales organization determines	The customer then
• The customer's needs • Provides Web page	• Provides info • Retrieves info • Initiates the sales process

TABLE 2.7. Advantages of Using Computer Technology

ADVANTAGES
1. Creates a customer community
2. Ease in processing info
3. Ability to build database
4. Expedites transactions
5. Use of electronic catalogs
6. Facilitates the selling process
7. Value

The Internet provides sales organizations with new opportunities to develop new markets. It helps buyers and sellers to locate one another, in negotiating terms of trade, and in executing secure transactions. Setting up a Web page is a good way for a sales organization to provide customers with consultative service.[18]

SELLING ON-LINE

Research shows that 22 percent of the public say they have made an on-line purchase in the past year and that the average Internet user spends approximately twenty hours on-line per week. The U.S. Internet use by job function shows that 19 percent have sales duties.

CULTIVATING CUSTOMERS ON THE WEB

Federal Express

After tracking packages, customers on Federal Express' Web site stay to get the latest information on FedEx news, special offers, and new services. The results have been a great marketing success for Federal Express.

They have achieved effective results by incorporating its on-line efforts with other marketing department programs. On every brochure, television ad, or print ad that carries a Federal Express phone number, its universal resource locator, or on-line address, appears as well.

The company's Internet efforts have extended beyond the marketing department. Federal Express' salespeople have found success developing customers using the Web site's tracking capabilities. The Internet allows salespeople to tell their customers where their packages are.

More than 65 percent of the company's orders are taken electronically. Larger customers can send and track packages through Federal Express's own network, called Power Ship. As the company's business has grown from 2.1 million packages shipped in 1994 to 2.4 million in 1995, it has been able to handle more inquiries without increasing the size of its call-center support staff. The sales force at United Parcel System has also used the Internet in a similar manner (see Figure 2.5).

FIGURE 2.5 Investing with Oppenheimer Funds

With over 55 funds to choose from, Oppenheimer Funds can help you pursue investment objectives ranging from conservative income to aggressive growth. Our broad spectrum of funds allows you to invest in mutual funds designed to fit your investment needs today, while maintaining the flexibility to make adjustments as these needs change.

To help you access the specific fund information you want quickly and easily, we've divided our fund information into five sections:

"We believe in providing shareholders top, long-term performance."

Investment Categories
Learn about the different investment options available within mutual funds, the levels of risk involved and which investment strategies may best help you meet your financial goals.

OppenheimerFunds Family
Discover all the funds that OppenheimerFunds offers, facts about the funds, the strategy for each fund, and how they have performed to date.

Prospectuses
Access the prospectus for the Oppenheimer fund of your choice for more complete information including charges and expenses.

Daily Net Asset Values
Check the latest closing net asset values of our mutual funds.

Performance
Find out the average annual total returns for the OppenheimerFunds family.

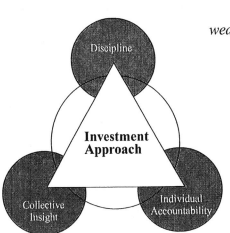

"The Right Way to Invest"
weaves three key elements into
one dynamic investment
approach:

Discipline assures the portfolio managers take their responsibilities to share-holders seriously, adhering to each fund's current stated objective and building on a foundation of trust to help meet their goals and expectations.

Individual Accountability makes each OppenheimerFunds portfolio manager responsible for their decisions about security selection, risk management and investment strategy - a strong incentive to provide excellent performance.

Collective Insight provides an additional dimension, assuring that a portfolio manager is backed up by a fully collaborative investment process. This means each manager is supported by an expert team of research specialists who constantly exchange investment ideas and information - so shareholders benefit from different backgrounds and perspectives.

For more complete information about the Oppenheimer funds, including charges and expenses, you may download and view a prospectus now, speak with your financial advisor, or call OppenheimerFunds at 1-888-470-0862. Please read the prospectus carefully before you invest or send money.

Shares of the Oppenheimer funds are not deposits or obligations of any bank, are not guaranteed by any bank, are not insured by the FDIC or any other agency investment risks, including the possible loss of the principle amount invested.

Oppenheimer funds are distributed by OppenheimerFunds Distributor, Inc., Two World Trade Center, New York, NY 10048-0203.

FIGURE 2.5 (continued)

Oppenheimer Funds launches first open-end mutual fund to provide broad exposure to commodity-linked investments
Oppenheimer Enterprise Fund Reopens to New Investors

Please note that we are not affiliated with the brokerage firm of Oppenheimer & Co., Inc., nor its affiliate Oppeheimer Capital. Oppenheimer & Co.'s Web address is www.oppenheimer.com.

For more complete information about the Oppenheimer funds, including charges and expenses, you may download and view a prospectus now, speak with your financial advisor, or call Oppenheimer Funds at 1-888-470-0862. Please read the prospectus carefully before you invest or send money.

Shares of the Oppenheimer funds are not deposits or obligations of any bank, are not guaranteed by any bank, are not insured by the FDIC or any other agency, and involve investment risks, including the possible loss of the principle amount invested.

Oppenheimer funds are distributed by Oppenheimer Funds Distributor, Inc., Two World Trade Center, New York, NY 10048-0203.

| prospectus | site map | questions | site comments | email us | lit request |

| NEWS | COMPANY | PLANNING | ADVISOR | SHAREHOLDERS | HOME |

Source: Reprinted with the consent of Oppenheimer Funds, Inc. All rights reserved.

SOME SUGGESTIONS FOR SELECTING SALES FORCE TECHNOLOGY VENDORS

The following are steps a company should take to make the process of choosing a technology vendor easier.

1. Define the needs and goals of a sales force technology system before approaching vendors.
2. Cut the list of vendors to about four or five by matching their features with actual needs. Inform vendors exactly what the needs are and ask them to send back proposals within a specific time frame.[19]
3. Demonstrations from the vendors or demonstration software or equipment should be requested when it is available.
4. Get testimonials from current customers of the vendors to establish if they have a reliable track record.
5. Feel comfortable with the final choice.

A company should ask itself such questions such as: "What kind of sales organization do we have?" "How computer literate are the salespeople?" "How much training will they need and what sales functions should be automated?"

PROFILE: Tony Williams, Regional Sales Manager, Phillips Industrial

"Sales force technology will play an incredibly important role in sales performance effectiveness. My salespeople are all armed with computer laptops, cellular phones, pagers, and the appropriate sales-related software. They are all well trained and proficient with this technology and it shows in their productivity. I'm not saying that sales force technology is a panacea, but it is a highly sophisticated tool that has helped my sales organization maximize its potential and perform better."

Source: Tony Williams (February 3, 1997). Personal Interview. Phillips Industrial, Mahwah, New Jersey.

SUMMARY

Sales force technology represents a variety of dynamic tools that can help the sales force. While these tools cannot replace the sales-

person and generate deals from customers, they can enhance efficiency and effectiveness levels. Sales force technology can range
from computer laptops, pagers, cellular phones, desktop personal
computers and software for contact management, database management and multimedia presentations. The key for sales managers to
remember is that these tools do not drive themselves and still need
the skill of management to get the best results.

Questions

1. What role does sales force technology play in the productivity
   of the sales force?
2. How should sales force technology be implemented?
3. What is the role of sales managers in handling how sales force
   technology is used by the sales force?
4. What is the difference between "contact specific" software
   and "database management" software?
5. What does the term "virtual mobile office" mean?
6. Explain the role of the Internet in the sales process and the
   benefits that it can provide.
7. What is the best way to select vendors for sales force technology?

CASE STUDY: KONTAC INFORMATION RESOURCES COMPANY (KIRC)

Pat Winters in her position as Northeast Regional Sales Manager
for Kontac Information Resources Company (KIRC) has lately felt
extremely frustrated over some internal problems. As her sales
department has characterized it "the media products division and
the marketing division are just not held accountable for their performance."

KIRC is in the automatic identification industry. They supply bar
code printers, input devices, network readers, radio frequency
equipment, interface software, and portable readers through a direct
sales force of about 120 people. The media products division that
supplies the label material to customers has been the source of
several problems for the sales department. These problems have

included incorrect packing lists being sent to customers, shipping instructions not followed, various materials orders shipped without notification, and an overall lack of communication. The marketing division is responsible for identifying high margin products that customers are interested in and developing marketing strategies to increase profit margins. The problem is that this is done without any real input from the sales department. Pat is frantic at this point because she feels that marketing is unaware that KIRC's customers are saying that KIRC doesn't respond to them fast enough. In addition, competition will be entering the region shortly, a factor that KIRC has not faced previously.

Actual Performance Last 12-Month Period January 1-December 31

Media Products	Automatic Identification Products	
(e.g. label materials)	(e.g. bar code printers, radio frequency equipment)	
1st Quarter $ 2,200,000	$5,900,000	
2nd Quarter $ 4,500,000	$10,500,000	
3rd Quarter $ 2,800,000	$6,500,000	
4th Quarter $ 5,100,000	$8,100,000	
TOTAL $14,600,000	$31,000,000	$45,600,000

Actual Performance Last 12-Month Period January 1-December 31

Northeast Region (Sales)

Connecticut	$ 3,700,000
Delaware	$ 1,900,000
New Jersey	$ 8,500,000
New York	$21,100,000
Pennsylvania	$10,400,000
TOTAL	$45,600,000

Last year the media business represented about 32 percent of total revenue while the automatic identification products generated about 68 percent. However, these problems create critical concerns when they occur because they have happened so frequently. Accordingly, the salespeople are spending an inordinate amount of time searching for answers to prevent losing their current customer base instead of selling to both these customers and developing new ones. Also, the amount

of effort being expended to save these customers and obtain pertinent information to retain them is starting to cost KIRC customers
and have a negative impact on the morale of the sales department.

Pat has attempted several times to have conference calls with
John Maxwell, the Regional Manager of Media Products and Karen
Mullin, Regional Marketing Manager, without much satisfaction. In
fact during one conversation John replied, "You think it's so easy to
get this stuff out, but I've got limited staff. Besides a lot of these
customers are just unreasonable with what they expect, anyway."
Both John and Karen have been defensive to Pat when she's tried to
discuss these problems with them.

Question

Pat is wondering if it is time to start screaming up the management
chain and how she should set measurements or objectives to get out of
this situation. Ironically, while KIRC is involved in a technology-related industry, they have virtually no sales force technology in use for
their sales effort. Accordingly, Pat is also wondering how she can best
incorporate sales force technology into the sales force to maximize
their sales performance results and improve coordination with marketing and media products. What should Pat do?

SECTION III:
GLOBALIZATION

Chapter 3

Strategic Issues
for an International Sales Effort

GLOBAL SALES ENVIRONMENT

The global economy may seem like an overused term, but this is an exciting time to do business globally. The fall of the Iron Curtain alone has made it a fascinating time to engage in sales activity internationally. Investment by the United States, Germany, Japan, and the United Kingdom in each others' economies is unprecedented. The United Kingdom has invested over $250 billion in the United States and in Japan, U.S. companies create and sell over $80 billion in goods and services. Some companies such as Singapore Airways, which is ranked as the number one airline in the world, have redefined the "competitive edge" due to courteous service and efficient flying performance. Luxembourg, as a tax haven, has become the largest banking nation in the world with more banks per capita despite a population of only half a million. Liberia has the world's largest maritime fleet, and Germany, due to reunification, looms as an economic superpower.

INTERNATIONAL SALES TECHNIQUES

Richard Horlick, managing director for Fidelity Investment's London office, offers several methods to help a global sales effort.[1] Horlick states that it is important to have a mission statement and corporate philosophy that makes a commitment to quality levels and performance. In Mexico, consumers rank service and the "personal touch" as important as price. They want attention before, during, and after the sale. To consumers in Mexico "Made in America" still means the highest quality.[2] Horlick also says that a lot of team building is necessary due to the complexity of global sales. In many cases this global sales activity is driven by ego and personal relationships and not the merits and costs. Nick Hodgson, the London marketing director of Thornton's Inc., has added that for global sales it is important to use visual aids to help the customer's understanding of product or service features.[3] The use of customer advisory groups and committees along with sales technological tools such as video conferencing, database management, and current industry software will help raise levels of sales efficiency. Strategic meetings within the organization between line managers, senior level managers, their economist and customer advisory groups are useful in order to decide the best strategic process to use for customers. The Securities Futures Authority in London proposes the obvious ability to develop personal relationships which can also lead to the long-term benefit of referral business.[4] The urgent rapid pace of cultivating clients and generating deals that is expected in the United States will not work in a global sales effort as effectively as using a more "slowed down" pace. See Table 3.1 for recommended conditions for successful global sales.

TABLE 3.1. Conducting a Successful Global Sales Effort

Sales organizations involved in global markets recommend these conditions to conduct a successful global sales effort.

- Communication between all world areas is critical
- Global Account Manager at the senior level
- Regular communications using e-mail and conference calls
- A lot of networking by interfacing with key decision maker
- Knowledge of culture, customer differences, local laws and customs
- Good communication between home, office, and sales outpost
- Consistent pricing policy
- Local person to handle marketing of foreign market
- Global sales strategy
- Technology tools
- Hiring from within the target country
- Team selling, since a team that has the ability to understand all clients' needs worldwide can work together to formulate the most effective strategy

Source: *Carter Sales Force Survey* (1996).

Contrasted with the direct sales force that is used in the domestic United States, overseas intermediaries and manufacturer's representatives are used. The intermediaries not only save money, but provide a dealer network that bears the burden of selling. Another customer-related matter that can assist a global sales effort is profiling customers. Since a global sales effort is an overseas investment with a smaller margin for error, this information is crucial. Before calling on a customer and doing business it is important to first find out if they want to work with foreign companies and if they have a prior positive international experience. Also, it should be determined if they are financially solvent through the review of some materials that show solid financial strength. Once a sales transaction has been underway it becomes important to get the customer to show some commitment to the given project. Assurances are fine, but in particular, a nonrefundable deposit to ascertain commitment and enthusiasm should be used, along with performing a customer product or service audit to assess customer needs and aspirations. This audit should examine the customer's structural strengths and weaknesses regarding finances and/or the product or service.

Last, *ISO 9000* provides a uniform framework for quality assurance that can be used worldwide. To qualify for ISO 9000 registration, a company must document its quality procedures and upgrade them where necessary.[5] Then the procedures are audited by a registered third-party auditor. If the audit meets the standard, the organization's quality system is certified and the organization is certified. This certification will help establish immediate credibility which can facilitate sales penetration in an international market.

HOW TO SELECT TARGET COUNTRIES

Certain specific micro conditions should be considered when selecting target markets to enter. Factors such as political risk, local customs, business practices, laws, and competitive presence should all be reviewed. For example, even though Europe remains full of opportunities for American companies, Disney parks, which are successful in the United States, have not found a strong niche with EuroDisney in France. While recent consumer spending in Mexico has declined, Mexican consumers have purchased about $50 billion worth of American cars, clothes, and computers.[6] Liberia had a civil war for a period of time since 1989, so while some firms may avoid this market based on the risk, others might find opportunity. Barings PLC collapsed when Nicholas Leeson, head of its futures dealings in Singapore, essentially in a sales role, suffered $1.36 billion in losses in derivative trading. Chris Bailey, Deputy Secretary and Press Officer for the Bank of England, has made some interesting observations about these losses. Bailey says that allowing bad banks to fail will send a message to sharpen other banks, thus allowing regulators to send out notice to firms that there are consequences for inadequate failure control.[7] Certainly a more stringent regulatory environment will have some bearing on the attractiveness of that market.

However, Brazil, which is considering constitutional amendments to expand foreign investment in its economy, may augment global sales opportunities for a firm. The Brazilian amendments are designed to abolish legal distinctions between foreign corporations and will allow foreign companies greater participation in their markets. These all present market conditions that can permit or preclude global sales penetration.

From a macro standpoint it is necessary to "define the market" by identifying market size in revenue and market and sales potential and other characteristics. For example, The European Union is already one of the biggest customers for U.S. goods and services. U.S. exports to Western Europe in 1994 totaled $100 billion.[8] When Canada and Mexico are added to Western Europe they total a gross domestic product of $10 trillion and population of 770 million people thus present incredible sales opportunities. In the first quarter of 1995, the European personal computer business grew by more than 28 percent, outpacing the United States for the first time in years. The 28 percent increase in PC sales was reflected in 3.49 million units sold, compared to 2.72 million units sold in the first quarter 1994. Despite a much bigger market in the United States, for the first time since the European recession hit in 1992, Europe was a much more active market for PCs than the United States, where PC business activity only grew about 23 percent. The number of home personal computers shipped in Europe grew by 44 percent and 24 percent for office PCs. The leading U.S. PC companies have market shares in Europe of 13 percent/Compaq, 9 percent/IBM, 7 percent/Apple, 5 percent/Hewlett-Packard, and 4 percent for AST Research, a California-based PC maker. This increase has been due to a strong European economic rebound, in particular in Germany, and to the belated demand for home PC's that has already hit the United States. In order to have an understanding of global market conditions and an overall sense of their business climate, it is important to "define the market" to effectively target a global sales effort.

HOW TO ENTER TARGET MARKETS

The efforts of the sales department and salespeople in global markets are not necessarily the only driving force responsible for sales opportunities.

Trade Agreements

Free trade agreements boil down to five core obligations: (1) phased elimination of tariffs on all goods, (2) liberalization of trade, (3) rules to protect investment and intellectual property rights, (4) services liberalization, particularly in the telecommunications, financial, and audio-visual sectors, and (5) a dispute settlement system to arbitrate commercial disputes and interpret the agreement.[9] These core obligations in trade agreements help to open up world markets. A global sales effort can certainly be facilitated by their existence. The World Trade Organization, which became operational in early 1995 and was designed with strict time limits for settling disputes, might also help market entry for sales efforts.

United States trade law specifically authorizes sanctions where there is government toleration of systematic anticompetitive practices by private firms that restrict access of U.S. products to a foreign market. That language is at the heart of Eastman Kodak Company's complaint which claims that anticompetitive practices that generally involved competitor Fuji Photo Film Company were industry wide and were at times conducted with the knowledge and participation of the Japanese government. After the United States, Japan has the second largest consumer market for photography products. Kodak believes that as a result of the alleged practices it has lost $5.6 billion in revenue in Japan. Eastman Kodak Company has accused Japan's Ministry of

International Trade and Industry, the Japan Fair Trade Commission, and rival Fuji Photo Film Company of choking Kodak's access to the Japanese photographic film and paper market.[10]

In a petition filed with the United States Trade Representative's office, Kodak alleged that Japan has created a "profit sanctuary" for Fuji by systematically denying Kodak access to Japanese distribution channels for consumer film and paper. Kodak cited "anticompetitive rebate schemes, resale price maintenance, and horizontal price-fixing" as practices that have "effectively locked Kodak out" of the Japanese market since the 1970s. Kodak has also sold private-label film under Japanese retailers' names there in an effort to secure shelf space for its more lucrative branded products. Prior to the private-label launch, analysts estimated that Kodak's Japanese market share at 9 percent for amateur film, compared with Fuji's U.S. market share at about 12 percent. So, this petition is just a part of Kodak's aggressive offensive to gain sales penetration of the Japanese market.

In addition to Kodak's complaints, Washington also has concerns about the sales consequences from a trade showdown with Japan. This can test ways in which America should deal with an economic rival. This trade fight is becoming a test for controversial "revisionist" views. The revisionists argue that Japan's economy differs fundamentally from that of other nations. Washington, they conclude, must force Japan to open its markets and adopt less adversarial trade practices. The antirevisionist's maintain that the United States cannot count on nonmarket forces to curtail Japan's trade surplus; this is inconsistent with a market economy. The revisionists hold that Japan's trade surplus allows it to pile up wealth and grow stronger at the United States' expense.[11]

The revisionists also believe that Japan's huge trade surplus will doom the world's free-trade system over time by forcing countries to adopt protectionist countermeasures. To prevent this, they want the United States and other countries to "manage" trade with Japan, using export restrictions, import targets, and similar practices to curb Japanese "adversarial trade." The underlying motivation for the revisionist is to get American companies better sales access to Japan's lucrative markets.[12]

U.S. trade policy has helped global sales penetration for American companies throughout the world. By joining the General Agreement on Tariffs and Trade (GATT) in 1986 and with the implementation of the North American Free Trade Agreement (NAFTA), sales barriers have come down and U.S. exports to Mexico have increased. Presently U.S. companies generate $33 billion in exports to Mexico with growth of 18 percent annually. This is quite favorable compared to overall U.S. global exports of 7 percent.

Acquisition/Merger

Acquiring a company or an interest in a company is a way to gain immediate sales penetration. Argentine brewer Quilmes Industrial SA, or Quinsa, has accomplished this in recent years by becoming a major player in Bolivia, Chile, Paraguay, and Uruguay with sales revenue of approximately $80 million and profit of approximately $85 million in 1994, but its participation in an unsolicited bid for Canada's John Labatt Ltd. represents a quantum leap in its foreign ambitions.[13] Buenos Aires-based Quinsa had committed to invest 312.5 million Canadian dollars (US$230.6 million) in a company formed by Toronto-based leveraged buy out firm Onex Corporation to buy all Labatt stock. If the transaction is completed under its current structure, Quinsa would become Labatt's largest shareholder with a 27.5 percent interest.

Quinsa is the largest beer maker in the southern zone of South America, with breweries in Argentina, Chile, Paraguay, and Uruguay. Its companies also produce malts, hops, crown caps, and mineral water in Argentina, and control the largest soft drink operation and bottle-manufacturing facility in Paraguay. Quinsa also controls malt and mineral water companies in Uruguay, and Quinsa, with Heineken, owns Cerveceria Chile, the number two brewer in Chile. They also recently reached an agreement to acquire 50 percent of Cerveceria Santa Cruz, a Bolivian brewery. These methods are commonly used to enter a market for sales presence.

Joint Ventures/Strategic Alliances

Under a joint venture agreement, a foreign company invites an outside partner equity participation in a new firm. Daimler-Benz AG, Germany's largest company, and ABB Asea Brown Boveri

Ltd., the Swedish-Swiss heavy engineering group, plan to merge their railroad-systems operations under an agreement that calls for Daimler to make a cash payment of $900 million to ABB.[14] The venture will offer a complete range of products, including electrical and diesel locomotives, high-speed trains, subway and light-rail cars, signaling systems and maintenance services. Daimler's rail operations are posting heavy losses and are about half the size of ABB's, which have been profitable for the past two years.

The companies have agreed to establish a 50-50 joint venture, which is subject to approval by their boards and by the European Union's antitrust officials. The venture would be the largest international provider of rail systems, with sales of $4.5 billion and an estimated 12 percent share of the world market. The next-largest competitors, with about 8 percent of the world market each, are also European. They are France's GEC Alsthom and Siemens AG of Germany. Daimler, best known for its Mercedes cars, has long sought to cut the losses at its rail operations, which are dragging down the performance of the subsidiary in which they are incorporated, AEG Daimler-Benz Industries AG. The companies' optimism is based on bullish predictions for the world's rail market, which is expected to grow 7 percent to 8 percent a year beyond the year 2000. Governments throughout Europe are looking to invest in new high-speed train networks, and have generally liberalized their rail markets and eased manufacturing requirements.

Strategic alliances are formed when two firms pool their particular skill or resources directly in a collaboration used to gain sales entry in a market. Typically, strategic alliances involve joining technology transfers, production technology or distribution access with each side contributing a different element to the venture. Volkswagen AG of Germany and Italy's Fiat SPA spent billions of dollars to acquire eastern European Communist era car companies such as Skoda AS in the Czech Republic and Poland's Fabryka Samochodow Malolitrazowych, known as FSM. GM looked at Eastern Europe as a way to lower its overall manufacturing costs while getting into new markets. GM is persuing a substantial expansion in Poland, having cautiously entered the Polish market in late 1993 with just $21.58 million of investment for a small assembly factory.[15] GM plans to discuss the timetable of the proposed expansion with car maker Fabryka Samacodow Osobowych, or FSO, with whom GM has a strategic alliance.

GM in this alliance would assemble 10,000 Astras from kits done with FSO and the alliance with FSO holds long-term advantages for GM. FSO currently holds nearly one-third of the Polish new car market and could provide an outlet for some GM products. GM's efforts to improve FSO's operations and pep up its product line also put it at the head of the line should it one day want to take over an efficient, restructured FSO.

Licensing

This involves contractual permission to use industrial property rights such as patents and trademarks. Some firms will trade technology and form a technology licensing agreement for market access. For example, a U.K. company, Hilson, supplies a key component in the air filtration systems used in a wide range of manufacturing processes. Since fertilizer manufacturers need to purify the air used in their processes before they emit it into the atmosphere, the filter cages that they produce require highly precise wire bending and welding technology. Hilson was doing well in the United Kingdom, but had limited success in the European continent since a filter cage may be light, but takes up a lot of volume, making it expensive to transport.

To enter the continental market Hilson needed a manufacturer on the spot. Through a French consulting firm, Advans, Hilson was put in touch with a French company, STPM, which specialized in precision wire products and wanted to develop new products. Since STPM did well on the European Continent, they would manufacture and sell the air filtration systems under a new brand name "Euro Cage." Hilson supplies STPM with "know how" and equipment and they receive a fee for the original technology transfer and continue to receive a royalty on each unit sold. Hilson has in this process extended their sales presence while STPM gains an entirely new product line and technological capability.[16]

Restrictive Domestic Forces on Exporting

U.S. exporters are facing potentially deep cuts in federal programs that help them capture business in Asia, Latin America, and elsewhere.

The U.S. Export-Import Bank, the Overseas Private Investment Corporation and many other trade-promoting agencies now pose a risk despite their traditional popularity with the U.S. business community. The Clinton Administration requested $3.2 billion to operate the programs for the fiscal year that started in October 1996, but Republican budgeteers prevented the funding from being anywhere close to that.

A key reason that these programs are at risk is that the U.S. Senate Budget Committee is expected to recommend slashing as much as one-third from the administration-proposed Ex-Im Bank authorization of $870 million for the 1996 fiscal year. Over a period of five fiscal years beginning in 1996, as much as $1.4 billion may be chopped off the bank's accustomed budget authority. Such cuts could cost the United States as much as $6 billion to $7 billion in export business during the five-year period. Many companies that depend on exports would feel the effect. Export-dependent companies such as Boeing, General Electric, Caterpillar Inc., and Westinghouse Electric are lobbying hard to defend these agencies against cutbacks. Much of the Ex-Im Bank's effort is expended for loan guarantees given to foreign buyers, on the condition that they buy U.S.-made goods. Although the bank normally assumes only a portion of the financing of any export transaction, an exporter might not be able to get the business without that vital Ex-Im Bank component.[17]

The United States has nineteen separate agencies involved in trade promotion. The Overseas Private Investment Corporation, among other U.S. agencies, provides political-risk insurance for U.S. companies investing in overseas projects. The Trade Development Agency underwrites the costs of feasibility studies that U.S. exporters must undertake in order to qualify for future business. The Commerce Department even acknowledges that without The Trade Development Agency's help, Raytheon Company, based in Lexington, Massachusetts, could not have won a $26-million contract to supply Hong Kong with an air traffic control system. According to Arthur Simonetti, an executive at the National Foreign Trade council, a Washington-based industry group, the Ex-Im Bank, and other U.S. trade promotion agencies are there just to make sure that U.S. exporters have the same support that their German, French, and Japanese competitors have.

INTERNATIONAL SALES OPPORTUNITIES

Two dynamic markets that can provide fascinating international sales opportunities are the European Union and China.

The European Union as a Competitive Force

The primary objectives of the European Union are to promote balanced and sustainable economic and social progress. It has been designed to provide the creation of an area without internal frontiers through the strengthening of economic and social cohesion and through the establishment of an economic and monetary union, ultimately including a single currency. The European Commission is the EU's executive. It initiates EU policy and acts in the general interest of the EU.

For example, the EU Commission is responsible for regulating certain sales-related activities, such as direct marketing. Direct marketing involves actions that provide direct access to the customer. The primary direct marketing tools are direct mail, door-to-door selling, and telemarketing. It would be essential for a firm planning a sales effort in Europe to understand the EU restrictions of a direct marketing campaign in Europe and what is specifically allowed.

The EU poses a restrictive force on sales competition within Europe since the European Commission can scrutinize outside firms that attempt to enter its markets.[18] Under EU rules, the European Commission has the power to block certain transactions or force restructured terms. The European Commission recently demonstrated this with its investigation into Dow Chemical Company's planned purchase of the former East German chemical works, saying the deal's government subsidy, which it estimated at 11 billion marks ($7.80 billion), appeared excessive. Dow agreed to take over the Buna, Boehlin, and Leuna chemical factories near Leipzig from Germany's Treuhandstalt, the agency charged with privatizing the assets of the former East Germany. The transaction, if completed, would significantly boost Dow's earnings over the next several years. Under commission rules, governments are free to make investments, but they can conduct bailouts only under strictly defined conditions.[19]

Fact Finding

As an example of how the fact-finding process can work for a global sales effort within the EU, Business Cooperation Centers (BCC) exist as sources of information to help small businesses increase their competitiveness. This is done by getting businesspeople in the EU partners, publicizing opportunities, assisting with the negotiation of cooperation agreements and helping with obtaining referrals for customers. There are several steps to follow when using the BCC. First, send a cooperation profile which is a self-description of the firm. Next, information is published in localized channels such as the industry press, bulletins, magazines, or databases and if the firm is interested they can contact the local publication or BCC central unit. Each cooperation is valid for six months with the possibility of six-month extensions and the BCC service is free. In addition, the EU has the Business Cooperation Network (BCN) which provides similar services as the BCC but is available for partners, intermediaries, or advisors. The purposes and services available when using a BCN include finding distributors for goods, transferring or adapting a new technology, granting or acquiring licenses, penetrating new markets, and taking part in community programs such as training, financing, or research.

There are always sources of valuable customer-related information available for a global sales effort at either the beginning or later stages of the sales process.[20] An effective fact-finding process should use local contacts that the firm may have in that market, along with the local chamber of commerce, the local embassy, customers already in the market, or a press officer of any government regulatory organizations in the country targeted for sales penetration.

Direct Marketing in the European Union

Direct marketing is a general term to describe a wide selection of techniques, using various media, that requires a direct response from the consumer (either the individual or business to business). Direct marketing can be used to sell products directly from distributors or producers. Selling and related practices have a long tradition in the European Union. The European Union has adopted certain legislation to protect customers during the selling process. Primarily, this involves a "cooling off" period of at least seven days that is available to customers should they decide to change their minds after a purchase.

Solutions to Defining Business Parameters in the European Union

Regulations affect advertising and direct marketing to an important extent, and still vary from country to country. Most EU member states have self-regulatory as well as regulatory standards and various forms of codes of conduct.

The principle of "Proportionality" is then used to resolve a business policy practice of one EU country that conflicts with that of another EU member state. Proportionality requires that the business measures adopted impose "*minimum restrictions*" on member-state governments or market operators, *while guaranteeing the "effective realization of the policy objective."*[21]

1. *Basic Rule:* The EU will try to resolve the identified problem with the lightest form of intervention in market functioning on national regulatory systems.
2. *Overriding Consideration:* All measures, when testing EU intervention, must be judged by their effectiveness in removing the targeted obstacle to free circulation. The EU must realize that "adopted measures" may not be "sufficiently robust" to overcome obstacles.
3. *Legislative Action:* EU legislative action may be avoided through reliance on voluntary self-regulatory measures such as codes of good conduct or undertakings by private parties.
4. *Significant Differences:* With significant differences in regulations between member countries, "harmonization" of specifications are required before a product that is made based on one set of specifications can be placed on all EU member-state markets.
5. *Basic Goals:* The EU market goals strive to ensure the minimum amount of uniformity concomitant with unrestricted cross-border business, and movement as well as to keep the internal market from being seen as synonymous with uniform and rigid legislation. The sales process in the EU faces various

regulations between member states that warrant some background knowledge prior to effective sales penetration.

China

Current Environment

A dynamic China has emerged, and as an economic force, it is entering and altering the global marketplace on its own terms (see Table 3.2). While Japan's trade deficit amounted to $14 billion, and while Europe's has doubled to more than $13 billion, China accumulated a $35 billion trade surplus with the United States last year. China's already large economy is set to double in the next eight years, making it the world's sixth largest. For Americans, however, China combines all the emotional issues: the fear of job losses, a human-rights record that still offends American values, and fears of military confrontation.

Until now, growth has come mostly from manufacturers that took advantage of the country's immense pool of cheap labor, where wages average around $100 a month. Increasingly, though, these companies are moving to more advanced products. Within four years, China expects to ship out $100 billion worth of electronics and machinery. It may soon become one of the world's biggest exporters of color TV's, auto parts, and cellular phones, and will also start offering engines, power generators, and computer tomography scanners. There are some infrastructure inadequacies in transportation, telecommunications, housing, water technology, and energy that may pose major obstacles

TABLE 3.2. China's Growth

	Gross Domestic Product Exports	(Billions of Dollars)
1991	375	75
1992	425	85
1993	510	90
1994	600	120
1995	650	160
1996	700	170
2000	950	200

to growth. However, despite China's macroenvironmental challenges, it has created lucrative sales and market potential. This has made it an attractive target for global revenue opportunities.

Potential market growth projections in China from the years 1995 to 2000 suggest that demand for products such as telephones, VCRs, air conditioners, beer, consumer electronics, washing machines, and detergents will grow rapidly. This is attributed to a greater number of households that have crossed the consumption threshold for these products, increased their income per household, and now have greater access due to advances in logistics and distribution. China could become the second largest economy in the world, in absolute size, by 2010.[22]

China's current growing population of 1.2 billion people, represents the bulk of tomorrow's world growth. China has successfully stimulated its growth through various creative economic policies. These have involved the development of economic zones, foreign investment incentives, and the encouragement of foreign investment that has accelerated growth. China's pharmaceutical market at $8.1 billion with an expected growth to $19 billion by the year 2000, is the sixth largest in the world. Sales competition between the five major vendors in the personal computer industry in China (Compaq, AST, IBM, Legend, and Hewlett Packard) continues to stay active. The Chinese government's one child per family rule gives children an exalted position in society, thus the major computer vendors are targeting them as a segment that can use computers for future personal advancement. China has become the second largest recipient of foreign direct investment in the world since 1993, with an inflow of $34 billion in 1994.[23] As China continues to grow rapidly as a superior global market area, it will be a major challenge for sales organizations to participate in that key area.

SOME REASONS TO SELECT CHINA

Shanghai

The Shanghai Pudong New Area has become a priority investment spot for foreign businesspeople. The development of Pudong in opening itself to the outside world is an important symbol of China's policy of reform.

Shanghai, a city located at midpoint of the so-called Asian Economic Corridor, is a major economic center in China. For more than a hundred years, Shanghai has always been an important gateway to the Chinese market for capital and merchandise transactions. Ever since the Chinese government made the decision to develop and open up Pudong in 1990, unprecedented changes have taken place there (see Table 3.3). The economic strength of the Pudong New Area has grown quickly with its GDP having increased at an average annual rate of 20 percent. The goal is to build a modern business center in twenty to thirty years.[24] The goal of Pudong's beginning in 1990 was to create a good investment climate; currently, it boasts 3,800 joint ventures. Some of the benefits of doing business there include a two-year income tax abatement and a 50 percent tax abatement in the following three years. For technology-related enterprises the tax abatement is extended even longer.

TABLE 3.3. All Foreign Investment in Pudong

	Projects	U.S. Dollars (billions)
1995	3501	9.1
1994	2663	5.9
1995	1628	3.3
1992	704	1.5
1991	170	.30

Tianjin

Ever since 1980, when the first enterprise with foreign investment commenced business, the investment climate in Tianjin has seen substantial improvement. At present, there are over 6,000 enterprises founded with foreign or overseas investment. The investment sphere encompasses industries such as manufacturing, agriculture, science and technology, advisory services, and real estate ventures. Being one of the major industrial and commercial cities in China, Tianjin is a hub of communication and a distribution center for domestic and foreign trade.

The Tianjin Trade Commission service center helps with the procedure to obtain a joint venture. Tianjin is an old coastal city that has a population of 9.3 million people. The Tianjin Economic and Technology Development Area (TEDA) was set up on December 6, 1984 and ratified by the State Council. It is an economic zone which enjoys the favorable terms and flexible policies for China's special economic areas, and its main function is to establish equity joint ventures, contractual joint ventures, and exclusive foreign investment enterprises. The objective of TEDA is to provide conveniences to investors, and to let investors make profits. Its developmental aim is to set up a world-oriented economic center spearheaded by international trade based on modern industries, and which is well coordinated with the development of finance and commerce. The Tianjin Port Free Trade Zone was approved in 1991. The Tianjin Port Free Trade Zone allows exclusive foreign-invested enterprises, equity joint ventures, and contractual joint-ventures as well as Chinese approved funded enterprises to hold sale promotion exhibitions, auctions, and other forms of international trade. These enterprises are also permitted to do import and export business in conformity with the regulations of the state. The city is also known for business activity in such fields as petrochemicals, metallurgy, light industry, textiles, electronics, mechanical machinery, and oil and gas development. Due to foreign investment over the past ten years, the city growth rate is about 14 percent annually. Foreign investment in 1996 was $40 billion.

The reasons for this growth are as follows:

1. A good environment for investment exists.
2. City government helps foreign investment with resources. Preferential policies are also available that help foreign investors set up factories and share preferential tax treatment.
3. Available labor personnel is favorable. For example, 10,000 undergraduates receive degrees annually, and industrial workers in the north and from rural areas in Tianjin are trained by specialized trade schools.
4. There is a basic need for foreigners to provide modern equipment and technology. With these types of partnerships enterprises will work quite well.

For example, the Huayuan Hi-tech Industry Development Co., Ltd. (HHID Co., Ltd.) is a comprehensive development and administration enterprise approved by the Municipal Government of Tianjin as a legitimate business body for the overall operation, development, and administration of Huayuan Hi-tech Industry Development Area (HHIDA). The purpose of setting up HHID Co., Ltd. is to establish and develop hi-tech industries in HHIDA, to complete the cultivating process of converting key laboratory inventions into industrial products, and to develop HHIDA gradually into a coordinated and comprehensive hi-tech district integrating research, development, production, trade, finance, consulting, training, and service. HHID Co., Ltd. is a group company with the full capacity for industrial development, construction, service, and trade.

Treatment and Customs Policies may apply as follows:

- For hi-tech enterprises in HHIDA that may be applicable, a reduced income tax rate of 15 percent will be applied. For newly-established hi-tech enterprises, the income tax will be exempted for the first two years of production.

- For foreign-invested production enterprises approved as hi-tech enterprises and with an operation period of more than ten years, the income tax will be exempted for the first two profit-making years and half of the income tax will be exempted for the following three years.

- Import customs duty will be exempted from raw materials and spare parts imported for the production of export products.

- Except those restricted by the state or other regulations, export customs duty for the exportation of products will be exempted.

- The import customs duty for importing apparatus and equipment which cannot be produced in China will be exempted for hi-tech enterprises and enterprises with foreign investment.

- Rapid depreciation is applicable to the apparatus and equipment used for the development of new technology and manufacturing of hi-tech products.

Investors are encouraged to invest in HHIDA and set up enterprises engaged in or related to the development, production, or processing of high-tech products and the application and utilization of technology in the following fields: Electronics, Aerospace Technology, Life Science, Material Science, and other new technologies.

Beijing

Beijing, the capital of China, has the unique role of being the political center of the world's fastest-growing country. As an historical and cultural city, it is the nation's hub. As an industrial city, it is second only to Shanghai and as an international city, it accommodates foreign embassies and international organizations. Furthermore, tourism has already become the pillar of the city's service sector, with tourism revenue accounting for more than 40 percent of the tertiary industry. This is even more significant considering the fact that the city's tertiary industry now makes up 47.6 percent of its overall income, and foreign exchange revenue from tourism and the number of foreign visitors to Beijing both account for a quarter of the national total. Beijing is the center for financial decision making and financial macrocontrol. All Chinese banks have their headquarters there and most foreign banks in China have their branch offices or agencies in the city. Also the State Planning Commission in Beijing is focusing on bringing five key industries— autos, electronics, petrochemicals, machinery, and building materials—into the twenty-first century.

Although the Beijing People's Congress meeting takes place annually for the municipal government, it is of greater significance than the previous ones due to the discussions it held on the development plans of the city. With the short-term five-year plan (1996-2000) and the long-range fifteen-year blueprint approved at the meeting, Beijing has entered a new stage of social and economic development. According to the Ninth Five-Year Plan, by the year 2000, Beijing's per capita gross domestic product (GDP) will quadruple that of 1980 and a fairly integral market economic system should be established. In order to achieve this goal, the municipal government has established the following outline:

- During the 1996-2000 period, Beijing's GDP will grow at an average annual rate of 9 percent.
- By the year 2000, the proportion of industry, agriculture, and the service industry will respectively account for 4.5, 45.5, and 50 percent of GDP.
- The total import and export volume of commodities will reach $9 billion.

- The rise of commodity retail prices will gradually go lower than the economic growth rate.
- Technological progress will contribute 50 percent to the economic growth and most of the city residents will receive at least a high school education.
- The population of permanent residents in Beijing, currently about 9 million, will be controlled to within 11.25 million.
- The per capita income of urban residents and the net per capita income of rural residents will both increase an average of three to five percent annually.

The Beijing Municipal Foreign Economic and Trade Commission routinely uses a delegation to visit nations to attract foreign investment in Beijing. The trade tour has already brought some investments into Beijing. The Osem International Ltd. from Israel signed a letter of intent to invest several million U.S. dollars on an industrial project in food production. Other successful foreign investment ventures in Beijing are discussed in Table 3.4.

Motorola

Motorola is an example of a U.S. corporation that has had success with customer development in China. It is one of the world's leading providers of wireless communications, semiconductors and advanced electronic systems, components, and services. Its major equipment businesses include cellular telephone, two-way radio, paging and data communications, personal communications, automotive, defense and space electronics, and computers. Motorola semiconductors power communication devices, computers, and millions of other products.

The fundamental objective of the company is total customer satisfaction. Motorola maintains sales, service, and manufacturing facilities throughout the world, conducts business on six continents, and employs more than 142,000 people worldwide. Motorola is well established in China as more than 10 percent of its sales are occur in China, and they employ over 6,000 Chinese associates. It is one of the fastest growing markets for Motorola in the world.

Motorola will increase its sales and market penetration in the China Market in the twenty-first century. Pagers do best because

TABLE 3.4. Foreign Investment Projects in Beijing

The Mitsubishi Stone Integrated Circuits Company, a Sino-Japanese joint venture, put down a total investment of $90 million to produce 120 million integrated circuits in Beijing. The Beijing Matsushita Color Kinescope company increased investment from 47.12 billion yen to 72.18 billion yen to manufacture 800,000 color kinescopes and 3 million display tubes each year. Both contracts were signed recently.

Beijing Nokia Mobile Telecommunications Ltd., a joint venture between Nokia Group in Finland and Beijing Telecommunications Equipment Factory 506, was officially inaugurated in Beijing. Following the production of digital and analog mobile phones for both GSM and E-TACS systems, the joint venture is now ready to produce base stations for the GS digital cellular networks. It has already secured several contracts and systems deliveries in Zhejiang and Yunnan provinces, and their mobile phones are sold throughout China. Headquartered in Helsinki, Finland, Nokia is a global telecommunication systems and equipment manufacturer, providing mobile telephones in most digital and analog standards. Nokia Group had net sales of $8.4 billion in 1995 and has approximately 34,000 employees worldwide. Beijing Telecommunications Equipment Factory 506 of Ministry of Posts and Telecommunications is under the supervision of Post and Telecommunication Industry Corporation. It is engaged in designing, manufacturing and distributing the telecommunication equipment. Both sides are confident that the joint venture will develop into an important contribution to the Chinese mobile telecommunications industry.

Up to now, the number of the Airbus-manufactured aircraft to be sold and leased to China has reached forty. In terms of passenger aircraft, Airbus products constitute less than 10 percent of the Chinese market, but in terms of wide-body planes, the company occupies almost half of the market. As a long-term plan, the company is attempting to win orders for half of the aircraft needed by China in the coming two decades. Their surveys estimate China will need 1,320 aircraft worth $100 billion between now and the year 2014. To win a bigger share of this market, Airbus has earmarked a $50-million investment to construct the CASC Airbus Beijing Training and Service Center. Being the longest range airliner in the world, the wide-body passenger plane, powered by four engines, can seat 280 passengers. Airbus has also signed an agreement with China Aviation Supplies Corp. (CASC) and Air China to supply A340s to Air China. Located near Beijing Capital Airport, the center will be the first training center of Airbus in Asia. It will function as a branch office, a training center, and a place to provide after-sale services.

they meet a customer technology need and they are affordable. Cellular phones are the next highest sold product and are more expensive. Motorola is changing some cellular phone features to make them more attractive to the Chinese consumer. For example, the width will be streamlined. Width is not a problem for Americans with bigger hands, but is far more inconvenient for Chinese users. Also, Motorola will add internal circuitry features and Chinese alphabet characters to make them more useful. These models are under way. Horizon, a new numeric pager, is a joint effort between Motorola Singapore and Tianjin Design Centers. The industrial design was evaluated by Motorola associates in Tianjin and Beijing to represent local consumer tastes. Personal computers are the least sold product because they are expensive as well as being a new product for China.

Motorola has also established a $12 million joint venture named *Shanghai Motorola Paging Products Co. Ltd.* The new joint venture is located in Pudong, Shanghai, and will use Motorola's advanced technologies to produce high-speed FLEX pagers. FLEX pagers, a world-leading advanced paging product featuring superior capabilities including antiinterference, roaming, multispeed automatic scanning and longer battery life, bring more benefits and better services to both the operators and the end-users. Shanghai Motorola Paging Products Co. Ltd. will cover the full scope of research and development, manufacturing, distribution, and postsales service of FLEX pagers. The joint venture will further improve its paging technologies and develop new-generation FLEX pagers. It will also speed up the localization process of its products and offer more opportunities to local suppliers. Annual output is expected to reach approximately 1 million units in the near future. The Ministry of Posts and Telecommunications in China has determined to use the FLEX high-speed paging rules of the U.S. Motorola Corporation as the coding mode and standard of national networked high-speed paging. The authorities of China's telecommunication industry have made this decision to bring their equipement into line with international advanced high-speed paging technology, as a way to speed up the development of the domestic wireless messaging industry.

Motorola Corporation and Leshan Radio Company Ltd. entered into an agreement for a joint venture named Leshan-Phoenix Semiconductor Company Ltd. That venture will become Motorola's semiconductor production center in China. The establishment of Leshan-Phoenix Semiconductor Company Ltd. marks that Motorola has taken a step forward in line with the principle of developing joint ventures in cooperation with China's electronics industry. With a total investment of $53.3 million, the joint venture will become a base in China for Motorola to produce semiconductor products, such as advanced surface mount small signal transistors. To ensure success, the joint venture will adhere to its principles by pursuing first-class international enterprise, winning customers, and marketing best management practices and quality service.

Motorola's sales in China and Hong Kong were $3.2 billion in 1995; this accounts for almost 12 percent of the corporation's worldwide revenues. In addition, Motorola receives income from the chips, pagers, and move cell phones it exports from Tianjin (see Figure 3.1). Motorola Corporation has strong brand equity in cellular phones and pagers. Although personal computer sales are low, the growth rate looks promising with purchases significantly up from last year.

With $1.2 billion, Motorola has the largest investment of any U.S, company doing business in China. Much of Motorola's investment is in Chinese workers. Workers at entry level positions are paid a salary of $125 per month, which is competitive for China. Motorola also provides a home ownership program for its employees in Tianjin and Beijing, which contributes to its standing and acceptance in China. [25]

Sales Process in China

In China, a joint venture agreement is the dominant entry vehicle. Through joint ventures, firms are getting impressive access in China's markets, with 80 percent of car sales, 90 percent of personal computers, and almost 100 percent of telecom equipment. The goal of a foreign joint venture in China is to guide the management of the ventures with the cooperation of local parties by sharing risks, benefits, and promoting market penetration.[26]

Several corporations and organizations have identified other strategic methods that help an effective global sales effort, particularly in China. These organizations include IBM, Merck & Company, Pepsico, Frito-Lay, General Electric, Motorola, Paine Webber, Oppenheimer Management Group, General Mills, Mars Inc., Hew-

FIGURE 3.1. The Future of China's Technology Market (1994-1999)

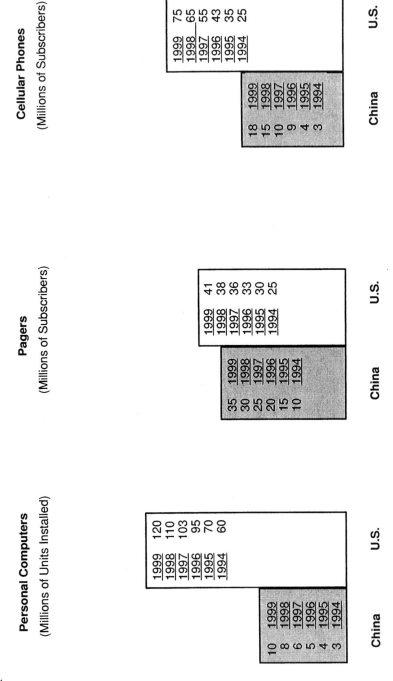

Personal Computers
(Millions of Units Installed)

China		U.S.	
10	1999	1999	120
8	1998	1998	110
6	1997	1997	103
5	1996	1996	95
4	1995	1995	70
3	1994	1994	60

Pagers
(Millions of Subscribers)

China		U.S.	
35	1999	1999	41
30	1998	1998	38
25	1997	1997	36
20	1996	1996	33
15	1995	1995	30
10	1994	1994	25

Cellular Phones
(Millions of Subscribers)

China		U.S.	
18	1999	1999	75
15	1998	1998	65
10	1997	1997	55
9	1996	1996	43
4	1995	1995	35
3	1994	1994	25

lett Packard, Shanghai Pudong New Area International Exchange Center, Tianjin Trade Commission Service Center, Asia American International Inc., Motorola, Price Waterhouse China Consulting, The Equitable, and The Sequa Corporation.[27]

Doing business in China means developing friendships and trust. It is important to get to know customers and let them get to know the sales force or those responsible for customer development. This takes time and it can involve attending functions, joining organizations, pursuing memberships, and performingin ways that demonstrate interest, involvement, reliability, and trust. These actions must occur first before business activity will take place (see Table 3.5). The key factor in reaching and selling to Chinese customers is the ability to identify product or service needs and affordability. Firms must conduct market research prior to entering China to understand the nature of the market and those factors that will help to reach and to sell to Chinese customers. It is also important for firms to have a strategy and a long-term plan to ensure that the product or service meets standards or customer expectations.

What criteria do customers in China use when judging the quality of products or services? As an example, in the beverage industry, a survey by Panorama Social Economic Research Company, Ltd. (PSER) revealed the tastes and trends of Chinese consumers. The survey showed that 60 percent of consumers rate a "natural" taste as their highest priority. The trend toward the natural represents the spread of a modern consuming psychology among the Chinese, which is the trend toward spending a larger share of income on health and pleasure and less on necessity.

On the basis of today's trends, pure and natural, health-improving drinks will probably gain a larger share in tomorrow's beverage market. Chinese consumers have traditionally considered beverages a summer product. However, with the change of lifestyle this notion has dramatically changed; the Chinese now enjoy drinking fruit drinks in winter as well. The PSER survey indicates that already 60 percent of consumers are now in the habit of drinking these fruit beverages during the winter months.

Although the PSER survey, conducted from June to October 1995, indicated that the older, well-established brands enjoy the largest share of the fruit drink market and the highest product identification,

TABLE 3.5. Strategic Customer Development Methods for China

Performance	China Sales and Marketing strategy
	Communication between managers and the sales force
	Corporate office support
	Team selling
	Be achievement-oriented and set up customer objectives
Technology	Use available technology tools such as:
	• Video-conferencing
	• Sales force technology
	• E-mail
	• Internet marketing (where available)
Customer Relationship Building	Networking by interfacing with key decision makers
	Listen to customer needs and share information with them
	Partnering and consultative selling with customers
	Interpersonal sensitivity
	Recognize and respond to marketplace change
Market Awareness	Knowledge of cultural differences and local customs
	Successfully interfacing with the government
	Insights into what constitutes value
	Ability to demonstrate financial return to economy
Staff	Employ a company representative who is knowledgeable about the local market and Chinese language
	Hire within the country
	Recruit and have highly capable people that have initiative and flexibility
Location	Have a physical local presence
	Regularly visit sales organization
Price	Consistent pricing policy

25 percent of the 1,000 consumers surveyed could not recall a single brand name without prompting. Consumers in China know their favorite flavors, but their brand loyalty appears low. However, American and European consumer products such as Coca-Cola or Pepsi Cola are very popular in China. After years of primarily purchasing goods from state-owned factories, when there is a choice, Chinese consumers almost always prefer Western brands; and often, foreign products fulfill an unmet demand. Western-style packages that bear English words also have a powerful allure in status-conscious China, because of the belief that foreign products are superior in quality to domestic goods.[28] For example, Coca-Cola entered a joint venture with a Chinese company to produce a fruit soda called Heaven & Earth or Tianyudi, which has effectively penetrated China's markets.

Ethical Dilemmas

Business opportunities are not the only consideration in pursuing customer development in China. Some of the problem issues range from the aftermath of the 1989 Tiananmen Square massacre: reports that orphans are systematically allowed to die, possible threats of military action with maneuvers off the Taiwan coast, poor treatment of its own citizens, and the imprisonment of U.S. Human Rights Activist Harry Wu. According to the International Intellectual Property Alliance, piracy in China of intellectual property, compact discs, and software totals $2.5 billion.[29] Should U.S. firms rush in "carte blanche" to do business in China despite these dilemmas?

By taking a socially responsible position while doing business in China, some U.S. firms may actually serve as a catalyst in helping China face various dilemmas. It could also facilitate China's economic transition from a planned economy to a market economy. For example, Motorola has developed a supporting educational program called "Project Hope." This helps the 200 million illiterate people in China, who account for 25 percent of the illiterate population in the world. The Project Hope program also helps the one million children in China, annually, who cannot afford to go to school. In addition, Motorola has launched the Employee Home Ownership Program to facilitate home ownership for their employees in Tianjin and Beijing, and they have invested over $300,000 for fellowships in universities in China in the past three years.

In China, the concept of "quanxi" not only means developing a network of good connections, but giving something back to the community. As Motorola has demonstrated, this should be a part of a customer development strategy in China since there is far more at stake than sales revenue.

PROFILE: Ying Xiao, Manager, China Consulting

"Americans are not aggressive enough in taking advantage of China's economy. There are plenty of lucrative opportunities to base a business venture in China. A key selling factor is building relationships, trust, and demonstrating value. To sell effectively in China you must get to know the Chinese people, their culture, and customs. You must also be patient and tolerant when it comes to developing a business relationship because it can take time. Even table manners and etiquette during meals become an important criteria to establish a business relationship in China."

Source: Ying Xiao (June 3, 1996). Personal Interview. Shanghai, China

SUMMARY

Global perspectives are an important dimension of doing business and customer dealings. It is important for the sales force to examine strategic issues for an international sales effort because it cannot only indicate new market opportunities, but can also show different creative and effective sales methods used in other parts of the world. Besides using "face-to-face" selling techniques, knowing "How to Select Target Countries" and "How to Enter Target Countries" can help penetrate international markets. Two markets, in particular, that could pose exciting dynamic sales challenges are the European Union and China.

Questions

1. What is "ISO 9000" and how can it assist a sales effort?
2. When Disney first entered the French marketplace with Euro

Disney, they did not experience as strong a niche as with their Disney park in Orlando, Florida. How would you have recommended they select this target market?

3. What is the "European Union" and how does the concept of "Proportionality" work?
4. Please describe the different ways a sales force can enter a target market.
5. What are the advantages and disadvantages of customer development in China?
6. Are there any actual examples of companies that have had sales success in China? Explain why.

CASE STUDY: MONAHAN'S CANDY

Monahan's is a well-recognized international brand. In developed countries it is regarded as affordable quality chocolate candy. Monahan's is real chocolate and therefore is not found among the very cheap compound chocolate candy, nor does it compete in the very top segment of the market with some Belgian and Swiss manufacturers.

In countries such as Indonesia, Monahan's, by default, finds itself in the top segment of the market. The lower purchasing power of the general population encourages a proliferation of chocolate compound/flavored confections at low price points.

In addition, Indonesia is in the tropics and real chocolate cannot survive in non-air-conditioned outlets as the heat-resistant characteristics are not good. The recipe needs modification if it is to stand up to the climatic conditions.

Monahan's wants to grow its brand and presence in Indonesia but does not want to compromise its name.

Options include the following (or a variation on these):

1. Do nothing. Continue to promote the brand in air-conditioned outlets, typically supermarkets, and wait for the buying power of Indonesians to increase to the point where they can afford to buy real chocolate.
2. Develop a compound chocolate product with heat-resistant characteristics suitable for sales outside of supermarkets of appropriate price points.

Either (a)   *Monahan's branded*

or (b)   *non-Monahan's branded*

3. Market a lower grammage unit of real chocolate to meet an acceptable price point that incorporates heat-resistant characteristics. Maintain strong Monahan branding.

Problem: Managing the Cost Effectiveness of Trade Spend

Description: In Indonesia, Monahan's chocolate candy business commands about 15 percent market share and is number two in the market. The leader, a local company, holds about 65 percent market share.

It is standard practice for manufacturers to buy shelf space in supermarkets. It is not mandatory, but if significant shelving is required, including gondolas, then a deal must be struck. This deal is usually negotiated on an annual basis.

In the case of the leading supermarket chain, which represents about 20 percent of the supermarket universe and 25 percent of sales, the industry ratio of net sales now averages 30 percent. A level of no more than 15 percent is regarded as healthy. This is the problem.

The breakdown of the trade spent is as follows (indicatively):

1. 70 percent shelf rental (defined on a store-by-store basis)
2. 15 percent promotional activities
3. 15 percent sales promoters

The solution should incorporate improving sales and reducing trade spending.

Question

The supermarket chain wants to see a year-by-year increase in spending. How can Monahan's candy effectively penetrate this market?

SECTION IV:
EFFECTIVE SALES FORCE
MANAGEMENT IN A VOLATILE
BUSINESS ENVIRONMENT

Chapter 4

Reengineering

SALES MANAGEMENT AND REENGINEERING

Volatile business conditions have led to drastic corporate downsizing in which sales organizations are expected to do more with less. Sales managers must also be more knowledgeable and possess a more demanding, myriad of business skills, many of which have not even been seen until recently. Many internal and external changes have occurred to organizations that have dictated the need to do business differently. In the external business environment, changes such as technology, globalization, catastrophic business crisis, a more frantic competitive climate, and more demanding, sophisticated customers are examples of some of the shifts in the business environment.[1] Internal changes to organizations have been in the form of reengineering accompanied by structural realignments and downsizing, greater emphasis on quality levels in product and service output, faster communication channels, and a more educated, skilled employee base with higher expectations from management.

By using reengineering, sales managers can make sure that the sales force is ready for any changes that may occur. This occurs by keeping their sales organizations in constant debate and by helping the sales force redesign their working conditions to serve the customer better. Sales managers should make sure that the sales force gets the training and education for the sales tasks they are assigned to perform.[2]

If used as a one-dimensional, quick-fix solution, reengineering will just lead to downsizing and poor strategic business results. More than 3.4 million jobs have been cut by Fortune 500 companies. The results of reengineering efforts have caused increased costs and decreased productivity. The obsession to look good at any price has cost organizations their most valuable resource—capable people. Reengineering that results in staff cuts to save money is not always in the best interest of the organization. The survivors may also feel loss, betrayal, and distrust and become less productive and avoid risk-taking situations. Middle managers alone have been the primary targets for over 20 percent of downsizing efforts.[3]

In a recent downsizing, Bell South projected the elimination of 3,000 employees exclusively in the sales and marketing functions. In fact, over a two-year period the average sales force experiences turnover of about 43 percent and reductions from downsizing of 20 percent. Some of this is due to office consolidations, shifts from the user of a "traditional door-to-door salesperson" to a more "integrated marketing" business type, or cost control.[4]

Reengineering is based on the concept of significantly altering existing models and thinking. It necessitates using dramatic improvements that are accomplished by reinventing the way in which work is done. It is through this method of radical improvement that makes reengineering so different and so compelling. Since reengineering finds better ways to give customers what they want while achieving huge advances in performance, it provides a competitive advantage that impacts the bottom line.

There is a human side to reengineering that helps to drive the entire effort. These human elements can involve vision for the future, new workplace values, involved leadership, teamwork, and customer-driven processes. The changes brought about through reengineering require new skills for people in the sales organization.

A definition of business-process reengineering is, "The radical redesign of an organization's operations and management to achieve strategic breakthroughs." Reengineering means starting over at the beginning by dismantling the way work is done, thinking "outside the box," and then recreating it in a totally new format. This is an effort that has long-term effects.

So if a reengineering effort is so demanding, what motivates an organization to use this process? Customers are a lot more knowledgeable and demanding than ever before. They know what they want and in today's competitive market someone can and will get it for them faster, cheaper, and designed specifically for their needs.[5] Reengineering can recreate the organization so that it becomes competitive, flexible, and moves with greater speed. Reengineering can mean survival.

Business-process reengineering projects have shown that some techniques and methodologies to achieving success involve the use of teams, benchmarking, organizational rationalization, business reviews, data/workflow analysis, redesign, and capacity planning. These are effective tools that can yield positive change.

Reengineering, also known as process innovation and core process redesign, is the search for, and implementation of, radical change in business processes to achieve breakthrough results. Its chief tool is a clean sheet of paper. Most change efforts start with an attempt to restructure existing processes. Reengineering, adherents emphasize, is not tweaking old procedures and certainly not plain-vanilla downsizing. Nor is it a program for bottom-up continuous improvement. Reengineers start from the future and work backward, as if unconstrained by existing methods, people, or departments.

Reengineering should be used primarily for major processes that play a significant role, such as customer service or sales activity. Effective sales reengineering attempts to achieve efficiency by asking: What are our core competencies? Where should we compete? What is our distinctive advantage? How do our customers define value? What changes should we make to adjust to changes in the marketplace?

The key focus with sales reengineering is to work on the process. There is the threat of bringing in changes and even possible job losses, due to competitive and marketplace forces. Then positioning to face these challenges in the form of good leadership, enhancing skills, and team involvement becomes necessary. The result, if successful, is achievement and empowerment.

The strategic approach to sales reengineering involves defining goals and the business process, listening to customers, benchmarking, using tools such as technology where appropriate, developing a reengineering plan of action, and monitoring and evaluating outcomes.

The sales manager can play an essential role during reengineering by bringing the customer into the process. Radical changes in the business environment have dictated the need for reengineering in organizations.[6] These radical changes in the marketplace have involved the following developments:

- technology
- sophisticated customers
- globalization
- company mergers and acquisitions
- rising business and sales costs
- impact of the "quality movement"
- communication volume and speed
- the need for adaptable, flexible, agile organizations

The sales manager's importance to the reengineering process can be to remind the organization that radical process innovation should consider marketplace perspectives and not just the internal perspectives of senior-level management and the company.

Reengineering can bring dramatic process improvements that are too often only demonstrated in individual process areas rather than in sales revenue results. In addition to giving employees and salespeople convincing reasons for the new design and the ability to provide feedback in the form of concerns and suggestions, management must also look outside the organization to the customers for direction.[7]

Times Mirror

Times Mirror Company's stock price nearly doubled as a new chief executive officer accelerated cost-cutting. Almost $800 million in restructuring charges were made, and 2,200 jobs were eliminated. The company repurchased 10 percent of its shares. For all of last year's drama, Times Mirror now faces a difficult task of rebuilding its basic businesses, which range from major metropolitan newspapers, including the *Los Angeles Times, Newsday,* and the *Baltimore Sun,* to professional-information publications and training services, to sports and outdoors-oriented magazines.[8]

The risks are high. "We are keenly aware that if we disappoint our shareholder, our stock price could drop sharply," says Mark H. Willes, Times Mirror's chairman, president, and chief executive officer. "We don't expect anyone to believe we will deliver improved results until we do just that," he adds. "To prosper, Times Mirror and its operations must grow," says the plainspoken executive who was selected from General Mills, where he was vice chairman.

Problems started when California's long recession hit the *Los Angeles Times* hard. From a 1990 peak, annual revenue has slid more than 10 percent to a little over $1 billion. Operating profit fell to a low of about $60 million in 1993 from a peak of more than $200 million. Daily circulation fell almost 20 percent, from a high or more than 1.2 million in 1990 and more than 2,000 positions were slashed.

Under Willes' push for performance, ten newspaper sections that provided mostly local coverage were eliminated. So were 930 jobs, about 14 percent of the work force in all parts of the operation. The organization is under almost endless change as it struggles for efficiency.

With newsprint prices climbing, Times Mirror estimates that its newsprint costs will increase by 25 percent or $40 million. The *Times* has moved to counter such trends. To save newsprint, editors have been asked to cut the space used for news by 3 percent. Among steps being considered are a merger of the paper's entertainment and lifestyle sections and elimination of the Monday business section.

SHIFT OF OPPORTUNITIES

Years of relentless downsizing, "right-sizing," and reengineering in corporate America are all aimed in part at shedding excess bureaucracy. It is certainly true that tens of thousands of middle managers have lost their jobs in recent years, and many face long, painful struggles in trying to gain employment. Even for many managers who stay employed, the flattening of hierarchies cuts promotion opportunities.

Yet other economic forces are offsetting these losses, and creating management work where it did not exist before. The "de-layering" seen in the great reengineering of corporate hierarchies spreads out management work and endows some rank-and-file employees with managerial responsibilities. Technologies that supplant workers require managers to oversee them. The growing complexity of white-collar work increases the need for management in some cases. A shift in management duties toward external dealings with customers, rather than just supervision of employees, blurs the distinction between managers and marketers.

The reality of reengineering is that many more people are in a decision-making mode, thus more people get elevated to a management category. Often changes in the marketplace create new managerial requirements.[9] As the health care business shifts toward managed care, American Home Products Corporation has restructured its sales and marketing procedures. Although the sales force has been cut by 30 percent, managers overseeing medical center accounts have increased fourfold, in part because such accounts require closer attention.

Examples of Reengineering Strategy

General Mills today is a trimmer, more focused foodmaker, with new top management, a reorganized sales force, and manufacturing plants. Mark Sanger, a twenty-one-year veteran of General Mills with a background in marketing, took over when longtime chairman and CEO H. Brewster Atwater Jr. retired.

"We don't want to be the world's biggest food company, but we do want to be the world's most innovative food company," he says. "Food categories are absolutely driven by new products, product improvements, and marketing innovations."[10] Consumers should see a flurry of "new" and "improved" products in coming months as the company seeks to reverse share losses in key categories. Breakfast cereals clearly are its most important category, providing 40 percent of $5.03 billion in sales despite an 8 percent volume decline. To reinvigorate its cereal sales, General Mills has made sugar-frosted versions of two old reliables, Cheerios and Wheaties. Sales to retailers during the first eight days totaled a robust $25 million.

Overseas, where General Mills was a latecomer, Sanger is pushing for rapid growth. Last year international sales accounted for 14 percent of the total. But, if the company exports more fruit snacks, that proportion could be 25 percent by the year 2000. General Mills already sells cereals and salty snacks through joint ventures, and will launch a third, desserts, in Latin America.

In the business world, fat is out and flat is in. Hierarchy breeds bureaucracy and removing it allows people to make their own decisions. This type of empowerment in turn improves efficiency. Many employees are becoming disillusioned by the disappearance of prospects for promotion and other traditional goals in their "de-layered" workplace. Flatter structures explode any illusions about career prospects which many employees are able to maintain in a more hierarchical structure.[11]

GTE's telephone operation generates $16 billion in annual revenues. With competitive challenges, GTE felt it had to offer significantly better customer service. Since GTE concluded that customers want one-stop shopping, it decided to provide one number to fix an erratic dial tone, question a bill, or sign up for call waiting.

The company started with repair clerks, whose job had been to record information from a customer, fill out a trouble ticket, and send it on to others who tested lines and switches until they found and fixed the problem. The next step was to link sales and billing with repair. It has given operators new software so their computers can get into databases that let the operators handle virtually any customer request. This not only eliminated unnecessary work, it has created a 20 percent or 30 percent increase in productivity so far.[12]

A computer company, convinced that customers needed more expertise from its sales force, poured tens of millions of dollars into reengineering its selling operations, training people in consultative sales techniques and outfitting them with costly electronic gear. It turned out that most customers did not care; what mattered to them was price.[13] Listening to what customers are actually saying and acting on what they actually need is an important component of reengineering.

The sales reengineering process can also start with a session listening to the individual priorities of the sales force to develop objectives regarding potential customers, providing a shorter sales cycle to the customer, or supplying salespeople better sales technological tools. Business objectives such as specific revenue results, business orders, and market share should be defined. Increased sales, technical knowledge, and the retention of key accounts with a sales reengineering project that gives clear, well-defined guidelines are essential.

Six Guidelines for Managing Change

Sales force involvement is a critical element for making a change effective and positive.

1. Create a statement of your purpose for doing business and of why the changes are necessary, in clear, memorable, and simple terms.

2. Communicate the changes repeatedly in different settings and through different managers, over time.
3. Answer questions quickly.
4. Provide opportunities for employee input on effecting changes in their areas of responsibility.
5. Be flexible and adaptive in making change a win-win situation for as many employees as possible.
6. Establish a workable timetable.

RESTRUCTURING THE IBM SALES FORCE

IBM experienced major changes during the late 1980s and early 1990s. Their competition was specializing and eating away at technology niches. Customers were looking for more specialized sales support and IBM primarily provided generalist skills. In addition, customers wanted highly responsive vendors at a time when IBM was slow to move due to their large bureaucracy.

During the 1980s and early 1990s IBM was structured by geography, using local teams assigned to customer accounts. These teams had generalist (broad-based functional) business skills and were highly dependent on the marketing support teams located at an area's central location. Whenever a bid was asked for by a customer, the local team had to go through many layers of staff for approval for any special bids or special system's requirements. This procedure could take weeks and the inability to respond quickly caused dissatisfaction with customers.

Customers were frustrated with IBM's high prices because they believed that IBM's competition offered comparably more affordable products. This led to the major restructuring of IBM in the early 1990s in which the corporation reduced their staff levels from a high of 400,000 in 1992, to a low of 225,000 in 1994.

IBM's Sales Structure

To improve its responsiveness and quality of support, IBM made many changes that capitalized on the size of the organization and its greatest resource, its customers and employees. Customer responsiveness was improved by giving salespeople greater authority and by retraining the sales force as specialists.

IBM was able to reduce costs by removing the various marketing support layers. Frequently, these individuals were managers in training, and did not have the skills required to support the field. They were used primarily as liaisons to the development or engineering work force. By reducing this layer and giving the sales force a more direct route to the development groups, IBM has reduced the response time for customer inquiries and this has allowed the development group to become more in tune with customer's needs.

IBM was forced to reduce its product cost structure due to shrinking competitive advantage and differentiation in its product lines. It reduced costs by removing the support team costs from the product and having the customer pay separately for support services. This change did cause problems with those customers who valued their support.

The restructuring efforts forced IBM to look at the sales force skill base and develop a strategy to protect its core competencies that deliver a competitive advantage. Static competitive advantage is no longer realistic. The dynamic changes that the technology industry is experiencing demand flexibility from a company if it is to remain competitive. To meet these changes, IBM has focused on its core skills, in which specialized individuals are constantly being trained. Many of the general skills were viewed as being nonstrategic and became outsourced to outside business partners.

IBM has developed a new sales method for account coverage. It has developed industry verticals where salespeople are trained to understand a specific industry and provide particular solutions to IBM customers. The territory sales areas, based on location, were eliminated and account coverage is maintained through the industry verticals. The following text outlines the steps in providing account coverage.

Accounts are now handled by the industry sales representative who is responsible for the ongoing efforts with the customer as well as for overall customer satisfaction. When a customer need arises, the salesperson will contact the appropriate systems specialists to assist in addressing the solution. The *team selling* concept allows IBM to match their expert with the customer's expert. For example, a salesperson who knows store systems and POS devices will work with the customer's store systems group, while an IBM communication specialist works with the customer's communication group. This type of approach has allowed IBM to provide better service to their customers through greater industrial and technical knowledge.

As a means to get the sales force more focused on customer needs, IBM has begun to regularly monitor customer satisfaction levels. All of IBM's sales force, administration, and headquarters personnel are evaluated and compensated based on customer satisfaction. IBM believes that its customer relationships, developed over the past fifty years, are its most important resource and that these relationships must be protected.

In another step to reduce costs, IBM shifted to a mobile work force. The introduction of a mobile work force and the development of industry verticals were both significant changes for the sales force. Salespeople could no longer meet with their management or peers on a regular basis to strategize; they did not have administrative support available to them to assist with daily tasks; and they no longer had the convenience or comfort of having their own cubicle. To successfully make this change, IBM had to provide the sales force with the proper tools.

All sales support individuals were given a notebook PC with a modem, and PC software to support their sales efforts. The software packages included a word processor, a spreadsheet, a presentation package, fax capabilities, daily planners with a directory, software update utilities, and a package to tie into IBM's mainframe systems such as e-mail, product, and customer information. These systems provided the sales force with the tools required to accomplish their customer support goals. Since the move to these systems was quite radical for IBM, it spent a great deal on training to assist the sales force.

IBM has also developed a new opportunity analysis software package to support the sales force in its new work environment. This system was designed to manage and improve account coverage by optimizing resources. Due to the reduction of the sales force, the salespeople now have larger territories and more customers. The opportunity analysis software was designed to assist the sales manager in prioritizing opportunities and allocating the proper resources to an opportunity.

The modified sales process works in this manner. Someone in IBM will be contacted about a customer opportunity. This person could be anyone in the organization. Based on the type of customer opportunity, it will be forwarded to the appropriate manager. This manager will either assign the customer opportunity to a salesperson or designate a business partner. If IBM does not offer a solution for this problem, the customer will be notified. Once the customer is contacted, the system will be updated to acknowledge the request. This step improves customer service by providing a response to all customer requests. It also ensures that IBM is maximizing all of its customer opportunities by using a tracking system. Once the customer is contacted, relevant information about the customer opportunity, such as, revenue potential, skills required, and time frame will be recorded in the system. A customer opportunity owner will be assigned to the account and this person is responsible for updating the system on any changes throughout the sales process.

This system offers many benefits to IBM, including improved customer service and improved resource optimization. One of the drawbacks is that the system is only as good as the inputted information. Despite this drawback, the system is viewed as a tool for better customer service. The ultimate measure of the success of the new sales process is having a system that maximizes IBM's profitability and addresses the customers' needs to their complete satisfaction.

The layoffs caused by IBM's restructuring created morale concerns. IBM has addressed these issues by investing heavily in sales force training. All sales support individuals go through three-week long training sessions. These classes focus on "empowerment," territory management, time management, and PC training. However, the flattening of the sales force infrastructure has also reduced the number of growth opportunities for the salespeople.

One of IBM's strengths in the past was the large size of its sales force. Many customers felt secure in knowing that IBM always had someone available to assist them. However, the cost of this service reduced IBM's price competitiveness. IBM was required to remove this support layer so that its price structure could remain competitive.

HEWLETT-PACKARD AND REENGINEERING

The Hewlett-Packard (HP) Telecommunications Sales Organization has recently decided to reorganize its sales districts in an effort to target two large telephone companies. A fourth sales district was formed in order to generate sales of specialized telecommunications equipment into these two companies. Hewlett-Packard has been successful in selling these specialized products into the rest of the telephone companies.

The market potential for specialized telecommunications equipment for each telephone company was determined to be $100 million a year. Based on sales to other telephone companies of similar size, HP's sales potential to each telephone company is 20 percent of the market potential or about $20 million a year.

HP has never been strong in selling products to the telecommunications services industry, especially the telephone companies. Any sales previously made to telephone companies was limited to their management information systems departments.

Recently HP has built several applications for the telecommunications industry specifically targeting the telephone companies. One such application is the HP Video Server. The Video Server is a component for the Video Dial Tone services that the telephone companies are trying to launch in order to compete against cable TV companies. It is capable of storing thousands of video movie titles and transmitting them simultaneously to hundreds of homes. This applications cost in the range of 3 to 15 million dollars depending on the configuration of the system. The sales cycle to sell this system typically takes one to three years. HP has been successful in selling this product to the other telephone companies.

Once accounts managers have been brought on board, they need to go through the HP orientation process. Although there is a significant time pressure to get new salespeople to generate enough revenue to meet the three-year sales objective. HP has lost new salespeople, especially from small companies that became overwhelmed with their size and bureaucracy. The new salespeople also needed to be trained on HP products but not in as much detail as the product specialists.

HP has recently issued notebook PCs to most of its sales force. These tools have improved productivity tremendously when large systems such as video servers and data collection systems are sold. It has helped in customizing sales presentations and creating sales proposals. However, HP still has not yet implemented a groupware application such as Lotus Notes.

Team selling requires coordination and communication among the members of the team. It is imperative to understand what each team member is doing in the account. The team needs to have a common database of customer lists and associated activities. When generating a proposal, various people, including the factory engineers, need to verify proposal information. Quotation of a system usually requires several layers of management signoffs. Various commitments need to be documented. A groupware application such as Lotus Notes will be able to address all these issues and more. Such an application, if implemented well, will increase the speed and flexibility as well as accountability of a large system team selling effort, and will give HP a competitive advantage.

PERSONNEL RESTRUCTURING

Reengineering does not just relate to a radical redesign of business processes in organizations; it relates to individuals in the sales organization as well. To properly reengineer it is important to have a job description and assess the actual job skills based on that job description.

- Is any professional training needed for management, interpersonal or computer skills?
- Stay aware of the general workflow of any adjoining divisions.
- Attend industry informational seminars and trade shows.
- Make positive business connections with external professionals.
- Keep an updated resume.
- Set a career path.
- Assist in the restructuring process.
- Keep a positive self-image by being confident.

Figure 4.1 diagrams an efficient sales organization.

FIGURE 4.1. Streamlined Efficient Sales Organization

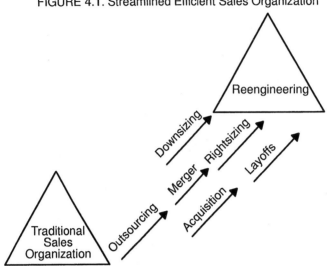

OUTSOURCING

Downsizing and outsourcing are opening tremendous opportunities for small companies.

The secret to making a deal is twofold. First, determine what a big company needs to increase sales or improve customer service; second, find the contact person and make a presentation. Large companies have realized that the world has changed and that many innovations are coming out of small companies.[14]

The core competence/concept helps top managers answer the fundamental question "What should we do?" And the business processes perspective addresses the question "How should we do it?" Some activities are performed so much better than the competition and are so critical to end products or services that they can be described as core competencies. When a series of activities are organized into a system that works better than the sum of its parts, this business process can also create competitive advantage, even if component activities by themselves do not.

Outsourcing involves contracting out significant support activities that would be prohibitively expensive or even impossible to duplicate internally. By identifying the firm's own resources based on a set of core competencies to distinguish itself from competitors and providing value to customer, outsourcing can decrease risk, shorten cycle times, lower costs, and create better responsiveness to customer needs.

In the process of outsourcing it is important to do the following:

- *Evaluate costs.* Try to determine just how much is being spent on a function and whether or not it can be done more cheaply by an outside company or individual.
- *Set objectives.* Realistically decide what an outsource partner can do for the company. Whether it is to cut costs, improve focus, or release resources, make certain the goals are attainable.
- *Be cautious.* Do not select an outsource partner without careful examination.
- *Monitor.* If you decide to outsource, set up regular performance reviews or similar criteria to measure the provider's performance. Outsourcing isn't an excuse to overlook an aspect of your business.
- *Be flexible.* Even after deciding to outsource, look at ways it can be improved. Do not be afraid to make changes in the ways a process is being handled.
- *Avoid jumping on the bandwagon.* Just because outsourcing is a growing trend does not mean it should be automatically embraced. If a change is not needed, do not make one just for the sake of it.[15]

PROFILE: Robert Palmer, Chief Executive Officer, Digital Equipment

"Reengineering and restructuring has to be a forward-looking corporate strategy. It is a way to strengthen the foundation for a company's long-term success. The reengineering process has relevance to sales, because it's done in response to competitive marketplace realities, customer needs, and requires agile, difficult action to achieve industry leadership."[16]

SUMMARY

Reengineering is a concept and tool that is the radical redesign of business processes. Its origins come from radical changes that have occurred in recent years in the marketplace. Accordingly, sales managers and the sales force should play an active role in a company's reengineering efforts, since they have direct dealings with customers and have an appreciation for marketplace perspectives and changes. Outsourcing is an activity in which companies more actively depend on competent resources from outside the organization to support their various functions.

Questions

1. Explain "reengineering" and why it has particular relevance to sales managers and the sales force.
2. What should an organization consider when experiencing "reengineering?"
3. Give some examples of sales organizations that have been "reengineered" and discuss how it was handled.
4. What is outsourcing?
5. Take the opportunity to develop your own plan for "personal restructuring."

CASE STUDY: COPELAND CORPORATION

Brief Description

Copeland Corporation (Incorporated in 1910) is a privately held manufacturer's representative in the plumbing and heating industry. They represent numerous manufacturers, under exclusive contracts, and trade throughout New England and upstate New York.

Copeland is divided into three major divisions designated as Wholesale Heating, Wholesale Plumbing, and Commercial. The largest of the divisions is the Wholesale Heating department followed by Wholesale Plumbing and last, Commercial.

They have offices in Buffalo and Albany, New York, Rocky Hill, Connecticut, Randolph, Massachusetts, and Portland, Maine. Their headquarters are located in the Randolph facility and they have distribution warehouses in Rocky Hill, Randolph, and Norwood, Massachusetts.

They are organized into six profit centers defined as Buffalo, Albany, Rocky Hill, Randolph Heating, Randolph Plumbing, and Randolph Commercial. The Buffalo and Albany profit centers are managed by the same person while the rest have individual profit center managers. All of their managers have more company responsibility than just that required to effectively manage their centers.

Copeland employs 128 people of which 30 are outside sales (12 commercial, 11 wholesale heating, and 7 wholesale plumbing) and 24 are inside sales (6 commercial and 18 combined heating and plumbing).

Ellen Voss is a VP of the company responsible for: (1) forecasting, sales, and marketing for the Wholesale Heating group. (2) the total Inside Sales group in the Randolph office. (3) communication on all heating issues for the whole company, and (4) control of all heating product pricing, margins, and selling programs for the whole company.

The Problem

The company needs to "reengineer," "refocus," and "revitalize" the outside heating sales force.

The heating and plumbing distribution business is changing rapidly. Although, it has been well behind other industries for years, it is quickly recognizing the competitive need to reduce operational costs and increase efficiencies. It is also enhancing productivity through technological advances, restructuring the inside support staff, and refocusing outside sales. In addition it is adding, and expecting from its vendors, diverse forms of value-added services. It is measuring the results of its activities to create benchmarks for itself which will raise the bar for industry standards.

Copeland is seeing consolidation within their customer base through acquisitions, mergers, and bankruptcies. They are also experiencing the consolidation of the product lines which those remaining customers are willing to stock, market, and sell.

Orders are no longer taken by the outside sales force. Rather, they are telephoned in, faxed in, or EDI-d in by wholesale customers. *Thus, the role of the outside sales force has changed and this has caused a highly talented and successful outside sales staff to now be unsure of their direction, feel resistant to change, and be fearful of their future.*

In addition, both the end user and the contractor have become more sophisticated. The contractor, like the wholesaler, is going through a cost-reduction metamorphosis due to increased competition, as well as the increased threat presented by the home centers. The outside sales force is being asked to take care of field problems in all their various forms (including those of the home owner) within the distribution channel. *This has led to a decrease in available selling time, a lack of focus on targets and goals, and an increasing frustration level at not achieving the numbers.*

Ellen's mode of operation is to allow the outside force to manage their own territories. As territorial managers they are responsible for all sales, revenues, and expenses connected to their account base. Ellen's role has been one of helping to set realistic goals and targets, guiding and helping as needed, and coordinating and transmitting incoming field information to their manufacturers in order to generate the sales tools needed.

Copeland is also changing as it evolves from a "family-owned" business to a small "corporation;" a move that they believe is necessary to face the shifting sands of their industry and the peculiarities of their market.

So, the problem is that the outside sales force feels remote. They are not in touch with all of the internal changes or the reasons for those changes. Despite repeated explanations and discussions in sales meetings, they still do not fully see, let alone understand, the changes taking place within their own customer base. They are therefore uncomfortable, unwilling to adapt, and resistant to change. They are unfocused and have become reactive rather than proactive to sales situations.

Question

This is a highly talented sales force. It is Ellen's responsibility to bring them through this time of difficult change. She is looking for ways to instill them with a creativity which will assure their futures. How would you advise her to proceed?

Chapter 5

Crisis Management

INTRODUCTION

The occurrence of a crisis and its aftermath can have a devastating effect on a company's sales. Crisis is a major, unpredictable event that has potentially negative results.[1] Crisis management routinely deals with issues affecting the virtual survival of the corporation. Sales managers are those people in charge of the sales effort and the various functional responsibilities of the sales force such as customer development, planning, controlling, budgeting, and decision making. They are particularly at risk when confronting a crisis and their inability to effectively handle the crisis can significantly change the ability of the sales force to generate revenue. Accordingly, sales managers should understand the dynamics of how to prepare for and manage "worst case scenarios." Like it or not, future events will most assuredly cause harm.

Traditionally, crisis management has been viewed negatively as "managerial fire fighting" or waiting for things to go wrong and then rushing to limit the damage. So, predicting problems not only requires a strategy to anticipate crisis situations like consumer protests or negative public relations. Crisis management also requires a plan of action once the crisis has occurred. For every $100 million in revenue, two incidents per year occur that call on a company's emergency response plan. For every $8 billion of revenue, there is one major loss per year, representing about one percent of annual sales. One catastrophic loss every ten years equals 1.5 times annual profit.[2] These catastrophic losses also include one or more serious injuries or deaths to employees. This is even more alarming considering that most companies do not even have a strategic system to anticipate and solve crisis situations.

About 50,000 U.S. companies reached the point of ultimate failure in 1989 as gauged by Dun & Bradstreet. By 1992 the number of failures had nearly doubled, to 97,000. Each year many thousands more head down the path to failure by losing ground to competitors or watching a key piece of business disappear.[3] Sales managers must develop cultures that foster and reward the management of crisis. They must continually update crisis management policies to ensure that they reflect changing industry dynamics.

Why do corporations fall short of objectives? Why do strategies that seemed eminently sensible turn out to be disasters? Just why do successful organizations, which once could do no wrong, suddenly begin to lose their way? As seen from the Barings Bank financial debacle, the role of sales management is crucial in today's global business arena role. Nick Leeson, as the trader who caused the Baring's Bank scandal, essentially performed in a sales role. To guard against billion dollar catastrophes and a host of lesser risks, the best line of defense is a solid crisis management process. Denny's was accused of ignoring six African American customers and had previously settled a federal suit for discrimination with African Americans in California. By 1995 Denny's had paid $54 million to these aggrieved customers.[4] Sales managers must fully integrate crisis management into business practices so that dealing with the crisis is not an after-the-fact exercise.

THE CONSEQUENCES OF CRISIS

Crisis can be characterized as a major unpredictable event that has potentially negative results. It can also be thought of as a turning point for better or worse. The crisis event and its aftermath may significantly change a sales organization and its salespeople, products, services, financial condition, and reputation. So, the real consequences of crisis events to sales managers can mean the loss of future sales and reputation, the loss of consumer confidence, prolonged negative publicity, exposure to lawsuits, declines in stock values and increases in operating expenses.

UNION CARBIDE

In the area of crisis management, few firms have experienced more than Union Carbide. In 1984, gases released from a pesticide plant of an affiliate—owing to a deliberate act of sabotage—killed about 2,000 people in Bhopal, India, and injured many more. The "crisis" as such obliged the company and its Indian affiliate to pay $470 million to the Indian government to compensate victims and survivors. The "crisis" also ultimately depressed the stock price so much that they were subject to an unfriendly takeover attempt. To fight it off, they had to sell off significant portions of the company and use the proceeds to pay a special dividend to the stockholders. To forestall another tragedy of such proportions, Union Carbide's management resolved to create the world's best episodic risk-management system (ERMS), one that ensures senior executive review of substantial risks. This incident really indicates what can be at stake with a crisis.

Starting in 1985, Union Carbide spent five years building a database of information that catalogs hazardous materials stored on site, size of storage tanks, vulnerability of local people to an explosion, and so on. Arthur D. Little, Inc. of Cambridge, Massachusetts, weighed the variables and ranked every one of the company's 1,400 operations. So, when the company initiated its ERMS program, responsibility was assigned to the senior line managers, not the risk manager. The company spent between $5 million to $10 million to develop its ERMS and spends about $1 million a year to manage it.

SEARS

Recently, Sears faced a crisis that caused the erosion of its customers' trust. In an attempt to boost company sales, Edward A. Brennan, Sears company chairman, implemented a new pay structure in 1990 for employees who earned commissions on their sales. A new emphasis was placed on sales quotas. In 1990, departments throughout the stores established new programs designed to generate more profits. The Sears Auto Centers implemented a new pay structure with an incentive system based on the number of parts and services sold. Sears had 868 auto repair shops located around the country, seventy-two of which were in California. The automotive unit accounted for $2.8 billion of Sears's $31.4 billion in 1991 retailing revenues. The commissioned pay structure instructed employees to sell a certain number of repairs or services per eight-hour shift and to sell a specified number of shock absorbers or struts every working hour. Sears rewarded employees with commissions, bonuses, free trips for top sellers, and the assurance of keeping their jobs.

Top managers who became overzealous in pushing sales performance failed to perform the proper management checks designed to ensure that "overselling" did not take place. This omission came to light on June 11, 1992, when the California Department of Consumer Affairs publicly announced its desire to revoke Sears's state license to operate its seventy-two California car centers. They alleged that Sears performed "unnecessary" service and repairs on its customers' automobiles. In December 1990, after complaints against the retailer had jumped by 29 percent, the state of California started its investigation of the Sears Automotive Centers. The Consumer Affairs Agency found that Sears charged an average of $235 for unnecessary repairs. Following California's action, Florida, Illinois, New York, and New Jersey also contemplated charges. In September 1992, Sears agreed to pay $8 million to resolve the California complaints. The settlement included paying the state of California $3.5 million for investigative costs and establishing a $1.5 million auto-repair training program. Also, over 900,000 coupons for $50 would be offered to consumers who purchased and had installed selected Sears automotive products or services between August 1, 1990 and January 31, 1992. In addition, Sears agreed to retain an independent organization that would conduct shopping audits at the auto centers to ensure that overselling did not reoccur. Sears also had to initiate a television and print ad campaign to explain and apologize for the car repair overcharges that cost them an additional $27 million.[5]

The failure to incorporate crisis management information into decision making will sooner or later result in one or several negative events. It may be a major incident, with associated costs, disruption of supply, and loss of market share, claims and litigation, higher costs than competitors due to inefficient resource use, or shutdown by an aroused public. Other crisis scenarios that can impact sales managers can be product tampering or recall, environmental accidents, protests by customers, negative media attention, computer breakdowns, or terrorism (see Table 5.1.)

TABLE 5.1. Strategic Systems in Crisis Situations

Companies that have a strategic system
to anticipate and solve crisis situations

38 %   62%

NO

YES

Source: *Carter Sales Force Survey* (1996).

CAUSES OF CRISIS

One particular cause of crisis is that senior executives too often do not understand the fundamentals of their business. They neglect to ask central questions, such as what precisely is their company's core expertise, what are reasonable long- and short-term goals, what are the key drivers of profitability in their competitive situation. It is a disturbing fact of corporate life in the 1990s that many senior people at very large companies have no idea what made their organization successful.[6]

Without an essential understanding of what the enterprise is all about, decision making becomes capricious and the company drifts. A&P's top bosses, failing to understand that regional market share was the key to profits, closed scores of stores in areas of the country the company once dominated; revenues and earnings plunged. Jostens, the Minnesota-based purveyor of class rings, yearbooks and other products to schools, boasts a thirty-four-year record of consecutive sales and earnings increases until, in the late 1980s, it diversified into computer systems, a field foreign to its senior executives. By 1993 the company was reporting a $12 million annual loss.

Another cause for crisis is corporate leaders who are proponents of streamlining efforts who then pump up their own bonuses while telling the troops to tighten their belts. It can be fatal to the cohesion, focus, and organization needed to respond to a crisis when cynicism and resentment build up because sales managers preach one doctrine and practice another. This brand of managerial hypocrisy goes well beyond pay and perks. Far too many sales managers ignore the human dimension of day-to-day operations, taking actions that violate unwritten rules as well as their stated intentions. They preach the importance of teamwork, then reward individuals who work at standing out from the crowd. They announce a preference for workers with broad experience then denounce job jumpers within the organization. They encourage risk taking then punish good faith failures.[7] Many future failures may take place because of the so-called new deal between workers and employers, in which traditional bonds of loyalty loosen or disappear. For example, the Leo Burnett advertising agency in Chicago, which works hard at employee retention by linking pay closely to performance, provides a more stable atmosphere than most other ad agencies.

Companies that offer employees a sense of long-term stability may satisfy customers and prosper at the expense of less effective competitors.

Poor customer relationship building can also be a cause for crisis. About 91 percent of unhappy customers will never buy again from a company that dissatisfied them and they will communicate their displeasure to other people. Some of the various reasons that customers become dissatisfied with a company are unsatisfactory product or service quality, high price, poor location, lack of attentiveness, complacency, not having a customer complaint system, or presenting a weak public image. In addition, about one-third of all dissatisfied customers leave because they were unappreciated; some of those customers will never complain to the company. So, the failure of sales managers to have a process to monitor and meet customer satisfaction needs can be devastating to a company.

A FRAMEWORK FOR CRISIS SOLUTIONS FOR SALES FORCE MANAGERS

Sales managers can help their organizations cope with crisis by knowing what to do before and after the crisis hits. Here are some steps to follow.

Phase One: Fact Gathering

Fact gathering is an extensive stage in the crisis management process. Certainly this is an important process to determine the best course of action when a crisis occurs. However, fact gathering should take place even before the crisis; actually it can be an ongoing process. Sales managers should determine the amount that their company spends in the region, their impact on the economy, awards and citations received, charitable donations, internal financial considerations, and the historical overview of the company. Information regarding customer dealings and in particular patterns of complaint by customers or regulators are important to know. All of this information from the fact-gathering process not only determines how to respond to a crisis but can have a preemptive impact with regard to those circumstances susceptible to a crisis.

Phase Two: Scenario Development

It is important for sales managers to develop the ability to anticipate and plan for crisis. This can be done by forecasting and developing scenarios with the greatest probability of occurring and estimating outcomes for alternative situations. A written crisis plan should be developed that discusses these things and helps the sales department respond quickly to crisis. Also, role-playing exercises should be given to the sales force to prepare for those contingencies. These scenarios and role plays need not distract sales people from other sales duties and can be done during a sales meeting once or twice a year. For example, the role play could be:

Simulated Drill: A reporter from *The New York Times* calls the office claiming that a man contacted him enraged that his daughter went into convulsions soon after drinking one of our soft drink products. How should this be handled?

The main purpose of the Scenario Development stage of crisis management is to have a process that can identify and address all the relevant elements of crisis readiness.

Phase Three: Communicating Our Message

This stage deals with assigning tasks and accountability and communicating this inside and outside the organization. The formation of a Crisis Management Team is an important tool to help sales managers cope with crisis. A problem with crisis management is that 43 percent of the time managers speak without authorization, 27 percent present incorrect data, and 22 percent take action that complicates the crisis. So, the crisis management team is essential to effectively communicate how the crisis is being handled. Sales managers need to either develop, or be a member of, the crisis management team. The structure of the crisis management team can be as illustrated in Figure 5.1.

The Crisis Management Team should determine who is the most appropriate person to speak for the company. It should develop communication plans to inform employees, decide how to keep customers informed of events, and help establish what media will cover the crisis and who will prepare drafts of news releases and press kits. A press kit addresses external communication by dealing with all potential players and the public. The press kit also deals with internal communication by notifying the Crisis Team members and calling a meeting, immediately sending a memo to all employees detailing the policy, having the press monitored, and possibly even setting up a 1-800 number to provide easy access for questions from the public. The media plays an important role, since in many instances they dictate the existence of a crisis and determine if it has taken place.

Effective crisis management programs establish an independent unit such as the Crisis Management Team, to ensure objectivity and avoid vested-interest specialization. Shared responsibility allows an

FIGURE 5.1. Crisis Management Team

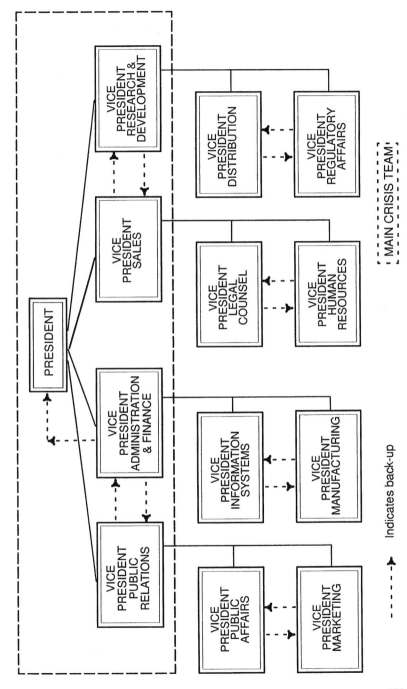

MAIN CRISIS TEAM

Indicates back-up

109

organization to pursue market opportunities aggressively without suffering from excessive adverse exposure due to a crisis. Companies can also establish a system of checks and balances involving sales managers, line managers, senior management, and the independent Crisis Management Team.

A SALES MANAGER'S PREVENTIVE FRAMEWORK FOR CRISIS

Problem Solving

Problem solving characterizes events that are not of crisis proportions, but that occur and have to be resolved. The sales manager's job is inherently a problem-solving job. This means determining how to improve morale, how to motivate salespeople, why sales performance levels are not where they should be, or how to get customers interested in the products or services that are being offered. Instead of selecting the first reasonable solution that becomes available, the sales manager should determine three things. First, defining the problem to differentiate facts from opinion and using all individuals as information sources will help state the problem explicitly. Next, alternate solutions should be generated to find a range of options. All individuals involved should propose alternatives, take into account long-term and short-term consequences and build these alternatives on one another in order to evaluate them in terms of their probable effects. Finally, sales managers should implement these solutions and have a monitoring and feedback system to assess their effectiveness (see Figure 5.2).

Sales Organizational Communication

Good interpersonal skills are no longer a luxury, but a bona fide qualification for effective sales performance. Sales managers spend about 30 percent to 50 percent of their time communicating with subordinates. Problems arise when sales managers believe they communicate more effectively than they do or subordinates believe these managers are more open to communication than they actually

FIGURE 5.2. Levels of Severity Facing the Sales Force

CRISIS MANAGEMENT	MAJOR UNPREDICTABLE EVENT THAT HAS POTENTIALLY NEGATIVE CONSEQUENCES
PROBLEM SOLVING	EVENTS, NOT OF CRISIS PROPORTIONS, BUT STILL DILEMMAS TO BE DEALT WITH
SALES ORGANIZATIONAL COMMUNICATION	ROUTINE, EFFECTIVE SALES ORGANIZATIONAL COMMUNICATIONS

are. Distortion, in which employees suppress information that may be interpreted to reflect negatively on themselves, can also take place with poor sales organizational communication.

To remain competitive and avoid situations that can grow into a crisis, sales organizations must have a responsible process for communicating, sharing information, and getting work done. Sales managers can overcome employee distrust by empowering the sales force, being supportive, open, and actively listening. To overcome distortion, sales managers can use "management by wandering around," keeping the sales force informed, and asking them for their input to maximize the sharing of information.

A Well-Defined Appetite for Crisis

A sales department must clearly define its appetite for crisis in every business area. It also needs a compensation program that rewards appropriate risk taking but discourages managers from taking inappropriate risks. With standards in place, sales areas can be held accountable for how they manage crisis. Making sales managers responsible for managing crisis fosters a culture in which assessing risk potential is an integral part of the decision-making process in product development, in responding to customer requests and in weighing new opportunities.

The problem is that too many companies are content to prepare their organizations only for the predictable snags. In recent years, one of the most common disasters stemming from management shortsightedness is getting stuck with yesterday's technology.[8] The manufacturer contemplating a new product line should be pondering new materials that his customers will be using ten years from now. The company that fails to buy new equipment that knocks a few pennies off costs per ton will almost surely surrender business to cheaper imports.

Staying close to the customer is the business mantra of the 1990s. Many companies continue to fail because they have lost touch with their most important customers. IBM was still pushing giant mainframes when the whole world was cutting costs. Companies that turn out products or services with a traditionally short life cycle are particularly vulnerable when they fail to detect and bend with shifting consumer attitudes. Whatever the business, staying in touch with customers often involves a lot much more than merely running market surveys and focus groups. Smart sales managers increasingly zero in on key customers who no longer want their product or service.[9] The theory behind such exit polling is that you can learn more from your mistakes than from your successes. GM would have known that it was failing ten years before it did if it had tracked customer defections at the right time.

Another customer-tracking technique that can help prevent a crisis is considering the needs of customers all along the value chain, not just the end user. Every company must please the whole series of customers and target audience. Depending on the business, this can be consumers, wholesalers, shippers, retailers, independent distributors, employees, stockholders and the financial community. Only by meeting the needs of each group can sales management remain informed. Former Ford chairman Red Poling, often found that talking with dealers was among the more high-profile proponents of sensitivity to multiple customers. Many companies fail customers because management simply has not trained or used its sales force properly. Salespeople should be allowed to focus on a specific category of customer—high-tech manufacturers, for example—to build expertise. Losing companies often make salespeople peddle a broad line of products to all customers in all markets or in a particular geographic territory. By failing to meet the "customized" needs and expectations of their customers, companies will find that over time they will lose these customers.

SOME SUCCESS STORIES

Rohm Company

Rohm Company, a Japanese firm, earned a record $267 million on revenues of $2.8 billion. Its 17 percent pretax earnings margin compares with approximately 4 percent for Japan's electronics industry as a whole. Rohm is Japan's leading producer of laser diodes, semiconductors that function like phonograph needles in compact disc players. Rohm is also the leading producer of the chips used in computer floppy disk drive motors.

In a country where businesspeople often wait for crisis to strike and then react, Rohm's management has demonstrated an ability to anticipate crisis. Most important, their managers assess the sales effort rigorously, even ruthlessly. In the summer of 1990, Japan's economy was still booming, as were Rohm's sales. Rohm's after-tax profit margins were slipping into the 2 percent range, which is not drastically low by Japanese standards. That same year Sony's net margins were around 3 percent, but Rohm's management was thinking ahead concerning what would happen to margins if sales started to slip.

Not content to wait for answers, Rohm's management shook up the company. They forced Rohm's salesmen to refuse unprofitable and low-margin orders.[10] This was almost unheard of in Japan, where suppliers tend to do just about anything to please a customer. To cut overhead they halted investment plans for some products; divisions were reorganized and jobs were cut. The production of some products, such as large-scale integrated circuits, were shifted to cheaper manufacturing bases in the Philippines and China, closer to their customers' operations. As a result of the changes, Rohm's sales rose by 21 percent, after-tax margins were 9 percent, and profits will grow about 10 percent annually over the next three years.

Honda

Honda has been rebuilding on the inside even as its once gleaming reputation was being muddied by charges that former sales executives were receiving payoffs. Richard Colliver, senior vice president of sales for Honda, has strived to restore trust in the field sales organization and mend fences with irate dealers.[11] One of Colliver's top priorities was regaining the faith of the vast majority of his 1,250 dealers who were not involved in the alleged payoffs. No dealers have been charged, although the FBI continues to investigate some forty dealerships.

Colliver inherited the mess when he arrived from Mazda. He was expected to clean up after his predecessor, S. James Cardiges, whose alleged fraud had already been uncovered by an internal Honda probe. Federal prosecutors now charge that Cardiges, a Honda sales executive, and his predecessor, John W. Billmyer, accepted cash and goodies as large as a $30,000 grand piano from certain dealers. Those dealers also felt compelled to lavish gifts on eleven other executives, most of them Honda and Acura zone managers. To its credit, Honda management is pouncing on the ethics problem. Its most forceful action has been to create a high-level management committee to oversee the appointment of dealers, a responsibility once vested in the sales organization. It will now require all senior managers to file financial disclosure statements.

OTHER TOOLS SALES MANAGERS USE TO DEAL WITH CRISIS

Technology's Role

As many companies have found, the growing complexity and size of funds under custody and management can make traditional risk-management methods obsolete. Thus advanced technology will be increasingly important in the management of crisis. This is especially true of the sales function.

Technology can magnify a single error when many people draw on faulty data in a widely available database. Companies too often fail to install any formal system for distilling and interpreting information from salespeople in the field. The right technology enables a company to obtain real-time information about clients, which is one of the most important capabilities needed to manage risky exposures effectively. For example, with the growth of derivatives, pricing becomes a major challenge. Many formulas that value derivatives are proprietary, making it difficult for custodians to provide independent valuation. Technology that can more clearly differentiate securities holdings is essential.

Companies also need technology to turn the surplus of raw data already available on clients into filtered information that sales managers can use to manage crisis more effectively. Technology helps determine the optimal level of a particular business activity. Various types of sales-related technology in the form of software are available. Some examples are:

Database Management	Relationship Management	
Lotus Notes	ACT	Goldmine
Access	Maximizer	Marketware
Excel	Telemagic	Sharkware

Mavericks

Crisis can bring out a maverick. No blueprints exist for maverick sales management and, by its very nature, maverick thinking defies conventional wisdom and cannot be premeditated. The brilliance of mavericks is evident in their ability to strike out on their own. Maverick managers stand apart by taking ideas such as a flexible workplace or open book management to unprecedented extremes.[12] Perhaps a maverick's greatest challenge is winning the support of employees. This is an important element to have because it is natural for salespeople to feel they are out there alone.

Great mavericks do not all think alike and their ideas can be unorthodox, but they do share an ability to stun the competition with their own personal brand of action. Unconventional leaders can be irritating, threatening, and disruptive for employees and competitors alike, but they are exactly what is called for in time of crisis. Mavericks are no longer oddities; for effective crisis management they are necessities because they will develop creative ways to resolve a crisis.

Customer Advisory Boards

A Customer Advisory Board is a tool that can be used by sales managers to prevent a crisis or minimize the damage should it occur. Customer Advisory Boards are a cost-effective way to find out from the marketplace how to become a firm they would do business with. The advisory board members, who are actual or prospective customers, cannot only provide a fresh perspective on how to prevent problems that can lead to a crisis, but on how to approach business opportunities. An important part of an effective board is the participation of the sales force and of sales managers. Their suggestions will help to target desired board members and frame the relevant issues to be discussed when the board meets. In addition, if they have involvement with the board they are also in the position to build relationships with the members.

The Customer Advisory Board can be comprised of CEOs and presidents or the functional executives that decide where they will direct their business. Members could be selected for their particular expertise. For example, a strategic planner with a good long-range perspective, or a technical expert that understands the features of a product or service might be a good choice. Customers want to believe that a company they do business with cares about them. The formation of a Customer Advisory Board shows this and helps to develop a rapport. This can be essential to early identification of any issues that dissatisfy customers that can lead to a crisis.

SYSTEM CHECKLIST

When a company has a comprehensive crisis management system, how can sales managers know it is working? Here are some clear indicators:

- Critical risk areas are identified.
- Reports are clear and concise.
- Crisis is automatically part of daily decision making.

- Crisis terminology is part of the vocabulary.
- Surprises are less frequent.
- Strategic advantages are identified.[13]

PROFILE: Dr. Larry Barton, Author of *Crisis in Organizations*, Vice President and Director of Issues Management, Motorola Corporation

"With the sales force, crisis management touches on both reliability and credibility issues. One key issue is the disruption of regular service. You can avert a crisis by asking if everything has been done to provide immediate support. So, the circumstances in today's business world dictate the need for a crisis plan and strategies. The sales force needs to be a significant part of the crisis management infrastructure that determines how an incident will be managed since customer pain can be high. It's easy for salespeople to say that because crisis management does not help me get business and in fact puts me in a defensive posture it's not important. But because crisis can have such devastating consequences to a sales organization's ability to generate revenue, the sales force and sales managers can't afford to operate in a state of denial. They must be the catalyst for their organizations to recognize the need for developing a crisis plan and implementing it appropriately."

Source: Larry Barton (March 12, 1997). Personal Interview. Motorola, Schaumburg, Illinois.

SUMMARY

Above all, crisis management must be viewed as an evolutionary process. In particular, the validity and appropriateness of risk policies need to be reevaluated constantly. In addition, sales managers must develop, and encourage top management to develop, a crisis management culture and philosophy that permeates the company. They should use crisis to their advantage and reduce the impact of a crisis. So, by being prepared, rehearsing options in advance, developing a crisis plan and identifying communications channels, sales managers can deal successfully with crisis. Hopefully, a crisis management proficiency will help instill the mind-set in sales managers that a crisis, when handled effectively, is an opportunity to show the marketplace how good they really are.

Questions

1. What is "crisis management" and how does it differ from "problem solving?"
2. What is the relevance of the "crisis management team" when responding to crisis situations?
3. What are some of the various tools that are available to sales managers for "crisis management?"
4. Select a newspaper article dealing with a "crisis" in customer dealings or sales situation and develop a plan to resolve it using the "crisis" framework.
5. Why does "crisis management" have importance to sales organizations?

CASE STUDY: GLOBAL OPTICS

Division Manager Faces a Flat Market

As Calvin Harris got off the phone with his immediate boss, Senior Vice President Bill Dunn, he thought to himself, "I must have been out of my mind to accept this job!"

Description

It all started four months ago in October when Calvin had been hired as New York Division Manager for Global Optics (GO). GO is one of the largest telecommunications firms in the United States. This is an industry that has grown dramatically since the breakup of AT&T in the early 1980s. However, in recent years the three Rs—Recession, Restructuring, and Reengineering—had a devastating effect on the industry. This has forced the industry to institute cutbacks and scramble after a shrinking and more selective customer base, particularly in New York.

Until recently, GO's New York office has been profitable. However, this might have been more attributable to a better economy than to any brilliant business strategy. In fact, other than one or two senior executives, it is even questionable if GO's senior level management really has the commitment to make the necessary organizational and strategic changes to impact revenue.

GO has an independent affiliate in New York called Global Technical Optics (GTO) that provides revenue also through telecommunication services. Management and employees that work for GTO are not really employees of GO since this is more of a contractual agency relationship. GO's senior management level in the corporate office in Baltimore, Maryland, signed GTO as an affiliate in the early 1980s when GO was still establishing its presence in New York after the AT&T breakup.

Greg Beck is the President of GTO and is known throughout the industry for his fierce competitive nature and nasty temper. Greg feels that most of the significant revenue-producing customers in New York, especially corporate accounts, are his. He has been known to protest any claims that GO and Calvin may have with these customers. Calvin has seen Greg have his way with GO's senior level management because of his ability to help their bottom line.

Calvin knows that because of his extensive industry and management experience he was recruited to establish a stronger market presence in New York. However, he is concerned in lieu of industry cutbacks, softness in the market, and the obstacles posed by GTO and Greg Beck. Calvin believes that a year of these adverse conditions could even close his office.

Questions

You are a former classmate of Calvin's who always did well in business classes. As a fellow manager, Calvin has consulted you for your expertise. Please thoroughly explain to him: Is this a crisis and how should he handle this situation? Also, how should Calvin accomplish his sales goals in the New York market?

Chapter 6

Legal, Regulatory, and Ethical Matters

LEGAL ISSUES IN SALES

Misrepresentation and Fraud

Misrepresentation is a false statement of a material fact on which a person justifiably relies to his or her detriment. If the misrepresentation is intentional, then it is fraudulent. This situation can occur in the sales setting. For example, intent to deceive is the characteristic that separates a fraudulent misrepresentation from an innocent one. One establishes intent to deceive by proving that the representation was false at the time it was made. Knowledge will be imputed to the party making the statement in which the party should have known that the statement was false or that the statement was made in reckless disregard of whether it was false or not. These distinctions are important to note because salespeople should understand the risks that may accompany "puffing" a product or service to get a sale. "Puffing," which builds up the merits of a product or service during a sale, may exaggerate so far to constitute fraud.

People may make false representations innocently (misrepresentation) or intentionally (fraud), through actions as well as speech. Concealment of material alterations or defects that would not generally be noticed is an example of fraud. Material facts influence parties in their decisions to enter contracts. Although silence usually does not constitute fraud, a duty to speak will arise in a situation if a person knows the other party believes a falsehood to be true.[1] Sales managers should be aware that these are situations that can relate to the actions of salespeople.

Uniform Commercial Code

The Uniform Commercial Code (UCC) represents another legal area that has important implications for sales managers. The UCC provides a uniform set of laws used for commercial transactions that is recognized in the District of Columbia and all fifty states except Louisiana. The UCC makes clear the laws relating to contracts and provides guidelines and commercial freedoms to sellers and buyers which gives them certain rights and duties.

UCC Section 2-105: Definition of Goods

It should also be noted that the Code applies to sale of goods. It is important to realize that the Uniform Commercial Code has liberalized the requirement of definiteness insofar as contracts for the sale of goods are concerned. "Goods" are defined in the UCC at Section 2-105:

The UCC provides:

1. "Goods" means all things (including specially manufactured goods) which are movable at the time of identification to the contract for sale ("identification" is the point in time in which the goods subject to the contract of sale are picked out or set aside) other than money in which the price is to be paid, investment securities and things in action ("things in action" are rights to recover money or other personal property through a court proceding).

Generally speaking, the term "goods" includes all movable things, any minerals or structures to be removed from land by the seller, any growing crops or timber to be removed from real property; and any other item to be removed from land so long as it is capable of severance without material harm to the real property.

Under the Uniform Commercial Code, an offer for the sale of "goods" may give rise to mutual assent upon acceptance by the offeree even though the same offer and acceptance would fail for lack of definiteness in the case of a subject matter other than goods. This could be found in contracts for personal services such as those of a plumber or lawyer.

UCC Section 2-204: Sale of Goods

The UCC provides:

1. A contract for (the) sale of goods may be made in any manner sufficient to show agreement, including conduct by both parties which recognizes the existence of such a contract.
2. An agreement sufficient to constitute a contract for sale may be found even though the moment of its making is undetermined.
3. Even though one or more terms are left open, a contract for sale does not fail for indefiniteness if the parties have intended to make a contract and there is a reasonably certain basis for giving an appropriate remedy.

UCC Section 2-305: Open Price Terms

Salespeople might occasionally leave the price term in a sales contract completely open or merely specify a procedure for determining price at some time in the future. The seller, on one hand, may believe that the market price is going to rise and so hope to sell at a higher price. The buyer, however, may believe that the market price is going to fall and so hope to conclude the purchase at a lower price. With a buyer purchasing inventory over a long period of time, the ability to buy at the lower price as the market price falls is crucial to remaining competitive with other dealers.

In recognition of the fact that "open price terms" are frequently necessary and desirable in business transactions, UCC Section 2-305 addresses this issue.

The UCC provides:

1. The parties if they so intend can conclude a contract for sale even though the price is not settled. In such a case the price is a reasonable price at the time for delivery if
   a. nothing is said as to price;
   b. the price is left to be agreed by the parties and they fail to agree; or

    c. the price to be fixed in terms of some agreed market or other standard as set or recorded by a third person or agency and it is not so set or recorded.

2. A price to be fixed by the seller or by the buyer means a price for him to fix in good faith. (Section 2-103 defines "good faith" on the part of a merchant as "honesty in fact and the observance of reasonable commercial standards of fair dealing in the trade.")

3. When a price left to be fixed otherwise than by agreement of the parties fails to be fixed through fault of one party the other party may at his option treat the contract as canceled or himself fix a reasonable price.

4. Where, however, the parties intend not to be bound unless the price be fixed or agreed and it is not fixed or agreed there is no contract. In such a case the buyer must return any goods already received or if unable to do so must pay their reasonable value at the time of delivery and the seller must return any portion of the price paid on account.

UCC Section 2-308: Absence of Specified Place for Delivery

While most commercial sales expressly provide for the place and method of delivery of the goods, many private sales altogether omit any mention of delivery place. Where either a commercial or private sale of goods fails to specify the place of delivery, the transaction will not fail for lack of definiteness because of UCC Section 2-308, "Absence of Specified Place for Delivery."

The UCC provides:

Unless otherwise agreed

1. the place for delivery of goods is the seller's place of business or if he has none, his residence; but

2. in a contract for sale of identified goods which to the knowledge of the parties at the time of contracting are in some other place, that is the place for their delivery.

Where the place of delivery is not specified in a sale of goods, the place of delivery is the seller's place of business, or if the seller has no place of business, the seller's residence, unless the goods are known to be elsewhere at the time of contracting.

UCC Section 2-309: The Time for Shipment or Delivery of the Goods

If the buyer and seller do not agree either expressly or impliedly on the time for delivery of the goods, UCC Section 2-309 provides that the time for delivery shall be a "reasonable" time. What is "reasonable" depends upon many factors, including the nature of the goods (perishable or nonperishable), the nature of the market, the transportation conditions, the purpose for which the goods will be used, and the extent of the seller's knowledge of this purpose.

UCC Section 2-310: Time of Payment for the Goods

Where the time for payment is not specified by the parties, payment is due under UCC Section 2-310 at the time and place where the buyer receives the goods. The UCC provides for payment at the time of receipt of the goods in order to facilitate the buyer's right to inspect the goods prior to payment as provided for in UCC Section 2-513. By deferring the buyer's duty to pay until the time and place of his or her receipt of the goods, the buyer can conveniently exercise his or her right of inspection just prior to payment. Where the parties provide for payment prior to receipt of the goods, the seller must make the goods available for the buyer's inspection prior to payment, although the seller need not give up possession of the goods until payment is received.

Stating the Quantity of Goods to Be Sold

Often a buyer of goods will contract for a seller's entire "output"; or a seller will agree to supply a buyer with all of his or her "requirements." Obviously, such contracts are inexact as to the quantity of goods to be sold, but they may be commercially desirable. A buyer, for example, may want to secure a source of supply that enables him or her to easily meet fluctuating market needs; the convenience of dealing with only one seller is an added benefit. A seller, on the other hand, may find that the assurance of a market for his or her goods makes for better planning and scheduling of business operations and helps save storage and marketing costs, thus making for higher profits. It may therefore be to a buyer's benefit to agree to purchase all of a particular seller's output or production of oil, lumber, etc.; and it may be to a seller's benefit to contract to provide all of a particular buyer's needs or requirements for tomatoes, green peppers, onions, or color television sets.

Even apart from the UCC, offers to supply "all your requirements" or to sell "the entire output of the factory" are generally considered sufficiently definite as to quantity or nature of the subject matter and will not fail for lack of definiteness. This is because the terms "output" and "requirements" provide objective standards by which the courts can measure the quantities intended by the parties, particularly where there has been a history of business dealings between the parties, or where one or both of the businesses have been established for a considerable period of time.

The language of the Uniform Commercial Code at Section 2-306, "Output, Requirements, and Exclusive Dealings" only strengthens this conclusion.

The UCC provides:

1. A term which measures the quantity by the output of the seller or the requirements of the buyer means such actual output or requirements as may occur in good faith, except that no quantity unreasonably disproportionate to any stated estimate or in the absence of a stated estimate to any normal or otherwise comparable prior output or requirements may be tendered or demanded.
2. A lawful agreement by either the seller or the buyer for exclusive dealing in the kind of goods concerned imposes, unless otherwise agreed, an obligation by the seller to use best efforts to supply the goods and by the buyer to use best efforts to promote their sale.

This concerns "exclusive dealing" contracts wherein a buyer and seller agree that the buyer will have an exclusive right to sell the goods of the seller in a particular area or under a franchise. By imposing upon the seller an obligation to use his or her "best efforts" to supply the goods, and upon the buyer an obligation to use his or her "best efforts" to sell the goods, Section 2-306 of the UCC provides an objective standard by which these factors can be determined and saves the offer and subsequent acceptance from failure for lack of definiteness.

Where Particulars of the Agreement Are Left for Future Determination by One of the Parties

Section 2-311 of the UCC provides that an agreement otherwise sufficiently definite to constitute a contract is not rendered invalid by the fact that it leaves particulars of performance to be specified by one of the parties. However, Section 2-311 also provides that "any such specification must be made in good faith and within limits set by commercial reasonableness." "Commercial Reasonableness" is not an obscure concept incapable of precise definition, but rather an objective standard measured by the sound business judgement of reasonable persons familiar with the customary practices in the type of transaction involved.

UCC Section 2-205: Firm Offers

The Uniform Commercial Code Section 2-205, "Firm Offers," creates an important exception to the general rule that an offer is revocable even though it contains an express promise that it will be kept open for a period of time.

The UCC provides:

An offer by a merchant to buy or sell goods in a signed writing which by its terms gives assurance that it will be held open is not revocable, for lack of consideration, during the time stated or if no time is stated for a reasonable time, but in no event may such period of irrevocability exceed three months.

A written offer to buy or sell goods made and signed by a merchant, and containing an express promise that the offer will be kept open for a period of time is a "firm offer" and cannot be revoked by the merchant for the time stated or for three months, whichever is less, or, if no time is stated, for a "reasonable" time, again, not to exceed three months. The effect of the UCC provision is that a merchant who promises in a signed writing that he or she will not revoke an offer to buy or sell goods for a period of time may be "stopped" from revoking the offer for up to three months regardless of whether the offeree has given any consideration for the promise not to revoke. The "signing" required is not a formal signature, but merely some authentication of the writing, such as initialing the clause containing the offer not to revoke.

If the offeree gives consideration for the promise not to revoke, a binding option contract exists rather than a firm offer, and the offer will be irrevocable for the time agreed upon by the parties without regard to the three-month maximum applicable to firm offers.

Apart from option contracts and firm offers, the general rule is that an offer is revocable at anytime up until the moment of acceptance. To be effective, the revocation must be communicated to the offeree prior to acceptance. Usually, the offeror directly notifies the offeree that the offer is being revoked. Any words or conduct by the offeror will serve to revoke the offer so long as a reasonable person in the position of the offeree would understand that the words or conduct constitute a revocation.

UCC Section 2-207: Additional Terms

Section 2-207 of the Uniform Commercial Code provides: Additional Terms in Acceptance or Confirmation

1. A definite and seasonable expression of the acceptance or a written confirmation which is sent within a reasonable time operates as an acceptance even though it states terms additional to or different from those offered or agreed upon.
2. The additional terms are to be construed as proposals for addition to the contract. Between merchants such terms become part of the contract unless:
   a. the offer expressly limits acceptance to the terms of the offer;
   b. they materially alter it; or
   c. notification of objection to them has already been given

or is given within a reasonable time after notice of them is received.

3. Conduct by both parties which recognizes the existence of a contract is sufficient to establish a contract for sale although the writings of the parties do not otherwise establish a contract. In such case the terms of the particular contract consist of those terms on which the writings of the parties agree, together with any supplementary terms incorporated under any other provisions of this Act.

Section 2-207 of the Code was primarily enacted to put an end to the "battle of the forms" between merchant buyers and sellers. The "battle of the forms" refers to the confusion that resulted prior to the Code provision from each party's use of his or her own sales and purchase forms.

To solve this problem with regard to the sale of goods, Section 2-207 of the Code provides that the offeree's injection of different terms will not necessarily constitute a rejection of the original offer not a counter offer that serves to terminate the original offer. Unless the original offer expressly limits acceptance to its terms, the additions to the offer will not prevent acceptance by the offeree but will be treated merely as proposals for addition to the contract. Where the transaction is between merchants, the new terms will automatically become part of the contract unless the new terms materially alter the contract or unless the offeror objects to the terms within a reasonable period of time.

Modification

Section 2-209(1) of the UCC provides that "an agreement modifying a sales contract needs no consideration to be binding." The theory behind the Section is that the consideration given to support the original contract also serves to support the modified contract. Of course, all of the Uniform Commercial Code Sections are subject to the "good faith" requirements imposed by the Code. Section 2-103 provides that the test of "good faith" between merchants or as against merchants includes "observance of reasonable commercial standards of fair dealing in the trade." Thus, the above Code Sections, particularly Sections 1-107 dealing with discharge of a claim or right and 2-209 dealing with modification of a sales contract, cannot be used in support of bad faith conduct.

The Bargain Theory of Consideration

Almost all agreements require consideration in the bargain theory sense in order to be legally binding and enforceable.

Bargain theory consideration requires two things:

1. The consideration or "something" given for the promise must be bargained for between the parties, i.e., the consideration must be the motive for the promise and the promise must be the motive for the consideration.
2. The consideration or "something" given for the promise must be legally sufficient. This is not to say that the consideration must be money or have economic value of any kind. Certainly money or money's worth is frequently given in exchange for a promise and is legally sufficient consideration. However, just as often, the "something" given has no economic value but is still legally sufficient consideration: all that is needed is a commitment by the promise to do something or refrain from doing something that he or she is not already obligated to do or to refrain from doing.

In order for bargain theory consideration to exist, each party must act because of what the other is giving to the agreement. That is, the promisor must make the promise because the promisee gives something by way of consideration, and the promisee must give something because the promisor makes the promise. In the example that follows, the motivation or bargain element is clearly lacking, and, as a result the promises made are neither legally binding nor enforceable.

Where either party promises to confer a gift upon the other, the motivation or bargain element is lacking because the party who promises to make the gift does not expect to receive anything in return. Because the promise of gift is not motivated by return promise or performance, bargain theory consideration is not present.

UCC Section 2-302: Unconscionability

In the UCC, unconscionability doctrine is directed to the prevention of oppression and unfair surprise. In its focus on oppression, it has obvious and strong links to duress; in its focus on unfair surprise, it has similarly obvious and strong links to fraud. One way of explaining the place of unconscionability in the body of contract doctrine is to describe it as the public face of a concern for which duress and fraud then appear as the private expressions. An unconscionable contract is one that shocks the *public* conscience. Duress and fraud concentrate, by comparison, on the effect of the coercive or fraudulent conduct on the contractual capacity of the affected party.

UCC Section 2-302 states:

1. If the court as a matter of law finds the contract or any clause of the contract to have been unconscionable at the time it was made the court may refuse to enforce the contract, or it may enforce the remainder of the contract without the unconscionable clause, or it may so limit the application of any unconscionable clause as to avoid any unconscionable result.
2. When it is claimed or appears to the court that the contract or any clause thereof may be unconscionable the parties shall be afforded a reasonable opportunity to present evidence as to its commercial setting, purpose and effect to aid the court in making the determination.

Thus, a contract that affords no meaningful choice to one of the parties but includes contract terms that are unreasonably favorable to the other party is an unconscionable contract that does not give rise to mutual consent. The fact that a party had little education and could not read the language of the contract is sometimes emphasized by the courts in finding unconscionability, as is the fact that the seller manufactured the contract forms using fine print. Excessive price also suggests unconscionability, particularly where the markup is two or three times the cost of the product, or where the product is sold at a price two or three times greater than the average retail price elsewhere. Finally, provisions requiring a buyer to waive some of his or her legal remedies or his or her right to a jury trial in case of later controversy over the contract also indicate unconscionability.

UCC Section 2-201: Contracts

The UCC tightly controls contracts that have to be in writing in Section 2-201.

The UCC provides:

1. Except as otherwise provided in this section a contract for the sale of goods for the price of $500 or more is not enforceable by way of action or defense unless there is some writing sufficient to indicate that a contract for sale has been made between the parties and signed by the party against whom enforcement is sought or by his authorized agent or broker. A writing is not insufficient because it omits or incorrectly states a term agreed upon but the contract is not enforceable under this paragraph beyond the quantity of goods shown in such writing.
2. Between merchants if within a reasonable time a writing in confirmation of the contract and sufficient against the sender is received and the party receiving it has reason to know its contents, if satisfies the requirements of subsection (1) against such party unless written notice of objection to its contents is given within 10 days after it is received.
3. A contract which does not satisfy the requirement of subsection (1) but which is valid in other respects is enforceable

    a. if the goods are to be specially manufactured for the buyer and are not suitable for sale to others in the ordinary course of the seller's business and the seller, before notice of repudiation is received and under circumstances which reasonably indicate that the goods are for the buyer, has made either a substantial beginning of their manufacture or commitments for their procurement; or
    b. if the party against whom enforcement is sought admits in his or her pleading, testimony or otherwise in court that a contract for sale was made, but the contract is not enforceable under this provision beyond the quantity of goods admitted; or
    c. with respect to goods for which payment has been made and accepted or which have been received and accepted.

While a sale of goods for $500 or more falls within the Statute of Frauds, far less of a written memo is required to prove the sale than is required to prove promises within the other five subject matter areas covered by the Statute. In the sale of goods situation, the only essential memo term is *quantity*, and even it may be misstated (although recovery, in that case, will be limited to the misstated amount). All that is required is that the writing afford a basis for believing that the oral evidence offered rests upon a real transaction and, of course, the writing must be signed by the party to be charged.

Conclusion

The following four principles regarding contract formation and execution by buyers and sellers must be remembered:

1. Definiteness is required because it is essential that offers (as well as acceptances) be clearly understandable: a court must be able to determine what the parties intended so as to meet their reasonable expectations with money damages or other remedies.
2. However, the requirement of definiteness does not demand that every detail of the agreement be spelled out with exact precision. Only "reasonable" definiteness is required, and an offer need not even spell out all the *essential* terms so long as the offer makes reference to some objective standard by which to fill in the missing particulars.
3. Insofar as the sale of goods is concerned, the Uniform Commercial Code has liberalized the definiteness requirement with provisions designed to "fill in the gaps" where essential terms such as price, quantity, or place of delivery are left open.
4. The trend in the law is to take the UCC approach with regard to all contracts, and not just contracts for the sale of goods. The courts are thus increasingly willing to read in or imply "reasonable" terms to fill in gaps in a contract so long as it is clear that the parties intended to enter into a binding agreement.

The relationship in America between personal freedom and freedom of contract is tremendous. The tone of the UCC seems to promote the freedom of contracts. Even if a term is left open it will not stop the completion of the contract. In light of this, sales managers should at least have a functional understanding of the UCC so that they can maximize their business dealings with vendors.

REGULATORY ISSUES IN SALES

Protecting the public from the wrongdoing or irresponsibility of companies that sell products or services has been the purpose of government regulation. The regulatory process is one of the most powerful ways in which the government can influence sales activity.

The main thrust in the United States is to encourage competition where a company's business policies permit efficiency and innovation. However, government regulation is used to protect citizens from hazardous products and various other risks to their health and welfare.

Antitrust policy is one example of government regulation that was developed to control concentrations of economic power in industry by reviewing mergers, disbanding large corporations, and lowering cooperation between competitors. Antitrust deals with those laws, agencies, and matters that promote competition. Anticompetitive behavior, such as collusion, can involve agreements among competitors to share a market, developing informalities, engaging in price discrimination or forming agreements to establish prices. The reason for antitrust policies and regulations is to prevent market dominance by companies using anticompetitive industry behaviors.

The Sherman Anti-Trust Act of 1890 and the Clayton Act of 1914 are federal laws that both outlaw all acts or contracts in restraint of trade. The Federal Trade Commission is a Federal Administrative agency that also outlaws unfair competition practices. Problems that can occur in this area that relate to sales issues are price discrimination, unfair pricing, price collusion by competitors and unfair competitive practices.[2] Sales managers should be aware of these regulatory policies when directing the efforts of the sales force, dealing with other competitors in their industry and developing business agreements with their customers.

Federal Administrative agencies have the authority to regulate the economic activities of individuals and businesses. The activities of administrative agencies impinge upon the rights of private individuals and regulate the manner in which such rights may be exercised. They have the power to prescribe generally what shall or shall not be done in a given situation just as legislatures do. These agencies determine if the law has been violated in a particular case and to take action against violators, even to impose fines and the equivalent of money judgements, just as prosecutors and courts do.

Regulatory commissions have existed in the United States for about one hundred years. They have particularly flourished during periods of great abuses, difficult economic times, or in times of reform. The sales manager is much more frequently affected by the administrative process than by the judicial process. The significance of the effects of the administrative process on sales managers can be most appreciated by discussing a few samples of authority exercised by the agencies:

Licensing Power: the agency controls entry into the given economic activity. For example, authority over rail, motor, and water carriers, and pipeline is given to the Interstate Commerce Commission (ICC). Powers in the investment field are exercised by the Securities and Exchange Commission (SEC).

Rate-Making Power: the agency possesses authority to fix the rates charged by companies subject to its jurisdiction. This authority is vested in those agencies which regulate utilities and carriers such as the Federal Power Commission (FPC) and the (ICC).

Power Over Business Practices: the agency is given authority to approve or prohibit practices employed in business. This is the primary power possessed by the Federal Trade Commission (FTC) over unfair trade practices and the National Labor Relations Board (NLRB) over unfair labor practices. Similar authority is vested in the agencies which regulate given industries. Thus the ICC must approve all railroad consolidations, closures, and issuance of stocks and bonds. It also has prohibitory power over discriminatory and other improper railroad practices.[3]

The regulation of businesses cannot be carried out effectively under a rigid separation of powers. Administrative agencies have been made the repository of legislative, judicial, and administrative governmental power. Far-reaching powers have been granted by Congress to many of the agencies and ordinary executive departments. This authorizes the agencies to promulgate rules, regulations, investigate and adjudicate violations. For example, the Department of Agriculture has the authority to regulate production through the imposition of maximum quotas for farmers. It can also regulate stockyards by fixing rates and charges and preventing unfair practices. State agencies can regulate their own state's internal commerce, so comparable Federal Administrative Agency powers are also available to these state agencies. Issues dealing with administrative regulatory agencies which may impact sales managers should be explored by sales managers, and not just attorneys.

It is usually rare to find a sales manager that is aware of the potential pitfalls in the area of administrative regulatory. Hopefully, a review of administrative agencies and relevant laws can at least serve as a guideline to resolve or avoid problems.

When Congress creates an agency it defines the field in which the agency will operate and the objectives that it will accomplish. This is known as the delegation doctrine. Any agency action outside the delegated field would, in an appropriate proceeding, be held as invalid. In *Yakus v. United States*, the only concern was to ascertain that the will of Congress had been obeyed.[4] Here, the legislature and judiciary combined to prevent the administrative agency from acting *ultra vires* or outside its scope.

In addition to challenging agency conduct, sales managers could also follow the advice of Title 5 Section 553 (e.) of the Administrative Procedure Act. This section gives interested parties the right to petition for a rule's amendment, repeal, or issuance. Even though one cannot force the agency to act or rule it is a good idea for sales managers to develop a dialogue with an agency. This might just involve basic action steps such as knowing the location and duties of Federal and Local agencies and developing useful contacts at these offices. Agency officials and inspectors have broad discretionary powers to set procedures and should work closely with management. From this dialogue, without crossing over the line of improper coziness or expecting special favors, a business may be able to negotiate or just wear the agency down.[5] Sales managers, either directly or through an attorney, should participate as much as possible in the agency process. This process has become increasingly adversarial, partly because so much of it has moved into the courts.[6] Accordingly, establishing a dialogue is more appropriate in administrative agencies than confrontation; the costly route of litigation and the courts should be used as a last resort.

ETHICS IN SALES

Anyone who wants to succeed in sales should be aware of the ethical issues that can arise. For a number of reasons, activities related to sales seem to have a greater frequency and level of ethical issues. Salespeople can face disturbing ethical dilemmas in business. These problems can entail bribes, dishonest advertising, cheating customers, overselling, unfair credit practices, and dishonesty in making or keeping a contract. Empirical research has explored recommendations for ethical decision making in the sales force. Previous analyses have proposed a variety of explanations as to why the sales function is particularly vulnerable. These reasons include the compensation system design, customer dependence on salespeople, unequal power in the transaction, the orientation of the salesperson, competitive forces, lack of sales supervision, salespeople pressure to achieve sales results, a lack of salesperson self-esteem, and even illogical or emotional customers.[7]

An effective sales manager should never do anything that he or she does not believe is right. Sales managers should also be instrumental in helping their own firms adopt ethical policies and plans. These ethical plans should include termination sanctions as punishment for employees or give promotions, raises, and bonuses for meeting objectives as rewards.

There is increasing evidence that the use of ethical policies and procedures in the sales force is beneficial to the whole organization.[8] In the case of commission sales in the auto parts and repair business, such a conscious design enabled the management of Pep Boys to motivate employees without encouraging unethical behavior.[9] An alternative system at Sears Auto Centers did not consider the ethical implications and resulted in a terrible scandal and controversy for Sears. One replacement auto parts business that was founded by two women as a demonstration of the policies and practices is now a firm generating $100 million in sales.[10] Their success is striking given that the auto parts industry is viewed as an unethical morass of kickbacks, bribery, and dishonest sales tactics and as a result has experienced declining sales.

Some answers may be found by having a process that asks the sales force to identify what they see as key ethical issues and then having them examine those ethical problem scenarios where the salespeople must respond. This can occur in a monthly sales meeting with ethical issues similar to the ones mentioned above. Then salespeople should identify those necessary ethical decision-making characteristics. This could mean a salesperson ignores the conduct, anonymously protests, publicly protests, asks others to get involved, or leaves the organization. Important to issues dealing with the ethical dilemmas in the sales position are the actions of management and certainly the sales manager's conduct. If their actions are inconsistent with ethical conduct and if they do not reprimand or punish such behavior, then why should the sales force behave with any integrity?[11]

SALES SITUATIONS INVOLVING ETHICAL ISSUES

A Framework for Understanding Ethical Issues

Ethics is a difficult concept to define, and thus, people appear to differ widely in their views of ethical issues and behavior. Studies have explored the reasons for these differences, and there is a possible consensus that environmental factors can influence the development of ethical awareness and response in individuals.[12] Other studies suggest the differences are more fundamental, even to the point of gender as a kind of moral determinant.[13]

Once a situation has been recognized as involving ethical dilemmas, those involved must still make a decision and take some action. Grappling with how that decision can be made determines a sales manager of strong moral character who can help organizations stand for something decent.

Utilitarianism

Utilitarianism as a formalized decision system is generally attributed to philosopher Jeremy Bentham (1748-1832) who noted that the most valued actions should be those that result in the greatest positive outcome for the largest number of people. This principle is a form of consequentialism that demands that choices be made by looking ahead to the assessment of consequences.

Deontologicism

Deontologicism is frequently associated with Immanuel Kant, who with his concept of the categorical imperative was striving to base actions on those precepts that could best be universalized. In Kant's view, since we can never be really sure what all the consequences of an action might be, we should ignore all the possible consequences in making our decision, and instead we should do that which we would want all others to do given the same circumstances.

The Golden Rule

The Golden Rule, saying "Do unto others as you would have them do unto you," or something like it, is at the core of the world's major religions, including Christianity, Judaism, Islam, Hinduism, Buddhism, Taoism, and others. This principle indicates that choices should be made by invoking reversibility, which results in not only setting limits on our own behavior but also encouraging us to promote the interests of others.

Although each principle provides guidance about how to make decisions in ethical situations, each principle also has drawbacks. For utilitarianism: we must approve the death of a dozen babies in a medical experiment if the result would be a drug that could save millions of other babies. For Kant: a schoolteacher must refuse to let a student undertake a tremendously creative project because then every other student must also be allowed the same thing. For the Golden Rule: a person must approve of an individual bribing someone with the understanding that, were he or she in the other's shoes, he or she would want to be bribed.

A Process for Ethical Decision Making

1. *Recognize that there is a moral issue.* A vital step to identify genuine moral questions that need attention from those that merely involve manners and social conventions.
2. *Determine the actor.* The question to be answered in this step is who is responsible—that is, who is morally obligated and empowered to do anything in the face of the moral issues raised.

3. *Gather the relevant facts.* Relevant information could include the way events unfolded, what happened, what else might have happened, who said what to whom, etc., as well as a look ahead to understand possible outcomes to the extent possible. This step, of course, must be completed in the time context of the situation.

4. *Apply the principles for ethical dilemmas.* After the choice between the different sides is clearly articulated, these principles can be applied to locate a line of reasoning that seems most relevant and persuasive to the issue at hand.

5. *Investigate the options.* Is there a third way through this dilemma? If so, a compromise or an unforeseen creative solution may be the best result for the situation.

6. *Make the decision.* Often overlooked, this step is required to move from the academic to the practical. Given moral courage and leadership skills, there is nothing more to do at this point than decide.

7. *Revisit and reflect on the decision.* When the tumult and shouting have died out, and the case is more or less closed, go back over the process and look for its lessons. This evaluation will strengthen decision-making skills and will help build lasting ethics expertise for the sales force.

PROFILE: John Moran, Author of *Practical Business Law*; Expert in Legal, Regulatory, and Ethical Matters in Business; and Associate Professor, Wagner College, Staten Island, New York.

"Ethical conduct must be a goal for today's sales force. Hard-sell and puffing techniques often prey upon customer's needs and desires by inflating their desires. Instead of using their expertise to educate customers, some salespeople have used their position to dupe them. Uneducated customers can be targets for smooth-talking salespeople who have superior product or service knowledge."

"Consumer credit laws, lemon laws, and warranties ensure that customers receive products and services that are merchantable and fit for the purpose that they were intended. Since the potential for commercial abuses by businesses exist, there must be policies for business regulation."

Source: John Moran (February 6, 1997). Personal Interview. Wagner College, Staten Island, New York.

SUMMARY

Changes such as the development of the Internet and the increasing ability of firms to access and use large amounts of customer-specific data are creating new dilemmas for businesses even as the same new technology enables employers to track the movement of unethical salespeople as they change jobs.[14] Salespeople, sales managers, and businesses in general, must create a positive professional climate in their firms.

Legal, regulatory, and ethical situations are more common than most people realize. It is likely that many of these situations will be encountered by anyone working in business, and in sales in particular. Salespeople for insurance, investments, and related services have been publicly singled out and criticized by the press for their legal, regulatory, and ethical transgressions.[15] Other situations that need to be prepared for close scrutiny of their legal, regulatory, or ethical issues include anyone involved with international business, anyone who gives or receives gifts in the course of business, or anyone who considers using fear as a sales tool.[16] These ethical issues are at the forefront in every type of business, and they are becoming more and more visible to outsiders.

When the relevance, importance, and prevalence of legal, regulatory, and ethical solutions are understood, it becomes more clear that advance preparation is critical for success. This preparation must include practice at recognizing legal, regulatory, and ethical issues, analyzing the important aspects of the issue at hand, choosing a course of action, and following through in a rational manner.

Questions

1. Why are "misrepresentation and fraud" issues for the sales force?
2. What role does the Uniform Commercial Code play in sales transactions?
3. Select three federal administrative agencies and explain what they do and how they have some bearing on regulatory matters in sales.

4. Explain how "utilitarianism," "deontologicism" and "the Golden Rule" still have relevance for the ethical conduct of today's sales force.

5. Ethical issues in sales are so commonplace that one of the easiest ways to find them is to look at business publications or newspaper articles. Find some articles dealing with ethical issues in sales and try to resolve them using the framework for understanding ethical issues.

CASE STUDY: KROL LTD.

Adam Carelli is employed by Krol LTD. as a precious metals trader. There are various aspects to his job, such as proprietary trading, quoting spot and physical markets for institutional and retail customers, advising financial consultants about the forecast on market direction, and providing physical inventory control. Krol LTD. stores thousands of gold, silver, and platinum bars for the firm as well as for their customers. At current market prices, the estimated value of their total metal holdings is $40 million.

Approximately three months ago, Adam first became aware of a very delicate problem. Some counterfeit silver bars were surfacing in the marketplace; the bars were being hollowed out and replaced with lead. The counterfeiters had done an excellent job and the only true method of detecting these lead-filled silver bars was by actually cutting the bar in half, thus destroying the bar. Each bar is refined and carries a certain hallmark, or brand name. In this case, the only false bars ever found were done by a refinery that at one time commanded a high premium for their products.

Adam sells various products to a customer located in Texas. This customer, from past experience, destroys all 100-ounce silver bars before she sells them. She had not been doing this for some time because she caused a jeweler to ruin a "melt." This resulted in a very big loss. Instead of detecting one or two bad bars, they were thrown into the melting pot and the entire population of the melt was thereby ruined. As it turns out, Adam was advised by his customer that she had gone through this painstaking loss, and that Adam should verify his population of 100-ounce silver bars.

Adam was shocked! After all, these bars have been in Krol LTD.'s depository for years. Adam researched this problem through his contacts in the market. The market was only somewhat aware of the problem. The firm that refined the bars believed that after the bars left their refinery, they were no longer responsible for the authenticity. Adam was flabbergasted and when he checked his inventory, he found that his company had a total of 5,100 100-ounce silver bars, at a current total value of $1.5 million. He did not know what was he going to do. After all, Krol LTD. could not take a chance on one of their retail customers possibly drilling into a silver bar to find it full of lead! He diagnosed the problem and decided the first thing to do was to alert his direct manager.

After examining all possibilities, they both decided to destroy every single bar that could possibly be contaminated. Krol LTD. could not risk any customer dissatisfaction of any product. Adam was afraid that many of the population would be contaminated. Adam was even more afraid that a contaminated bar could possibly leave Krol's vault without anyone knowing it. As the situation stands now, they are almost finished destroying all the bars. Adam sells them to a customer who cuts them in half for examination. Of course, Krol LTD. is obligated to return payment to customers for any bad bars they may find. Adam believes he has discovered that 0.03 percent of their bars had been counterfeit. They are three-quarters of the way through the original 5,100 pieces.

Of course, this problem led Adam's senior managers to question the remaining balance of inventory for the firm, as well as their customer holdings. As far as Adam knows, there have never been any other false bars found, from any other refinery, be it gold, silver, or platinum. Krol LTD. had an ethical responsibility to react to this crisis situation, or else take on the risk of a contaminated bar leaving the vault in the hands of a trusting customer.

Question

Did Adam Carelli and Krol LTD. handle this situation in an ethical manner? Why?

Chapter 7

Sales Force Management and Diversity

SALES FORCE DIVERSITY ISSUES

Sales management today faces tremendous challenges. In particular, the change in demographics has driven diversity issues. To generate revenue, companies need to develop a sales effort that takes into account sales force diversity issues. Companies that fail to do this are at a competitive disadvantage. Salespeople and sales managers that do not understand the culture of African, Hispanic, and Asian markets and use women and minorities to their fullest potential will not grow in the 1990s or the twenty-first century. Managing diversity is becoming one of the most pressing business issues that sales managers must face today. As the U.S. labor force becomes more diverse, it is important for sales organizations to effectively respond to diversity issues in order to attract and keep talented salespeople.

One of the reasons for the growing awareness of sales force diversity issues is the changing demographic picture in the U.S. work force. Where the American labor force was at one time primarily represented by white males, we now see:

1. Greater number of women,
2. More minorities entering the work forces,
3. An increase in the age of workers,
4. A greater number of people with disabilities, and
5. An increase of gays.

What if a company has an African-American salesperson and his or her sales manager senses that clients may show discrimination against this salesperson by refusing to do business with him or her? Or, if they have a female Hispanic sales manager who is avoided and made to feel isolated by others in the company? This chapter will discuss these and additional issues and the action steps that can be taken to avoid problems and maximize success in the sales department.

Diversity is a demographic reality that is defined as those immutable human differences that are inborn or exert an important impact in our own lives. The six primary elements of diversity are age, ethnicity, gender, race, sexual orientation, and physical abilities. They form the image that we have of ourselves and the world. However, diversity can involve any variety within a particular group based on cultural differences or any other recognizable differences that lead to values and norms distinct from the majority's.[1] Diversity should be used as a holistic approach to developing and maintaining a work environment that works for all employees, including white males.

Multiculturalism involves one culture reflecting the mixture of diversity. Managing diversity involves efforts to create an environment that works naturally for the total diversity mixture. The focus here is on the mixture, with managing defined as empowering or enabling employees. With this focus people can celebrate those things that make them different and still be able to perform and progress in the sales force.

Firms should actively assimilate women and minorities into the sales force. Diversity involves all kinds of differences between people, especially with respect to gender, race, and ethnicity. Sales managers are expected to meet their company's objectives through sales performance, profit margins, and customer base growth. To accomplish this, sales managers need qualified people. This requires sales managers to make their departments more efficient and effective. In addition, a career in sales is in many cases an essential step for promotion and senior management advancement (see Figure 7.1).

Companies may feel that sensitivity and action concerning diversity is not necessary. However, the federal government does not agree. The Glass Ceiling Commission was formed by Congress to study barriers to advancement for minorities and women. Their recommendations stated that these barriers are based on attitudinal or organizational bias that prevents qualified individuals from advancing within their organization and reaching their full potential.[2]

FIGURE 7.1. Some Issues That Can Be Faced by Sales Managers

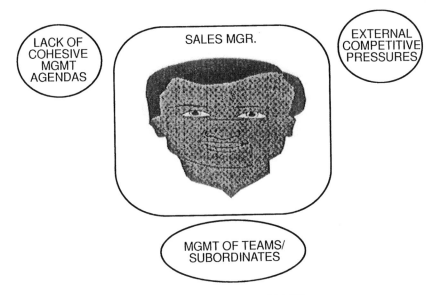

TO RESOLVE THESE ISSUES

THE SALES DEPARTMENT MUST EMBRACE DIVERSE PERSPECTIVES

Typical barriers include:

1. The lack of management commitment to establish systems, policies, and
2. Practices for not achieving workplace diversity and upward mobility.

Barriers also involve pay inequities for work of equal or comparable value, sex, race, and ethnic-based stereotyping and harassment, unfair recruitment practices and lack of family-friendly workplace policies. The Commission's recommendations focused its attention on barriers to the advancement of minorities and women and promote work force diversity by building public awareness of specific behaviors, practices, and attitudes that either cause or prevent the advancement of minorities and women to leadership and management positions. It also recommended concrete policies to Congress for improving and expanding employment opportunities for minorities and women. Their action will encourage businesses and organizations to develop and execute an agenda that promotes equal employment opportunity, work-force diversity and cultural change.

The Way It Is

On the basis of the U.S. Department of Labor, Bureau of Labor Statistics, between 1990 and 2005 there are significant projected labor force increases based on sex, race, and Hispanic origin expected by the year 2005. The civilian labor force for African Americans is expected to increase 24 percent, Hispanics by 43 percent, Asians and other racial minorities by 43 percent, and white females by 19 percent. Considering that the overall labor force is expected to increase by 17 percent during the same period, it will be women and minorities that account for the majority of the growth. Marketing and sales occupations are projected to result in continued growth from about 14 million positions in 1990 to about 18 million in the year 2005.[3]

It is interesting to look at this issue in terms of sales occupational patterns (Figures 7.2 and 7.3). For example, based on 1992 U.S. Bureau of Labor Statistics' averages, from the 14 million people employed in sales occupations, 6 percent are African American. Out of this 6 percent, only 2 percent reflect African-American males. Those of Hispanic origin represent 6 percent, with 3 percent males and 3 percent females in sales. Other racial minorities in sales, excluding African Americans comprise 3 percent. White females represent 42 percent of sales positions. Similar figures for related management positions, such as marketing, advertising, and public relations, show African Americans holding 3 percent of these positions with males occupying about 2 percent. Managers of Hispanic origin also occupy 3 percent and other racial minorities excluding African Americans hold 1 percent. White females comprise 32 percent of these management positions.

Last, according to a study by Catalyst, a women's research group, women only make up 26 percent of the business-to-business sales force compared with 46 percent of the work force as a whole. The study also shows that only 14 percent of the sales managers were female. In all of these cases the percentage of women and minorities

FIGURE 7.2. People Employed in Sales Positions (1992 Figures)

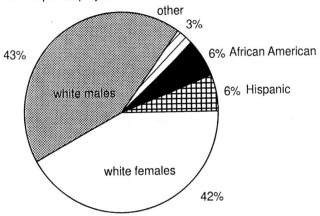

Total: 14 Million Salespeople

Source: Based on data from the U.S. Department of Labor, Bureau of Labor Statistics.

Copyright 1995, by Tony Carter

FIGURE 7.3. People Employed in Related Management Positions (1992 Figures)

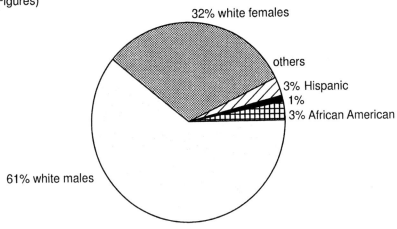

TOTAL: 516,000

Source: U.S. Department of Labor, Bureau of Labor Statistics.

Copyright 1995, by Tony Carter

FIGURE 7.4. Earnings of Sales Executives

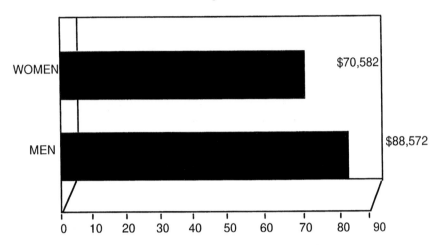

Source: Based on Compensation Survey in Search of Equity, by W. Kenan, *Sales and Marketing Management Magazine*, November, 1993.

Copyright 1995, by Tony Carter

in sales positions is far below their percentage in the total population. The Catalyst study has found that women in sales in all industry groups face barriers in advancement. The study showed that sales could provide both men and women the possibility for high earnings and superior training, independence, and the opportunity to work with people (see Figure 7.4). However, the study also points out that women are discouraged by the prospect that sales is a male-dominated field, there is little support for women, and there are no visible sales managers.[4] A recent executive survey of 544 sales and marketing executives stated that women earned $70,582 annually, compared with $88,572 for men. Not only is this 80 percent of what men make, but the figure actually lowers to 77 percent when total compensation figures, such as bonuses, commissions, and benefits are also considered.[5] These sales occupation and salary disparities for women are alarming when compared to two recent surveys. One study conducted by *Sales & Marketing Management Magazine*, asked its readers, "Who is better at sales, men or women?" While 70 percent of the respondents rated the sexes the same, 17 percent said women performed better and 13 percent said men. Seventy-five percent of the respondents in this survey were men.[6] Another survey, conducted by the National Association of Purchasing Managers, rated the sexes equal in overall selling performance.

With regard to minorities in sales, Tony Williams, an African-American sales manager for Phillips Industrial, an international company that sells technical equipment, notes that issues of diversity are important for managers, salespeople, and customers to acknowledge. Williams has observed, "Customers still show surprise when on the phone my voice is articulate, but I show up." He adds, "Once my competency is established, any perception problems get worked out quickly." However, he states, "Problems with perception do persist when for example, I'm in small towns in the deep South trying to transact business and I find myself getting stared at."[7]

Given the low number of African Americans in sales management and sales positions one may wonder: Why does this occur? They are not just running into a "glass ceiling" but one made of cement and steel. As Williams points out, "Within my organization the older crowd seems resistant to me, and even with certain clients you can tell they are not used to seeing capable blacks." According to a study done by Andrew F. Brimmer of Brimmer and Company, Inc., in 1991 disparate treatment of African Americans in the work force cost the American economy about $215 billion in lost income and lost productivity.[8] Much of this problem appears to be related to continued discrimination that limits their access to higher paying jobs. For example, the slow rate at which African Americans are being absorbed into sales managerial and professional positions results in an income deficit and their underutilization. A full use of all groups in the U.S. labor force would result in a gain in the total output of goods and services (see Figure 7.5).

What Is at Risk

Companies searching for the competitive edge encourage sales force diversity by preparing for competition in an increasingly multicultural marketplace. Sales managers in high performance organizations should value diversity as a pragmatic strategy for sustaining growth in a competitive business climate and changing labor force

FIGURE 7.5. Cost of Lost Income and Lost Productivity of the Disparate Impact of Discrimination Against African Americans in the Work Force (1991 Figures)

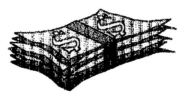

$215 BILLION

Source: Study done by Andrew F. Brimmer and Company, 1991.

Copyright 1995, by Tony Carter

composition. Dartnell's Survey of Sales Force Compensation shows that between the average compensation of a sales trainee of $40,000, field expenses of $16,154, and benefits of $7,548, there is an annual investment of at least $63,702. The investment can total as much as $471,395 when a salesperson leaves a company after 7.4 years, the average tenure of a sales rep with a company.[9] As a result, selection, retention, and sound management practices become critical. Management cannot afford to squander the talents that can be utilized from these groups as sales employees and managers (see Figure 7.6).

IMPACT OF LITIGATION ON SALES MANAGERS

Besides the cost of lost investment resulting from the poor handling of diversity issues, companies can incur the expense of legal action. Sales managers can protect their organizations by creating a work environment that makes salespeople aware of the legal and business consequences resulting from diversity issues. At the least, it can cause low morale, absenteeism, turnover, low creativity, and low productivity. At the worst, it can result in costly lawsuits, criminal penalties, large compensatory awards, bad publicity, and the destruction of a corporate image that may have taken years to create. For example, the average Fortune 500 company can expect to lose $6.7 million a year, or nearly $300 per employee, due to sexual harassment alone. Corporate America will spend more than

FIGURE 7.6. What Is at Risk

Average Compensation of a Sales Trainee - $40,000
Sales Expenses - $16,154
Benefits - $7,548
Annual Investment - $63,702
Average Tenure of a Sales Representative - 7.4 years

Source: *Dartnell Sales Force Compensation Survey* (1996-1997).

$1 billion over the next five years just to settle sexual harassment lawsuits. Both corporations and sales managers can be held legally responsible for their employees' conduct with regard to diversity.[10]

Knowledge about the following information can facilitate healthy working relationships and guarantee a better environment for all salespeople in the organization:

1. *The Civil Rights Act of 1964* states in Title VII that in any employment activity an organization may not discriminate on the basis of race, color, religion, nationality, or sex (which also includes pregnancy, childbirth, or related conditions).
2. *Affirmative Action (Executive Order 11246)* imposes obligations on employers with federal contracts to make efforts to recruit minority applicants. It involves an undertaking to remedy the under utilization of women and minorities through the express consideration of race or gender.
3. *The Age Discrimination in Employment Act (ADEA)* prohibits age discrimination against individuals who are at least 40 years old.
4. *The Americans with Disabilities Act (ADA)* proves that it is

unlawful to discriminate on the basis of a medically recognized physical or mental handicap.

5. *The Equal Pay Act* applies to victims of pay discrimination regardless of gender. The victim must prove that his/her work was equal to the work of an employee of the opposite sex, that it was performed in the same establishment and that they were paid less. Then the employer must justify the system based on merit, seniority, or any factor other than sex.

6. *Sexual Harassment* falls into two categories. The first, known as "Quid Pro Quo," occurs when an employer conditions the granting of economic or job benefits upon the receipt of sexual favors from a subordinate. The second category involves a sexually discriminatory "Hostile Environment" created by unwelcome sexual advances, requests for sexual favors, and other verbal or physical conduct of a sexual nature.

7. *Racial or Ethnic Harassment* involves a working environment charged with racial or ethnic hostility created or tolerated by the employer. Such a hostile environment occurs when workers of a particular heritage are subjected to higher levels of criticism, or crude or practical jokes. It can also involve being exposed to racial or ethnic insults, jokes, or graffiti.

These laws were created to allow people of all sexes, races, and religions, including white males, equal opportunity and access to the work force. They have even influenced company policies. For example, DuPont has a policy that harassment of any type will not be tolerated regardless of whether the initiator is a DuPont employee, customer, or business associate. DuPont communicates its policies to its employees, including salespeople. Sales managers that accept the principle of sales force diversity must create an environment within the sales force that understands the needs and concerns of a diverse department so that everyone gains a competitive edge.

ATTACKING THE PROBLEM

In determining how executives directing the sales and marketing effort should address diversity issues within their companies, several things should be realized. First, managing diversity does not

involve lowering performance standards, providing special programs to make white males feel guilty, replacing affirmative action,
developing women and minorities at the expense of white males, or
a short-term strategy. Instead it entails understanding the needs of
each individual, having the courage to make the right personnel
decisions and creating an environment where teammates will
respect each other. The essence of managing diversity is recognizing and capitalizing on the value of diverse work force, using new
ideas, new perspectives, and wanting everyone to maximize his or
her potential.

Diversity issues that occur with a sales effort can be effectively
handled through the use of good management skills. In the case of
the African-American salesperson who must call on prejudiced clients, it is essential for management to reinforce its support by
initiating *one-on-one* meetings. Through collaboration and dialogue, these meetings provide an opportunity for the sales manager
and salesperson to monitor and address issues of concern to the
salesperson. In fact, using *joint sales calls*, where they visit a client
together, is also helpful. Team building and even mentoring can
help women and minority salespeople, as well as sales managers.

Team building involves activities and a sense of cooperation that
encourages salespeople toward consensus decision making. It also
enhances team performance and improves communication and relationships between members of the sales force. A *mentor* is a professional person, usually one at an executive level in an organization,
who acts as a counselor, advisor, and professional guide to a less
experienced person, often in the same organization. It is helpful to
the growth of any professional to have access to this kind of guidance. In the work environment it is essential to career advancement
and job security to align with someone who is successful and knows
what to do next. "On-the-job" mentors also fulfill a very important
career enhancement and psychosocial function. This means that the
mentor takes such an active role in the protégé's career growth that
the protégé feels even more a part of the organization. To foster
diversity in the sales force, it can be advantageous to have access to
someone who has done it all before. Mentors, formally or informally provided by the company, or sought out by women and minorities in sales positions, not only help with their performance, but

also with career development by sharing their insights, development, and expertise.

Diversity management training is another method that can be used to prepare sales managers for the changing composition of the sales force. Most proactive companies are those who have embraced diversity training for their employees, especially those in sales. Intensive training should particularly be directed to sales managers, as nothing changes until managerial behavior changes. Several themes that diversity management training should address are the following:

- The need for sales managers to be concerned about demographics, diversity organizational benefits, and their own management effectiveness
- The problems that arise when diversity is not adequately managed, including litigation implications, high turnover, reduced productivity, poor attitude, workplace stress, and poor communication
- The skills required to manage diversity

There are many ways in which companies implement diversity training for sales managers. At IBM, diversity awareness has been incorporated into traditional, customer-focused sales training. A particular module of the training challenges salespeople to look at situations from their customer's perspective and offers role-playing exercises that confront multicultural issues. At Seafirst Bank in Seattle, diversity training for lending officers took the form of a series of one-day seminars on workplace diversity. The program included a self-examination exercise that encouraged participants to look inward at their perceptions of themselves and others. Some aspects of Seafirst's training include films, video segments, facts and figures on diversity, case studies and group discussions.[11]

Sales managers should acquire the following skills from such training:

- *An understanding of the sales manager's own biases and stereotypical assumptions about others and how these affect decision making.* For example, how is the female population perceived? Are ambitious women seen as "too pushy?" Are Asians seen as more docile and passive than other ethnic groups?

- *Improved problem-solving and listening skills geared to those from other cultures.* Local community leaders from the NAACP, Latin and Asian-American Community, and Anti-Defamation League, or women's organizations could also be used to educate sales managers about these various groups as well as cultivate relationships with the local marketplace. This is an important component in developing these skills because many sales managers may not have a background in dealing extensively with these particular groups.[12]

- *Increased awareness of the employer's unwritten rules of success and the skill to communicate them.* This will not only educate the sales managers, but provide a necessary dialogue with local people and groups. Finally, success factors should be discussed and encouraged among the sales force. This can involve the use of sponsors and mentors as sources of tutelage, advice, and inspiration. Achievement, professionalism, and a demonstrated competence in performing the job should be the basis of career advancement, regardless of race, ethnicity, or sex.

- *Counseling skills for communicating performance and career development information.* This will encourage access to job opportunities and identify the attributes, characteristics, and factors that lead to success.

- *Team-building skills in order to reinforce sales professionalism and trust.* This will make salespeople aware of the values and lifestyles of their colleagues from other cultures and to acknowledge their own prejudices.

- *Transforming the work environment skills that help to make an ambiance conducive to diversity.* This will instill and provide an appreciation for diversity and good community relations.

- *Patience, since there are no quick fixes or easy answers in managing diversity.*

Some firms have found that assigning accountability to management may be a way to work on diversity issues. This accountability can be linked to a compensation plan reward system that compensates managers for successfully handling diversity efforts.[13] Colgate-Palmolive links pay for diversity performance to show that the company values diversity. These efforts focus primarily on women and African Americans. By assigning individual objectives for all managers, including sales managers, such as attracting women to Colgate at all levels, the company will reward its managers for successfully achieving this. Corning, Inc., uses the annual performance review process to evaluate how diversity matters have been addressed. This process not only evaluates how women and minorities were considered for job openings and promotions, but also evaluates complaints filed against a manager. At Corning, all employees, including those in sales, are expected to attend diversity seminars to increase their awareness and sensitivity of issues concerning women and minorities. Federal Express has a task force on women and minorities in sales management. They publish an article in their own sales newsletter "Sales Perspective" that discusses their diversity efforts with the entire sales organization.

Another way to manage diversity is by utilizing total quality management (TQM) principles. The key concepts of quality management are closely linked to those of managing diversity.

The principal goal of *total quality management* is the overall improvement of the organization that, in turn, increases the reliability of service to the customer and raises customer satisfaction. Managers and employees cannot focus constructively on improving quality to customers until they understand the importance of meeting requirements within and across departments and functions. Organizations function most effectively when sales goals are aligned with the organization's goals. Organizations are more successful in uniting different groups in the pursuit of common goals when individuals feel secure that their differences are valued.

Empowerment is an element of total quality management that expedites the overall improvement of the sales department. Salespeople feel *empowered* when they are allowed to participate in decisions affecting their work. Effective performance requires trust and open communication among team members. Diversity issues that are poorly managed can undercut trust, sabotage communication, and create barriers to the sales force's ability to achieve its potential. Sales managers are becoming more responsible for creating effective teams of employees who are unlike themselves in gender, race, religion, culture, language, education, values, lifestyle, and family relationships. In total quality management, effectively managing a diverse labor force becomes an integral part of enabling salespeople to achieve to their full potential.

Women and minorities must also aggressively seek out sales

career opportunities and bring competitive qualifications as candidates. Once on the job they must request support from the company to provide the performance expected from them and take an active role in their own development (see Figure 7.7). As an example, an Asian-American sales manager should not only establish a network with other Asian professionals in order to share their experiences on performing and coping on the job, but anyone that can share information and corporate norms.

WOMEN IN SALES MANAGEMENT

Research shows that salespeople's response to the leadership styles of their sales manager may depend on the gender of both the manager and the subordinate. There is some evidence that male subordinates may react to newly appointed female sales managers

FIGURE 7.7. How Women Can Use Mentoring to Help

GAIN A SENSE OF BELONGING

INSIGHT ON WHAT TO DO

PROFESSIONAL GROWTH

CAREER ADVANCEMENT

BETTER PERFORMANCE

JOB SECURITY

Copyright 1995, by Tony Carter

PROFILE: Vice President of Trading for a National Brokerage Firm

A vice president of trading for a national brokerage firm started out as the only woman in a group of seventeen men.

She attributes her rise through the ranks to "Never asking anyone to do anything that I wouldn't do myself." She adds, "It is important to make a business relationship with co-workers a partnership so that if my department is busy they know that I will pitch in and help them."

It was a slow grind upward and it took a great deal of patience to watch less-experienced men get promoted over me. I remember one such incident—someone who had less time on the trading desk, unmarried with no college education, was given a promotion and raise that I felt should have gone to me. I was told, off the record, that he was given preference because he was a man and after all, someday he would have a family to support. Although I'd completed a bachelor's degree and was working on my master's, the question I was invariably asked at every interview was "How fast can you type?"

It is very important to have a mentor. The person who acted as mine was thrust into the situation. It was a matter of necessity—they needed someone to learn the job fast, so that someone could cover if a trader was out. Fifteen years later, we still work together and he's the head of my desk, but it was a bumpy start.

I believe that gender is still a factor in the workplace, but certainly far less than it has been. We're still dealing with an "old time boy's club" out there, but we've gone from being tolerated to being accepted and on occasion—welcomed. So, it is important to dispel the myths and prejudices against women in the business world. Businesswomen are resourceful, flexible, and assertive. My advice to other women is to try to resolve difficulties yourself before enlisting help from others—namely, management. Above all, act professionally.[14]

with unwarranted hostility. The historic norm was that women who competed against men were unfeminine. However, more recently there is growing evidence that both male and female subordinates are quite satisfied with their female sales manager's supervision. The research also showed the following.

1. Men appreciated supervision by considerate sales leaders. The reason may be that men view their work with their female sales managers as an extended family or social relationship.
2. Women valued charismatic leaders. The reason may be that women may classify "considerate treatment" from female sales managers as an inhibiting factor in the masculine world of selling.[15]

A basic tenet for the twenty-first century will be to properly manage the firm's limited personnel resources. Executives will be unable to sufficiently fill the available sales management and sales positions and avoid potential lawsuits in the future without effectively recruiting, keeping and managing women and minorities. But, the responsibilities for successfully dealing with diversity issues lie both with the corporate world and women and minorities themselves. As Joyce Miller, former Executive Director of the U.S. Department of Labor's "Glass Ceiling Commission" has said "All companies should have a diversity program to address, confront, and meet these issues, but the key is having competent women and minorities in the first place."[16] Ray Habib, Director of Sales for Everything Yogurt, considered one of the top ten franchises for the 1990s, acknowledged for its commitment to women and minority franchises, made some interesting observations. With his company now entering global markets, Habib claims, "We find all types of people do well with us, but our emphasis is on the selection process." He adds, "We find the quality of the people, their track record, appearance, communication skills, professionalism, and ability determine success."[17] Given the highly competitive environment in which sales departments are expected to generate results, perhaps finding salespeople and sales managers in this way goes beyond being the right thing to do. It may even make good business sense. See Table 7.1 for statistics regarding diversity training.

TABLE 7.1 Diversity Training

50%	50%
YES	NO

Source: *Carter Sales Force Survey* (1996).

SUMMARY

The twenty-first century will continue to bring widespread changes throughout Corporate America. The implications of these changes for the sales profession will be that most of the new entrants into the work force will be women and minorities. They are significantly underrepresented and underutilized in sales and sales management positions, which will grow. Corporations that value diversity and fully utilize women and minorities as a productive resource in the sales effort will be the businesses that will be competitive and survive.

Questions

1. Why is managing diversity important for the sales force and what bearing can it have in the future?
2. What did the "Glass Ceiling Commission" do?
3. If you, as a sales manager, wanted to create as productive an environment as possible for women and minorities on the sales force, what would you do?
4. What are the characteristics of a good diversity training program for the sales manager?
5. What role should women and minorities in sales play in managing diversity?
6. What is at risk from a business standpoint if a sales manager does not handle diversity issues effectively?
7. What is at risk from a litigation standpoint if a sales manager does not handle diversity issues effectively?
8. Can you identify any companies in which the sales managers uses effective measures for handling diversity issues and describe what they are doing?

CASE STUDY: BOSTON TRUST

Sales Management Diversity in the Large Corporation

Walter Roberts was transferred from Boston Trust in Detroit, Michigan, where he functioned as Sales and Marketing Manager. Walter was actively recruited and promoted by Boston Trust in Boston, Massachusetts, to fill a newly created position as Northeast Sales Manager. This occurred while he was pursuing a Juris Doctor and Masters in Business Administration. Upon completion of his JD and MBA, Walter relocated to Boston to occupy this position.

He believes that his new department is leading a shift in the company to become more market driven. In addition, he is not only the highest ranking black officer in the company, but he is the only black manager in the entire company. Walter believes that he is paving the way for the future development of more black managers in the company. Even though he feels that he is highly qualified, he feels a great deal of resentment from all levels of employees that he either: does not deserve the position because he did not work through the ranks in Boston; or, must be a "yes man" to high management levels in order to have been selected.

Boston Trust has offered financial services to the business community and individuals since 1874. The environment of the company is stodgy and most employees have been with the company ten to twenty years. Boston Trust is one of the largest and most profitable financial services companies in the United States and, in particular, Boston. However, over the past six years it has steadily been losing its market share.

Description

Brian Nelson is Walter's immediate manager and Walter reports to him. Brian has been with Boston Trust in Boston and worked his way up the ranks since he received his MBA ten years ago. It was not Brian's idea to have Walter transferred from Detroit. Since his arrival seven months ago, he has treated Walter in a distant, mistrusting manner. Walter has not found him to be an effective communicator. While he always claims to be too busy to meet with Walter, he always seems to have time for others. Brian would not initiate these meetings. He will not take the time to provide feedback on Walter's performance.

Brian can be very moody and makes everyone aware of it when he is in a bad mood. He belittles people in meetings and in private and unless you are in agreement with him or working to support his ego, you are perceived as a threat. These are some of the comments that he has made to Walter:

- When Walter asked him what he thought of a presentation he gave, Brian replied, "It was OK. Why do you ask? Are you insecure or something?"

- At a manager's meeting, in front of the attendees and Walter, he said, "He won't be here long; he won't make it past March."
- Brian has told other managers that Walter has been prescribing cures without knowing the illness, as a result of being asked to speak about his observations of the organization.
- Brian has mentioned a few times in meetings in front of Walter why a person in a similar position was fired, and that he had better watch himself. (Walter's conduct had not warranted such a warning.)
- Finally, Brian teases women managers in particular at meetings and uses vulgar language toward them, yet they go along with it. Walter has been the only manager to stand up to him when he has either attacked him in meetings or has interfered in his department.

Calvin Mason is Regional Manager for the Northeast and Brian Nelson reports to him. Calvin is the person responsible for Walter's transfer to Boston. He was impressed with Walter's performance a few years ago when he was Regional Manager for the Southwest. Calvin is very bright, intuitive, and well educated, with a JD/MBA. He cares about people and believes in what the company stands for, which is quality and good service. Although Walter does not get many opportunities to talk to him, when he does, Calvin gives him some encouragement. He has said to Walter on a few occasions, "You will be the first black manager of a major city in this company." Calvin Mason evaluates employees on job performance and not how hard they laugh at his jokes.

Question

Walter Roberts has come to you as a fellow manager to discuss the frustration that he feel in Boston Trust. How would be describe his situation and what types of things would you advise him to do in order to alleviate his problem?

CASE STUDY: HUNTER CORPORATION

Factions in the Sales Department

The Hunter Corporation, which is located in Jackson, Mississippi, manufactures environmentally compliant powder coatings for servicing in the automotive, architectural, and general industrial markets. They also manufacture structural steel components including truss girders, bar joints, metal decking, and other specialized products. Hunter has three manufacturing plants that employ 750 people. Last year their annual sales were about $100 million. Jill Cameron has been Hunter's sales manager for the past seven years. She has recently been preoccupied with two dilemmas in the department.

Morgan Stevens and Ken Brewer are the only two senior account managers in the department. Morgan is the only African American out of a sales force of twenty-four people. He began working for Hunter seventeen years ago in Production and Operations. Eventually, he was promoted to the position of Production Supervisor. After thirteen years in Production, he decided to pursue an opening in the Sales Department. On the basis of his technical knowledge and good interpersonal skills, he did well with customers. For the most part, customers have respected his competence. After two and one-half years in the department he was promoted from Sales Rep to Senior Account Manager. One of Jill's concerns is that she has recently heard secondhand from other reps that some clients that Morgan calls on do not want to deal with him because he is black. In reality, this is something that Morgan has dealt with since he has been in the department, but Jill has only heard about it recently. He has never discussed this situation with her.

Jill's other concern deals with certain allegiances being formed within the sales department. Hunter's sales force is composed of an extremely independent and aggressive group of people. However, because most of these individuals have been successful using their own styles and techniques, it has been difficult to bring them together for the purpose of solving specific account problems or discussing national multilocation accounts. National multilocation accounts generally involve two to four salespeople depending on the geographic location of Hunter's customers. When the sales department works together it is still not in a unified way, but with some people siding with Ken Brewer and others siding with Morgan. While Ken and Morgan do not have any particular dislike for each other, they have never really had any particular use for each other either. Actually, both of them are still responsible for perpetuating these factions. Jill has made efforts to continually place salespeople in team settings. The results of these efforts have shown less than expected productivity and communication. In these team settings the salespeople are just "going through the motions" of team activity—enough to satisfy management.

Question

So, now Jill finds that she has been spending a great deal of time trying to figure out how to solve these two dilemmas. How should she handle them?

SECTION V:
CURRENT SELLING SKILLS
AND TOOLS

Chapter 8

Sales Planning

MANAGEMENT FUNCTION OF SALES PLANNING

The sales plan is one of the toughest functions of a sales manager's responsibilities. Sales planning is difficult because it is hard to predict what business events will occur in the future. The ability to identify future conditions in the marketplace, how active a company will be, what staff levels it will need, or the actions of competitors can be difficult to predict with any degree of precision. Documenting this plan creates a degree of accountability rather than just being able to say "I've got our plan all in my head" (see Table 8.1). No business understands the importance of effective sales planning better than the competitive soft drink beverage industry. PepsiCo's net sales totaled $30.4 billion, with 71 percent of its revenue generated from the domestic U.S. market. Coke's net sales totaled $18 billion, with 71 percent of its revenue coming from global markets. PepsiCo will alter its global strategy in the future, targeting emerging markets, such as China, India, and Eastern Europe.[1]

Sales managers who direct growing business activity annually have the ability to know their customers well enough to design a sales process that meets their needs. Customer sophistication and price and value sensitivity are strong factors in both retail and business-to-business customer buying behavior. Wal-Mart changed its business design by offering inexpensive access to a wide range of nationally known products. Wal-Mart made shopping easier by offering lower prices than other department stores and using logistics to cut an average of two hours off shopping time.[2]

Effective sales managers must not only focus on the sales force achieving their goals, but on the whole process. Thinking and acting

TABLE 8.1. Use of a Written Plan

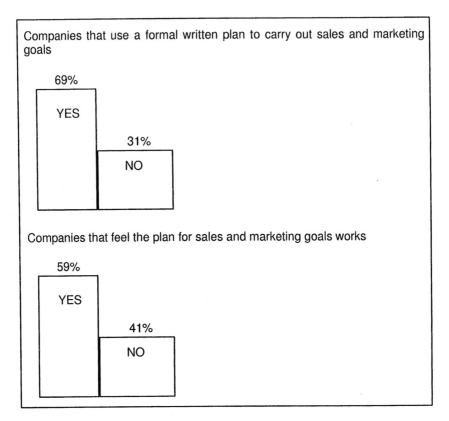

Source: *Carter Sales Force Survey* (1996).

with a strategic perspective is the key to successfully impacting the sales process. Accordingly, sales managers can coach their salespeople to build up strategic skills in the areas of planning, customer relationship building, teamwork, selling, follow-up selling skills and negotiation.[3]

Format of the Plan

The sales plan determines what direction the company will take as it attempts to reach its sales objectives. It also depicts how the sales force will implement its efforts. The ability to identify revenue and customer opportunities provides the means to effectively develop a focused sales plan. The sales plan should be a relevant, evolving document that states the company's direction. This is accomplished by using the following sections in the sales plan.

Mission Statement

This section briefly discusses the philosophy of the company toward business and values. The mission statement is usually no longer than half a page to one full page.

Sales and Marketing Objectives

These are the goals that the sales force will try to accomplish in terms of the directiion of the organization.

MARKET DYNAMICS

This section deals with the macro environmental conditions that may be out of the organization's control, but still have to be identified because of the threats and opportunities that they can pose for the sales force. In this section the domestic U.S. economy and local state or city economies could be examined. Industry conditions should also be reported on as well.

Market Segmentation

This is the process of dividing the total market for a product or service into various subgroups divided by common characteristics (see Figure 8.1). Examples of this can be seen in the computer notebook/laptop computer industry. Business executives, salespeople, business students, overnight delivery truck drivers and family members are various customer segments with different characteristic and uses for the same product. Identifying these segments and their needs will give the sales force a better understanding of what specific features and benefits to emphasize when asking these cus-

FIGURE 8.1. Segmentation

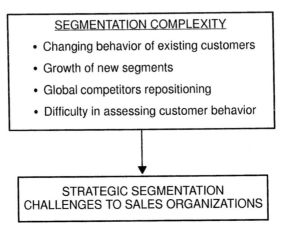

tomers for business. Segmentation gives the sales force a competitive edge, a customer relationship building process, the ability to identify customer opportunities and meet customer needs, and maximum use of sales-related resources. Customers can be segmented by location, age, gender, income, ethnic background, personality, or lifestyle.

COMPETITION ANALYSIS

This section provides a critical profile of other firms in the same industry. These competitors can be examined in terms of their staff levels and quality, company philosophy, geographic scope of where they do business, products, or services and financial condition. The key benefit to having a competition analysis is that it allows an organization to determine its own *competitive advantage* also known as a *distinctive competency,* which are unique advantages over competitors. In addition, competition analysis points to strengths that competitors have that might be duplicated or can at least be monitored.

This is an extremely critical section of a sales plan, because while the sales plan's purpose is to determine where the sales organization is going, this section says how it will get there. To be competitive, sales strategies must be developed that are different from rivals and provide unique value. Firms can outperform their competition if they can establish sustainable distinctive competencies. The key to effective sales planning is to incorporate strategies in the plan that create comparable value to customers at a lower cost or provide increased value or both. Sales strategies should use an understanding of the firm's resources, environmental forces, and management's values and objectives.[4] Sound sales strategies are also important because they reflect a customers place in the company's mission, goals and purpose.[5]

FINANCIAL CONDITION

This section should provide actual performance figures from the prior year and most important, projected figures for the upcoming period. This should include projected revenue figures and expenses, ideally month by month. Sales managers should identify customer activity-related costs from production-related costs. Then, they should explore different ways to reduce sales costs required to perform various activities. This type of cost analysis by sales managers can show exactly what sales-related activities are linked to the generation of sales revenue and the allocation of resources.[6]

* * *

SAMPLE SALES PLAN

New York National Division Sales Plan
TABLE OF CONTENTS

Mission Statement

Market Dynamics

- National Economy
- New York City Economy
- Market Opportunities and Threats
- Recommendations and Other Suggestions

Sales Goals

Customer Segments

- New York Market Segments

Competitor Analysis

Strategies and Tactics

- Target Accounts
- Target Segments

Appendix

Mission Statement

The purpose of the New York National Division is to assist local customers with the successful completion of transactions outside of the local area and to effectively develop accounts of contacts in order to generate national business.

Market Dynamics

National Economy

Market conditions are improving in Houston and Dallas. Although vacancy rates in Houston and Dallas remain among the highest in the country, businesses there are benefitting from a Texas economy that is diversifying beyond oil, from a moratorium on new construction, and from corporate relocations to the area, particularly in the Dallas Market.

Major cities in the Northeast, hit much later by the rolling recession, have fundamental advantages that may help ride it out. Overbuilding has not been too severe, and the economy is diverse. Some areas in Seattle, San Francisco, and Sacramento have prospered. In Los Angeles, cutbacks in aerospace defense work may have weakened their economy.

New York City Economy

The City's economy is out of a recession, but not in a strong recovery. The real estate market has contracted, tourism is slowing, hotel occupancy rates have fallen, unemployment has skyrocketed, and inflation has jumped. New York City is coming out of a cyclical downturn in its economy, so the City should see some recovery in the future.

Market Opportunities and Threats

Opportunities

- Corporations restructuring may be selling off assets such as real estate and/or getting financing to generate cash flow.
- Troubled properties may drive activity for banks and life insurance companies.
- Explore potential from foreign (European/Korean/Japanese) lenders and investors as well as Domestic Pension Funds.
- Focus on national corporate prospects that moved outside of Manhattan to such areas as Long Island and northeastern New Jersey.
- Smaller competitors and agents should fall out of the industry due to the slowdown in activity.

Threats

- A continuing slowdown will affect revenues.
- A declining stock market could affect retail and industrial activity.
- Interest rates continue to increase.

Recommendations and Other Suggestions

Recommendations

- Continue to target and develop seminars for key accounts.
- Provide entertainment, such as sporting events, theater and dinners.
- Continue focus and clear direction of the sales effort. This should involve improved quality of sales calls, better use of time in scheduling calls, paying better attention to "A" accounts, sales/marketing/product knowledge training for the salespeople.

Other Suggestions

- Continue ongoing technical training of staff.
- Instill customer responsiveness and teamwork in staff.
- Be willing to have legal and technical staff adjust posture depending on relationship with customer and circumstances of deal.
- Constantly review various approaches to price on national deals.

Sales Goals

1. To increase your share of business activity in your market, key target accounts need to be identified and sales progress monitored quarterly.
2. In 1999:
   a. Identify your office's ten best customers.
      Manager will contact each customer quarterly.
   b. Evaluate the feasibility of hiring additional sales representatives with industry experience. Implement a "targeted" sales effort on customer segments sharing the cost with branch/county operations.
   c. Assist the salespeople in converting prospects to customers.
   d. Make calls on key targeted accounts, especially those in which the transactions are large and complex, and where a sales representative has not been successful in securing the business in the past.
   e. coordinate all sales activities on a monthly basis with *local* and *state* efforts.
   f. Implement updated sales incentive programs for salespeople who develop business activity.
   g. Where possible, make joint calls to improve the service commitment to the customer.
   h. Coordinate promotional activities with branch and regional operations in order to benefit from shared expenses.
3. Customer Presentations
   a. Professional customer presentations need to be planned for the first half of the year which continue to stress the financial strength and service/product capability.

4. Control of Promotional Expenses
   a. Promotional expenses need to be planned and targeted on key accounts.
   b. Salespeople should belong to organizations only if they actively participate and if business is obtained from members of the organization.
5. Service Objectives
   To achieve the highest service level possible within the office.
   a. Office will exhibit customer service attitude; employees will be responsive, courteous and professional.
   b. *All* orders are to be followed up in writing containing as much information as possible.
   c. On canceled, closed, or pending (ninety days) transactions, the customer should be billed promptly and branches should be paid their charges.
   d. Customer service surveys should be taken to monitor the level of customer satisfaction.
6. Personnel Development
   a. Each employee will set specific goals designed to enable the office to achieve its contribution toward the sales objectives. Performance goals are to be set jointly with the sales manager and this should also address skill enhancement.
   b. Each company employee is to receive at least one performance appraisal a year which is to be completed by the manager or direct supervisor. Salary increases will not be approved without an accompanying performance appraisal which has been reviewed with the employee.
7. Training
   a. Employee training should be a continual process in each office including on the job training under supervision and group training sessions on office procedures, customer service procedures, sales skills training, service/product knowledge, etc.
   b. Regular staff meetings should be held to keep communication flowing to all employees.

c. Specific goals should be established for each employee which will increase their ability to work with customers more effectively.

8. Internal Company Relationships

a. Communicate goals and objectives, including key customers and prospects we plan to target.

b. Communicate service expectations so that issuing offices are in a better position to satisfy the customers' needs.

c. Be willing to meet with and discuss service and sales coordination on a regular basis to avoid conflicts.

9. Projected Sales Revenue

New York National (Estimated Month-by-Month Revenue)

January	700,000
February	600,000
March	750,000
April	800,000
May	800,000
June	800,000
July	550,000
August	550,000
September	250,000
October	115,810
November	200,000
December	500,000
TOTAL	$6,615,810

Customer Segments

Primary Segments	*Secondary Segments*
Developers	Major Local
	Small
	National

Lenders

Banks
Mortgage Bankers
Finance Companies
Insurance Companies
National Lenders
Pension Funds

Attorneys

General Practitioner

National Accounts

Corporations
Franchises

Brokers/Agents

Large Independents

Competitor Analysis

Company Name:

Key Staff:

Strategies/Philosophy:

Recent Performance

Geographic Scope

Sample Sales Plan
STRATEGIES
TARGET ACCOUNTS/KEY ACCOUNTS
TARGET SEGMENTS

KEY ACCOUNT/ TARGET ACCOUNT	STRATEGY SELECTION	TACTICS	PERSON RESPONSIBLE	COST	DUE DATE
Miller Corporation	Growth	Educate and inform Miller staff on financial strength; conduct seminar on financial strength	Simone Mayer	$2,000	February
Account Manager: Joe Eisenberg	Service	Improve technical and pricing awareness	Wendy Salustro	$10,000	Ongoing
	Personal Attention	Lunches	Robert Hynes	$1,000	As special occasions arise
			TOTAL COST	$13,000	
Palin Inc.	Keep customer informed and renew	Identify contacts and have lunch with key staff	Sara Thomas	$500	Spring
Account Manager: Myles Reed		Regular meeting with key staff	Paul Yi	-0-	Quarterly
			TOTAL COST	$500	
Raymonds	Improve awareness	Identify key attorneys that handle national transactions	Arturo Pereyra	-0-	January
Account Manager: Johan Swildens	Keep customer informed	Regular meetings and correspondence with key staff	Marc Lavine	-0-	Quarterly
		One-on-one lunches	George Henman	$1,000	Quarterly
			TOTAL COST	$1,000	

Sample Sales Plan
STRATEGIES
TARGET ACCOUNTS/KEY ACCOUNTS
TARGET SEGMENTS

KEY ACCOUNT/ TARGET ACCOUNT	STRATEGY SELECTION	TACTICS	PERSON RESPONSIBLE	COST	DUE DATE
Malewicz and Krol Account Manager: Stacy Sherman	Improve awareness of technical servicing ability	Servicing Accounts Administrator	Meera Godbole	$10,000	Immediate and continuing (sales calls, phone contact, mail outs)
		Improve account awareness of technical proficiency	Richard Bender	$2,000	Immediate and continuing sales calls, phone contact, mail outs)
		Develop closer ties with attorneys	Adam Pinkert	$1,000 Semi-Annual Lunch	April
	Entertainment	Sports and Theater	Philip Hartz	$2,000 <u>Qtr</u>	Jan., Mar., June, Aug.
			TOTAL COST	$15,000	
Walter Corp. Account Manager: Linda Hadley	Get to know VP's and attorneys that handle transactions	Correspondence and phone contact with Harold Dean on a regular basis	June Rutman	$500	Ongoing
	Good National service involvement	Pre- and post-closing follow-up on files	William Manger	-0-	Ongoing
	Equitable pricing	Monitor pricing info and needs	Christina Villa	<u>-0-</u>	Immediate and continuing
			TOTAL COST	$500	

Sample Sales Plan
STRATEGIES
TARGET ACCOUNTS/KEY ACCOUNTS
TARGET SEGMENTS

TARGET SEGMENT/ ACTIVITIES	STRATEGY SELECTION	TACTICS	PERSON RESPONSIBLE	COST	DUE DATE
New Business Segment	Build Relationships	Regular Meetings	Laura Lee	$-0-	Monthly
Segment Manager: Carolyn Cirillo	Consultation	Marketing and management advice	Yuko Ishizuka	$3,000	Ongoing
			TOTAL COST	$3,000	
Marketing Communications	Advertising Media	Development for key segments	Christine Lavelle	$15,000	Jan. 1995
Project Manager: Martelic Coble	Press Releases, successful projects and promotions.	Increase awareness	Yashuiko Kobayashi	-0-	Quarterly
	Improve sales force technology	Upgrade computer notebooks		$18,000	
	Customer Mailings	PR awareness to key segments	Sumita B. NY National Staff	TBD	Ongoing
	Trade Associations	Memberships in major associations	Isabelle Prevost	$4,000	Ongoing
	In-House Communications	Lead Report		-0-	Monthly
		Internal Newsletter		-0-	Monthly
			TOTAL COST	$37,000	
		Total Target Accounts, Target Segments and Target Projects cost	$60,000		

Sample Sales Plan

FINANCIAL CONDITION

AREA: NEW YORK NATIONAL DIVISION

PREVIOUS YEAR ATTN: SALES MANAGER

	ACTUAL	PLAN
Revenue	4,959,758	5,657,740
Interest Earned	10,009	18,685
Other Revenue	949,840	838,055
Other Agents	70,138	290,750
Commissions	- 58,472	-189,420
NET REVENUE	5,931,273	6,615,810
Taxes	459,656	527,094
Staff Costs	2,735,321	2,520,421
Contracted Labor	68,960	64,300
Computer Equipment	233,231	341,446
Occupancy Expenses/Rent	426,585	426,682
Office Equip/Tele/Supplies	250,211	286,871
Purchased Services	112,989	51,300
Advertising and Promotions		73,988
40,514		
Travel and Entertainment	26,685	85,100
Automobile Expenses	26,542	33,875
Other Expenses	119,530	91,035
60 percent Interest	30,369	37,500
TOTAL EXPENSE	4,564,067	4,506,138
RESULTS W/O INTEREST	1,367,206	2,109,672
CONTRIB. MARGIN	23%	3%
CONCENTRATION EARNING	655,301	739,000
RESULTS WITH INTEREST	2,022,507	2,848,672
CONTRIB. MARGIN	31%	39%
NUMBER OF EMPLOYEES	976	1,011

End of Sample Sales Plan

DEFINING THE MARKET

There are various terms which help determine sales opportunities in the marketplace. Without identifying opportunities in terms of revenue, it is difficult to develop the sales plan and relevant sales strategies and actions. The ability to "define the market" is essential to creating an effective sales plan and should drive the strategic thrust of the sales plan. The key concepts that help to define the market are:

- *Market Potential* - The projected amount of revenue that can be generated by all firms in a given market, under ideal conditions.
- *Sales Potential* - The projected amount of revenue that can be generated by a single firm in a given market, under ideal conditions.
- *Market Forecast* - The projected amount of revenue that can be generated by all firms in a given market, under realistic conditions.
- *Sales Forecast* - The projected amount of revenue that can be generated by a single firm, under realistic conditions.
- *Market Share* - The percentage of business available to a firm in a given market compared to other firms in that same industry.

For example, based on this chart, in Los Angeles in the year 2000, the market potential is $75 million, the sales potential is $9.5 million and market share for the Walter Corporation is 26 percent. The key to getting "potentials" into realistic forecasts is through using various methods which help "massage the figures."

REVENUE PROJECTIONS BY REGIONAL AND LOCAL MARKETS
(MILLIONS OF DOLLARS)

	1998			1999			2000		
	TOTAL	WALTER CORP.	%	TOTAL	WALTER CORP.	%	TOTAL	WALTER CORP.	%
Total U.S.	$1,023.3	$140.7	13.8%	$1,138.4	$160.5	14.1%	$1,170.7	$224.1	19.1%
Western Region	$237.1	$11.8	5.0%	$278.8	$14.0	5.0%	$290.7	$54.7	18.8%
L.A.	64.0	4.4	6.9	74.0	5.2	7.0	75.0	19.5	26.0
San Francisco	30.0	2.7	9.1	35.0	3.1	9.0	35.0	3.3	9.3
Anaheim	18.0	0.7	3.8	22.0	0.9	4.0	24.5	2.2	9.0
Phoenix	12.0	0.5	4.2	12.0	0.5	4.2	11.7	1.0	0.5
San Diego	10.0	0.3	3.0	13.0	0.6	4.5	14.0	1.2	8.8
San Jose	7.1	0.2	3.4	6.8	0.2	3.2	6.5	0.2	3.1
Other	96.0	3.0	3.1	116.0	3.5	3.0	124.0	27.3	22.0
Northeastern Region	$164.0	$22.0	13.4%	$193.3	$26.0	13.5	$213.3	$29.2	13.7%
N.Y. City	51.0	6.2	12.1	62.0	7.4	12.0	68.0	8.4	12.3
N.E. Jersey	30.0	3.3	11.0	35.0	3.9	11.2	39.5	4.7	11.8
Boston	10.0	1.8	18.0	11.0	2.0	11.5	11.5	2.1	18.2
Hartford	2.7	0.5	16.5	3.5	0.6	17.0	4.2	0.7	17.0
Rochester	2.3	0.1	3.0	2.8	0.2	5.0	3.3	0.2	6.1
Other	68.0	10.1	14.8	79.0	11.9	15.0	87.0	13.1	15.3

Methods

- *Historical Data* - This explores the history of sales activity in a particular market and bases future performance on this track record. A drawback of this method can be changes in trends in the marketplace, such as the October 1987 stock market crash.
- *Sales Force Assessment* - Since they have frequent direct client contact, ask the salespeople what they think the marketplace will bear. A drawback here may be the temptation to give self-serving projections.
- *Test Marketing* - Allows actual use of a product by customers in a specifically targeted area to monitor product popularity and future use. A drawback with test marketing is that it can be expensive and once the product, which may even be experimental is in use, it is no longer a secret from the competition.
- *Management Assessment* - This is similar to Sales Force Assessment, but instead asks the managers to share their experience and scope of knowledge to determine what the marketplace will do.
- *Focus Groups* - This uses ten to fifteen representative customers from a business market and asks them a range of questions to determine what the market may do and how to get customers to do business with them.
- *Regression Analysis* - One such method involves statistical analysis based on "The Sum of the Least Squares Method." While the other methods are more qualitative, this is a more quantitative-based way to determine sales projections (see Figures 8.2 and 8.3).[7]
- *Systematic Tracking* - In a more complex marketplace, demand has become harder to predict. Accordingly, it becomes necessary each year to update and revise the process of determining potentials and forecasts to see how the system compared to actual customer demand.[8]

Reference guides, such as the *Survey of Buying Power* that is published annually by *Sales & Marketing Magazine* or various federal government reports, many of which are free, provide market data that point to and help develop market and sales potentials and forecasts. Determining the potentials and forecasts is critical because once they have been defined, then strategic sales decision

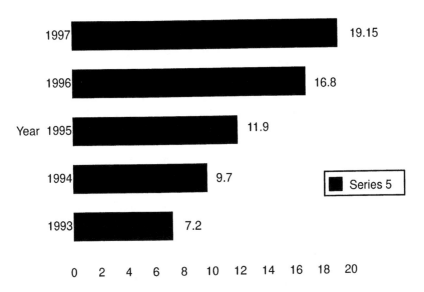

FIGURE 8.2. Year Predictions

making becomes much easier for sales managers. This means selecting sensible sales strategies based on market, segments, or specific account revenue opportunities, determining performance goals by assigning more realistic quotas to salespeople and more effectively focusing on territory potential based on revenues (see Table 8.2).

PRICE DETERMINATION

With price determination, the challenge for sales managers is to reach both a price and customer value definition that is workable for the company and the marketplace.[9] This can be determined by what the market is willing to pay and the price structure that other firms use in their particular industry.

These are some strategies that can help sales managers with the pricing process:

1. Develop a collaborative effort between sales, senior level management, and other functional areas in the company. Being close

to the customer, the sales force can offer suggestions concerning their price sensitivity to upper management. The marketing department could point to the need to raise prices based on the need for greater profit margins, or production could explain certain manufacturing expenses that should be factored into the price structure.

2. Explore different pricing approaches that may provide a competitive edge. Cost Plus pricing uses the product or service cost as a starting point and adds in an adequate profit margin.

3. Competition-based pricing, which can mean pricing to meet competition, pricing below competition, or pricing above competition.

4. A quantitatively based method that can give a price level or a price starting point is break-even analysis.

This calculation looks at: $\dfrac{\text{fixed costs}}{\text{selling price-variable costs}}$

Example: $\dfrac{\text{fixed costs} = \$50,000}{\$100-\$50} = 1000$ units as the break-even point

$$\text{Sales price (unit)-variable costs (unit)}$$

This is the output point where revenue equals costs and which identifies that output point that must be met before costs exceed revenue. Break-even analysis is a good quantitatively based method that can help sales managers determine pricing levels. It also draws attention to the cost activity involved in the process of doing business, which should help sales managers stay in touch with the relevant costs in the sales process.[10]

Before initiating a price structure, sales managers should communicate to the sales force that dropping price should not be a sales strategy of first resort. This is something that happens frequently based on the ability of salespeople to use pricing as a way to increase sales which does not always translate to profitability. Some customers are so price focused that they may not be worth the effort.

Many companies have extensive information on sales activity, market share, distribution volume, and the benefits of advertising

FIGURE 8.3. Sales Predictions

YEAR	TIME PERIOD (x)	SALES ($ Millions) (y)	squared x	squared y	x*y
1993	1	7.2	1	51.84	7.2
1994	2	9.6	4	92.16	19.2
1995	3	12.6	9	158.76	37.8
1996	4	16.8	16	282.24	67.2
1997	5	**19.5**	25	380.25	97.5
1998	6		36	0	0
1999	7		49	0	0
2000	8		64	0	0
2001	9		81	0	0
	Sum of x 10	Sum of y 46.2	Sum of Sq x 30	Sum of Sq y 585	Sum of x*y 131.4
	Mean of x 2.5	Mean of y 11.55			

N=4 $b = (N*sum(xy) - sum(x)*sum(y))/(N*sum(squared(x)) - square(sum(x)))$

b= 3.18

$a = mean(y) - b*mean(x)$

a= 3.6

Forecast for 1997:   19.5

FIGURE 8.3 (continued)

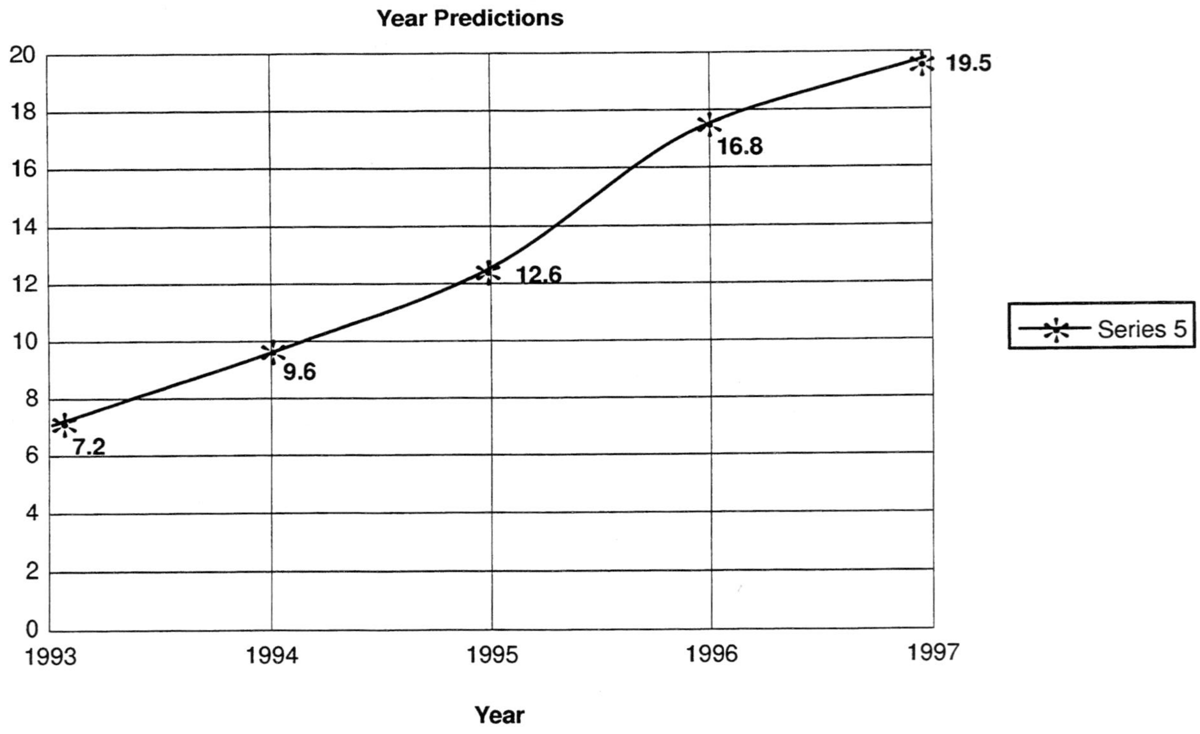

Year Predictions

Series 5

19.5

16.8

12.6

9.6

7.2

1993   1994   1995   1996   1997

Year

20
18
16
14
12
10
8
6
4
2
0

TABLE 8.2. Various Basis for Sales Force Territory Assignments

- Experience level of salesperson demand of territory

- Personal preference of the salesperson

- Automated territory mapping systems which identify territory opportunities

- By customer size and volume

- Based on density of potential business and proximity to manufacturing plant

Source: *Carter Sales Force Survey* (1996).

TABLE 8.3. Knowledge of Pricing Matters

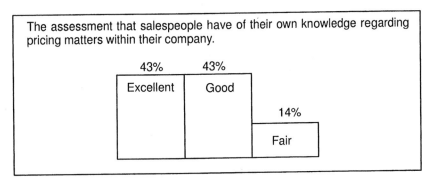

The assessment that salespeople have of their own knowledge regarding pricing matters within their company.

43% — Excellent
43% — Good
14% — Fair

Source: *Carter Sales Force Survey* (1996).

on sales. However, tracking measures on pricing performance are not usually done. A price tracking system should graph information on pricing performance. Comparing competitor's prices on a line graph can show a firm its pricing performance in relation to its industry.[11]

Pricing must work in conjunction with other company considerations. This means looking at costs as a basic component of price, the customer who determines if that price along with product or service quality is receiving superior value and sales objectives.[12]

PROFILE: W. R. Bennett, Business Development Manager, Monsanto Company

"Today's highly competitive and demanding business environment, really requires a clear, useful planning process. While it's important to listen to customers, sales managers have to devise a plan that addresses how your products meet their needs. Business conditions today see sales organizations forming more partnerships and alliances with customers, reducing the size of their sales force, and relying more heavily on sales force technology and electronic commerce. The sales plan must be devised in a manner that allows a sales organization to meet its routine tasks, yet anticipate and respond to any new business demands."

Source: W. R. Bennett (November 14, 1996). Personal Interview, Monsanto, New Orleans, Louisiana.

SUMMARY

Planning, while a difficult function of sales management, is extremely critical for the strategic focus and direction of the sales force. By "defining the market" and determining the potentials and forecast it becomes much easier for sales managers to make tactical sales decisions and develop effective sales strategies. With an understanding of the marketplace, in terms of revenue figures, it also becomes easier to write a realistic sales plan, set sales quotas, and determine territory potential. Pricing considerations should also be a role of sales managers and this should be based on internal costs, sales objectives, and customer and competitor information.

Questions

1. Why are sales plans considered one of the most difficult functions of sales management?
2. What are the various components of a good sales plan?
3. There are various benefits that can be derived from segmentation. What are they?
4. What is the key purpose to a sales organization in conducting a competition analysis?
5. How does the process of "defining the market" work?
6. What are the important considerations in developing a pricing structure?

7. Using the sum of the least squares example given in the chapter, calculate the sales predictions for the years 1998 through 2001.
8. Emarch Corporation wants to establish the "break-even" point" from a particular computer product that they sell. They have determined that their fixed costs are $170,000 and their sales price per unit and variable costs per unit to be $150 and $100 respectively. Please calculate Emarch's break-even point in units.

CASE STUDY: SALES MANAGEMENT OF DRUG PRODUCTS

Mary Danuta's First Steps as a Sales Manager

This morning Dr. Calvin Stanley, President and CEO of Genet-Pharm, announced at the senior scientists' meeting, "I just want to let you all know that I believe we are in the midst of an exciting era for this company. I really think our research and hard work has paid off with the development of our new drug products." GenetPharm is a biotechnology firm located in southern New Jersey employing about fifty people. Most biotech firms are small and entrepreneurial in nature-averaging between forty to two-hundred employees. Genet-Pharm was started seven years ago and until recently was principally engaged in research and development. They have recently developed drug products in cancer therapy and have received F.D.A. approval to manufacture them. It now plans to actively market these drug products.

Biotechnology has been a growth industry in the corporate world. The biotechnology industry handles the development of new products in the diagnosis and treatment of diseases. For a few valid reasons biotech firms are usually funded by venture capitalists or large pharmaceutical companies. First, the profit margins that can be realized are quite lucrative. This is especially true in the case of venture capitalists who are involved with the public offering of a biotech firm. Second, while large pharmaceutical firms will work on a diversified drug product base, typically many biotech firms will only focus on a specific drug product. Such an affiliation can allow a large pharmaceutical company a "big payoff" if the biotech firm's efforts are successful without the pharmaceutical company having to allocate their own resources to do that research internally. Last, many of the internal bureaucracies that can hamper innovation for large pharmaceutical companies are really minimized in small, streamlined biotech operations.

Mary Danuta has been with GenetPharm as a Research Scientist in the lab for seven years. She has a Masters Degree in Microbiology and has recently received an Executive MBA degree. She wants to use her lab experience and business degree outside of the lab and GenetPharm has given her the opportunity by appointing her to a newly created position. To effectively promote the cancer therapy drug products, she's been made sales manager for all of New Jersey. GenetPharm will target physicians, pharmacies, and hospitals as customers. GenetPharm hired an outside independent market research firm to identify some data. They determined that Mary's territory in New Jersey has about $1.5 billion available in total revenue for drug products.

Within the three primary customer segments independent physicians control, through prescriptions, about 52 percent of this figure with pharmacies and hospitals actually spending about 20 percent and 28 percent respectively. GenetPharm wants to penetrate about 2 percent of this market. The annual sales budget given by Dr. Calvin Stanley, which includes salaries and other sales and promotional expenses, is $389,700. Mary will basically have to start from scratch which will include developing an effective sales effort and creating a sales department. From the Survey of Buying Power in *Sales and Marketing Management Magazine* and other sources, Mary pieced together an analysis of territories throughout New Jersey and was able to formulate the following table:

__TERRITORY__	__% OF TOTAL DRUG PRODUCT SALES__
Atlantic/Cape May	5%
Bergen/Passaic	19%
Jersey City	7%
Middlesex/Somerset/Hunterdon	11%
Monmouth/Ocean	12%

Newark	21%
Trenton	4%
Vineland/Millville/Bridgeton	2%
Other Counties	19%
New Jersey	100%
Estimate of Total Sales Revenue Available for Drug Products in New Jersey	$1.5 billion

Question

Advise Mary about what she should do.

Chapter 9

Personal Selling

IMPORTANCE OF SELLING

Effective selling is the latest and best area for capturing customers. While product quality has always had to be great just to be competitive, the next place to compete is in sales and customer service. The consulting firm Bain & Company has developed research showing that boosting a company's customer-retention rate of 2 percent has the same effect on profits as cutting costs by 10 percent. Effective selling means directing the entire organization, from manufacturing to finance, on sales and customer service. It needs the involvement and attention of top management and requires building relationships with customers. For example, General Electric has engineers stationed full-time with some of their customers. The process of effective selling uses salespeople to solve customers' problems, not just take their orders.

Customers also want sellers who can develop strong relationships because of the intense pressure to form partnerships with their own customers. Today's smarter, tougher, more demanding customer has less patience than ever for the hard sell and more opportunities to take his or her business elsewhere. This ability is essential to success in business today, when customers are increasingly looking for business partners. The quality top salespeople possess is empathy; customers greatly value this because it allows salespeople to see the world through the customer's eyes.

Sales, like many other business activities, has experienced significant changes in how companies conduct themselves. To survive and grow, companies must implement powerful changes not just in the way they meet the needs of their customer base, but also in the way they cultivate new business.

Psychologists have identified two different underlying goals that people pursue in achievement situations. A learning goal orients people to improve their abilities and master the tasks they perform. A performance goal orients them to achieve a positive evaluation of their current abilities and performance from important others. A learning goal orientation stems from an intrinsic interest in one's work. This involves a preference for challenging work, a view of oneself as being curious, and a search for opportunities that permit independent attempts to master material. A performance goal orientation stems from an extrinsic interest in one's work—the desire to use one's work to achieve valued external ends.

SELLING SKILLS

Under a learning orientation, also referred to as a *mastery orientation,* salespeople enjoy the process of discovering how to sell effectively (see Table 9.1). They are attracted by challenging sales situations and not unduly bothered by mistakes. They value the feelings of personal growth and mastery they derive from their job.

TABLE 9.1. Effective Selling Methods

Sales organizations that deal with "key accounts" (prestigious accounts that actually or potentially yield high revenue) give these suggestions to effectively sell to them.

- Understand the key account's mission and objectives
- Sell to all levels and functional areas
- Develop strategic alliances and partnerships
- Build a solid relationship with all decision makers
- Understand and service them since they cannot be taken for granted
- Tailor the selling approach around the specific value the product or service offers them
- Build customer satisfaction with each contact
- Be professional
- Know your competitive advantage
- Provide value-added service
- Understand how they use your products
- Create a key account program
- Review results on regular basis
- Be creative, ask questions, and learn their business

Source: *Carter Sales Force Survey* (1996).

Under a performance orientation, also referred to as an *ego orientation*, salespeople seek favorable evaluations of their skills from their managers and colleagues. They are reluctant to experiment with new approaches, fearing these behaviors will result in poor outcomes and consequently negative evaluations of their abilities and performance.

There is research that indicates that salespeople are concerned about not only performance goals but also learning goals, and that these two goals differentially motivate their work behavior. Most sales motivation and evaluation programs attempt to instill a performance orientation. They focus on setting sales targets, offering salespeople incentives for achieving or surpassing these targets. Similarly, most research on sales performance has suggested that performance improvements occur through instilling a performance orientation that causes salespeople to work hard. Sales performance depends considerably on developing a learning orientation. This orientation, like a performance orientation, motivates salespeople to work hard while also motivating them to work smart. This involves salespeople planning, after-sales calls, and having the confidence to try a wide variety of sales approaches. Sales performance depends on working smart, not just working hard.

Sales managers should consider their subordinates as potential learners. Even those salespeople who are relatively low in self-efficacy are motivated by a learning orientation to work hard and smart while a performance orientation can demotivate salespeople low in self-efficacy.

THE MECHANICS OF SELLING

Need: a customer want or desire that can be satisfied by a product or service

The key point about a need is that the customer recognizes it as such and states it that way. For example:

> "We do *need* to find a way to . . . "; "I would *like* to find a way to fix . . . "; "I *could use* a way to improve . . . "; "We have been *interested in* . . . "; "I *am looking for* a solution to . . . "; "I do *wish* we had a way to . . . "

Opportunity: a customer problem or dissatisfaction that can be addressed by a product or service

Opportunities lack a clear statement of the customer's want or desire to solve the problem or to alleviate the dissatisfaction. When a solution is clearly desired, you are dealing with a need. When there is no stated desire for a solution, you are dealing with an opportunity. For example:

> I suspect we're not helping our image to our clients if there is an error in the report we ordered.

> I'm afraid some of our recent closings have not gotten across the fact that we're a first-rate operation.

It is important to spot the difference between opportunities and needs. When a customer describes a problem or dissatisfaction, that is an opportunity to get the customer to state he or she would like to find a solution. When the customer makes that statement, a need has been uncovered, and the customer has recognized it.

Satisfying Customer Needs

Selling is a process of uncovering and satisfying customer needs. But in order to do an effective job of satisfying customer needs, it is important to understand the difference between features and benefits.

Feature: a characteristic of a product or service

Benefit: the value of a feature to a customer

Selling Mechanics involve the following:

Opening: to gain customer attention and permission to continue

Probing: to gather information and uncover customer needs

Supporting: to satisfy customer needs with benefits

Closing: to gain customer commitment

Each stage may detour, but this format is important to keep in mind.

Opening: Is the time for introductions and the purpose of the call. Use language that compels their interest. *Probing:* Involves the skill of asking questions to gather information and uncover needs.

FIGURE 9.1. The Mechanics of Selling

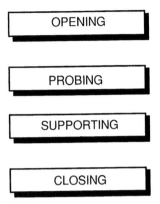

Opening

Opening involves the following two stages:

1. Introductions
2. State the purpose of the call

Stating the Purpose of the Call

Use language that will make the customer feel that the meeting may be worthwhile. For example: "I'd like to take a few minutes to describe how our company can increase your billable hours by saving you time at closings."

Using a Bridge to Position the Purpose

Bridge: "John Mills at Palin, Mills suggested I give you a call. They are really pleased with the way we have been able to increase the profitability of their closings, and John said you had a similar practice."

Purpose: "I'd like to take a few minutes of your time to explore whether our service might help your firm as well."

Using a General Benefit Statement as a Bridge

1. A description of an assumed general need.
2. A description of a general benefit of a product or service which meets this need.

For example:

Bridge: "In these times, physicians like yourself have been looking for ways to increase the profitability of their practice. _____ developed a way to increase your billable hours by saving you time."

Purpose: "I'd like to take a few minutes of your time to discuss whether our service may be of benefit to your practice."

Probing

Probing is the skill of asking questions to gather information and uncover customer needs. There are two types of probes: *open* and *closed*. Open probes encourage the prospect to respond freely. Key words that can be used are: who, when, what, where, why, how, tell me. Closed probes limit the response to a yes, no, or a choice among alternatives that you supply. Key words that can be used are: do, does, is, are, have, has, or which.

Stating the Reason for Probing

Prospects often resist being asked questions. In order to eliminate this obstacle, it is a good idea to prepare the customer. For example: "I'd like to ask you a few questions now, to see just how we may be able to help your firm. Is that OK?"

Supporting

A support statement is made when the following occur:

1. A need has been uncovered, and
2. There is a clear understanding of the need.

Support needs, *not* opportunities. Probe until you are sure you understand the opportunity which you can later satisfy with a benefit *(supporting)* if it turns out to be a need.

How to Support

1. *Acknowledge* the customer's need.
2. *Introduce* the appropriate benefits that will satisfy the need.

Customer: "What I want is a service that can help me be more profitable." (Need)

Salesperson: "You're absolutely right, increasing profitability is more important than ever in this marketplace." (Acknowledgment)

"Our service has been developed to help firms like yours to increase your billable hours by saving you time. Using our service will mean more profits for your firm." (Benefit)

Words that can be used to begin a support statement can include: "I agree, you need to . . . "; "You're absolutely right about . . . "; "I can see how that can be a problem . . . "; "Exactly . . . "; "I understand your concern about . . . "; "I couldn't agree with you more . . . "

Handling Skepticism

When a prospect questions or doubts that a product or service will provide the benefit, then it could be helpful to make a proof statement. A proof statement is made by citing a proof source. A proof source is any reference or piece of information that proves the benefit in question. Some tactics can involve: explanations, citing numbers of statistics, telling success stories, citing data from research studies, magazine articles, professional journals, and testimonial letters, presenting brochures or other print material.

Words that can be used to begin a proof statement are: "Mr. Prospect, you will get . . . "; "I can understand why you'd be interested in . . . "; "Let me explain further how we . . . "; "We've done some research on the subject of . . . "; "You may be interested in what we've done . . . "

Caution: Do not support the skepticism. *Do not agree* with the prospect and then offer proof. It's like saying: "Yes, you're right. Now let me tell you why you're wrong." For example:

Prospect:	"Come on. Everybody says they can save me time. The trouble is, nobody really does."
Salesperson:	"I know that it's easy to promise to save you time, but _____ really does do it. In fact a recent survey of our clients showed that virtually everyone has seen an improvement since switching to _____. We can show the potential savings to you as well."

If the prospect accepts the proof, he or she then accepts the benefit. If you are not sure, probe to find out. If he or she still rejects this then probe to find out why and offer a second more acceptable proof.

Handling Indifference

The indifferent prospect *does not see the need* for a product or service because of: satisfaction with a competing product or service, satisfaction with an internally developed system or procedure, or with the usual way of doing things, no perceived need for your type of product or service.

Therefore, *probe to uncover unrealized needs.* Example.

Prospect:	"That's interesting. But as I said, we use _____ Manufacturing, and I'm very happy with them."
Salesperson:	"Let me ask, have you ever had problems with getting a quick decision on a question?"
Prospect:	"Well, now that you mention it, there have been a couple of problems . . ."
Salesperson:	"Oh? Tell me about them."
Prospect:	"Well a few times they've had delays in getting an answer to me. They always say it's because they have to get clearance from headquarters."
Salesperson:	"Doesn't that kind of a problem end up either costing you money or taking up extra time for

you and your clients?" (This question sets up recognition of the need.)

Customer: "Yes, it does."

Salesperson: *(Now probe to confirm the need)* "Would it help if you could deal directly with the company headquarters location that was always able to give you a quick decision on various issues?"

Indifference can be extremely difficult and awkward to handle. The goal is to say something to keep the conversation alive, but without being perceived as being pushy. Key phrases include the following:

- "I see, it might be of no interest."
- "I understand, you don't need . . . "
- "Okay, that doesn't seem to be an important area for you."

After acknowledging, use a general benefit statement: "I see, it might be of no interest. On the other hand, several of the cost-saving features of our service may be worth looking at."

Probe: "Can we look at some of the alternatives?"

Handling Objection

Two types:

1. Easy: *Misunderstandings* about a product or service, caused by a lack of information.
2. Difficult: *Drawbacks* of a product or service, which exist whenever there is an inability to directly satisfy the customer's dislike of or dissatisfaction with the product or service.

Misunderstanding (Easy)

Handle in the same way as an opportunity: First, probe to confirm the customer's need. Then, make a support statement to clear up the misunderstanding. Example:

Prospect: "Look, I don't have time to deal with getting decisions from an out-of-town operation."

Salesperson: "What you're saying, then, is that saving time is important to you and that you need fast decisions on underwriting issues?"

Prospect: "That's right. My time is valuable and I need fast answers."

Salesperson: "That's very understandable. And _____ has been set up to give you exactly what you need. Our branch is colocated with the state headquarters office and all decisions are made right there. You'll be able to get fast decisions from us very easily."

Drawback (Difficult)

Minimize the importance of the drawback and make the prospect aware of benefits that outweigh the drawback. *Remind* the prospect of benefits already accepted. If necessary, *probe* to uncover needs. Key phrases include the following:

- "Let's take a look at your total requirements." "Let's review all the factors involved in your decision." "Let's take a look at time savings in detail." "Well let's think about what we've agreed is important to you."

When you feel you have been able to minimize the importance of the drawback to the prospect, pause and wait for a reaction. It is important to recognize that this last objection can be the key to closing the sale and that customers often object in response to a competitor's offering, or because a superior applies pressure to get a better deal.

A last-minute objection can also be a pressure tactic designed to "get the most" from each supplier. Whatever the reason, the reaction should always be the same: Use the objection to help close the sale. Here's how:

1. *Probe the objection.* See what is behind it. If the customer previously agreed to whatever he or she is now objecting to, remind the customer of previous meetings, discussions, or correspondence in which the issue was discussed and resolved. Raise the question of what or who is now reopening the issue. Find out why it is being raised now.

2. *Watch for competitive "incentives."* Often competitors add incentives to attract customers. These "incentives," however, are often added at the expense of something else. The competitor is frequently trying to direct the customer away from your proposal by attracting him or her to something you haven't offered. Review the competitive proposal to find out what the competition is and is not offering and inform the customer.
3. *Sell the new players.* If other people in the customer's organization have now become involved in the decision, identify and sell to their needs, too.
4. *Conditionally close the sale.* To handle the last objection, find out specifically what will satisfy the customer. Ask a "What will it take?" question, such as: "Since you're not satisfied with the $1.89 price per unit, what price do we have to match to get your next 1,000-piece order?"

According to a study by the Advertising Research Foundation, 35 percent of purchasers said they took up to 90 days after the initial inquiry to buy, while 28 percent said they placed an order between three and six months down the road, and 10 percent said they waited for six to twelve months to buy. The same study revealed that, when it comes to future purchases, only 13 percent said they would buy within three months, and 44 percent said they would require six to twelve months to decide. When customers make a decision to buy a product or service, they want to take action. The last thing they want to hear is a lot of needless detail.

Closing

When a prospect gives a buying signal close.

1. Summarize the benefits which the customer agreed were important during the sales call.
2. Formulate an action plan which requires the prospect to make a commitment.

Summarizing the Benefits

Summarize only those benefits that the prospect agreed were important. Words that can be used to begin to summarize are: "We agree that ... "; "Yes, our service *will* ... "; "Right. You *will* save ... "; "We've talked about ... "; "We've seen that ... "; "It's clear that ... "; "Clearly, you would ... "

Formulating an Action Plan Requiring Commitment

In some cases, the next step in the sale may not require a prospect to instantly place an order. The goal may only be trying to get the prospect to agree to try a service the next time they have a need for it. The prospect may agree to do this, but the salesperson has no way of ensuring that this will be done.

In these situations, the chances of actually getting the sale can be increased by moving the prospect to a higher level of commitment. For example, get the prospect to tell you the exact name of his client so that you can enter this in your back office files in order to further expedite the process. (Bank Name, Client Name, etc.) Make a definite appointment to call the prospect back after an agreed time period, just to make sure the anticipated transaction is moving ahead smoothly.

Final Thoughts on the Mechanics of Selling

Prepare for a sales call by qualifying customers and anticipating sales challenges, objections, and opportunities before meeting with clients. This also involves obtaining background information about the customer, dealings with competitors, and any special issues prior to the sales call. Try to match the image of a successful salesperson. Personality studies show that 93 percent of feelings and attitudes are communicated through body language and only 7 percent with words. Do not overreact to obstacles since they are a regular part of the selling process. Do not automatically assume every obstacle is a major hurdle. Always take the time to make customers feel appreciated. This can be done by simply saying: "We appreciate your business." This means a great deal to customers because research shows that the main reason customers become dissatisfied and give their business to another company is due to the lack of feeling appreciated.

To avoid unnecessary future problems, it is important to take care of customer complaints as soon as they occur and allow customers channels where they can make complaints. When clients ask for special treatment such as Saturday delivery, rush orders, or personal service, be cooperative, but also let them know that it is going above and beyond the call of duty so they will feel obligated to do a favor in return. This will lead to good sales results from clients satisfied customers are one of the best sources of leads and referrals.

CONSULTATIVE SELLING

A growing number of sales organizations are adopting a problem-saving approach toward working with customers. Selection decisions are increasingly based on the ability to contribute to the overall success of the customer's business. Many sales organizations have adopted *consultative selling* as a way of positioning themselves as attractive business partners. While there are many variations of consultative selling, essentially this selling strategy focuses on the role of the sales force as a source of knowledge and ideas in addition to products and services.

The *value added* is in the relationship between the salesperson and the customer, not just in the product or service capability but in offering a consultative approach to dealing with customers. This may mean that a company assists their customers with marketing tips or uses their technology experts to teach customers how to use their own more effectively as a business tool. If customers acknowledge that a salesperson or someone in their company has a high level of expertise and it can help them, then it is worth more to that customer.[1]

Evidence suggests that consultative selling is evolving beyond being based on product-related knowledge. A number of sales organizations are investing in acquiring comprehensive knowledge of customers' customers. Firms are giving their salespeople an intangible asset that enables the salesperson to be a high value-added business partner.[2]

LISTENING

Despite the acknowledged importance of listening, many consider it to be the number one weakness for most salespeople. Few empirical studies have focused on the effective interpersonal listening of salespeople.

Listening is an important, active process where salespeople can strategically draw customer information to accurately determine selling opportunities. The use of a 70/30 rule, which is something that is akin to the 80/20 rule in marketing (20 percent of the customer base generates 80 percent of the business activity in units or revenue dollars), should be used in sales listening situations. The 70/30 rule says that salespeople should listen 70 percent of the time and avoid the natural temptation of controlling the sales call by talking too much. The remaining 30 percent of the time that is used by the salesperson to talk involves strategic dialogue based on verbal and nonverbal communication from the customer.

Knowledgeable, prepared salespeople develop more meaningful relationships by listening to customers than salespeople who do not. In addition, memorized "sales scripts" used when opening, closing, or probing during sales calls free the memory from the clutter of what to say to customers and when to say it, in order to listen better. Sales managers should emphasize the need for salespeople to develop strong "listening" skills.[3]

A great deal of anecdotal literature supports the importance of including nonverbal cues, the notion that listening in selling must be an active rather than a passive activity. Emotional skills, such as empathy or the ability to read interpersonal situations, help salespeople become good collaborators, and networkers, thus getting the cooperation they need to reach their goals.[4] Behaviors such as nodding, eye contact, and simply not interrupting demonstrate that the listener is interested in the speaker's message. As a result, the speaker is often encouraged to share more information. Effective listeners tend to note nonverbal as well as verbal cues, interpret present messages in light of the speaker's prior comments and actions, and do not allow their emotions to cloud their interpretation of the messages. Perhaps more important, effective listeners listen emphatically, and hold their evaluation of the speaker's message until it is complete.

In addition, anecdotal literature stresses the need to concentrate during the evaluation state. Several behaviors such as note taking, listening as if you plan to report the discussion to others, or mentally seeking the speaker's underlying organizational structure are often suggested as techniques to enhance concentration. The key to the final stage of the listening process is to offer a positive response through verbal and nonverbal cues such as nodding, questioning, restating, and summarizing using facial expressions and body language.

TEAM SELLING

As the selling process becomes more complex, and as customers expect higher levels of service, team selling is becoming more prevalent. *Team selling* occurs when sales and nonsalespeople, under the direction of a leader, coordinate sales strategy and information. The team can consist of anyone in the firm whose knowledge of a product, customer, or industry can be used to the seller's advantage.

Three types of "teamwork situations" are: (1) the entire selling team works exclusively with single national or international accounts; (2) national account executives work with one or two geographically dispersed accounts serviced by field sales representatives; and (3) salespeople work with large accounts that cut across sales district boundaries, but no national account executive serves as coordinator. These team situations describe relatively permanent teams that are defined through assignment to particular customers.[5]

The sales team is not limited to large key accounts and complex customers. The sales team is a customer-focused group whose primary objective is to establish and maintain strong customer relationships, however, this team can also play a transaction-servicing role. The sales team has salespeople assigned to specific customers. Ideally, membership in the sales teams should be stable, with team members being selected from inside or outside the sales organization. The recent emphasis on team selling reflects a useful travel in sales tactics. However, sales teams are not appropriate in all situations. For example, a working group can suffice if performance goals can be met through a sum of individual contributions, and if potential team members and/or the organization are not willing to risk the constructive conflict, mutual trust and interdependence required to develop a real team. An organization with a poor work performance ethic would probably have trouble getting a real team to develop. A cooperative spirit and high level of task focus must be present for sales teams to be effective.[6]

NEGOTIATION

The process of negotiation for the sales force and customers should allow both sides to get what they want. Negotiation is essential for success with customer dealings. The sales manager should provide salespeople with effective methods for engaging customers during a negotiation scenario. Negotiation skill, as much as technical business knowledge, administrative ability or other management skills, has influenced the ability, of sales managers to achieve results. Effective negotiation is the ability to work with people, understand them, and relate to them.[7] If the salesperson and customer can reach agreement in a way that meets the needs on both sides, then the parties are negotiating effectively. The key to this is to approach negotiation as a problem-solving situation, which means finding real problems, creating new solutions, and reaching mutually satisfactory agreements.

Negotiation Methods

This involves several elements:

1. Problem solving negotiation, where both sides win, should be a key goal during the process. Salespeople must attempt to work out problems and differences with customers and not narrow terms down to just one issue, such as price. Look for the full range of attributes that give customers value. Try to avoid the winner/loser negotiation. A cooperative attitude can best assist this process.
2. The assumption that all customers want the same things is no longer true. Accordingly, salespeople must find out what their customers want, even if it is not what they want to hear. They should ask questions and probe to uncover this relevant information.
3. Detailed preparation is important so that any anticipated issues may be identified prior to the negotiation. This basically serves as a rehearsal so that there are as few surprises as possible.

4. Sales managers should help the salespeople develop realistic expectations and starting points for achievements in the negotiation. For example, teams of two or more people improve the overall quality of creative problem solving during negotiations. Teams with even moderate cohesiveness were able to outbargain solo's because they increase the overall value of the deal being negotiated. Teams are also better at finding more issues to use for making tradeoffs and concessions.[8]

5. Mental composure is an important element of negotiation. While it may seem that there is more pressure on the sales force to sell than on the customer to purchase in a negotiation, both sides are under pressure to get what they want. Accordingly, salespeople should not get themselves trapped into "emotional blackmail" from threats. When under attack from an irate customer during a negotiation, just listen and focus on constructive ways to resolve differences and neutralize negativity.

6. At the completion of a negotiation in which the customer does not get everything that was wanted, the customer should still be congratulated. Avoid making the cusomter feel bad about giving in; rather, the customer should feel that something was won. This instills goodwill for possible future business dealings.

7. There are two schools of thought on "up front" offers. One proposes to ask in the beginning for all of the initial demands and more than is expected; then work the terms out. This provides a full position from which to compromise. The other position is to begin with fairly moderate demands and a flexible attitude to initiate the negotiation process.

8. Having an "objective" focus on the relevant negotiating issues can keep salespeople from being distracted and from losing customers. Some context of what the long-term implications from the negotiations will be is helpful to prevent salespeople from getting lost or overwhelmed in the process. It is also important to keep track of all issues under discussion and to assert the needs of the sales organizations.

9. However, the use of emotional, subjective appeal during a negotiation by a salesperson to get customers more involved in the sale, and can help on an emotional level.

10. A key issue is to keep in mind that while frustrating and difficult, everything should be done to close a deal. However, once every possibility has been exhausted, it may then become necessary to walk away from the deal.

Negotiation Skills

Various issues should be recognized before and during the negotiation.

- *Knowledge* - Superior knowledge or information about the other side is an incredible advantage during a negotiation.
- *Time* - The side in the negotiation that needs to either purchase by a certain time or sell by a certain time usually has a disadvantage in negotiation concessions. A customer's time pressure is a key issue during a negotiation.
- *Urgency* - This involves a certain level of business necessity that dictates the need to sell or buy something now or desire that dictates preferring or wanting something now.
- *Believability* - This entails the ability of salespersons to make the other side believe what is being said and to know when they are being bluffed.
- *Closure* - Closure involves knowing when the right balance exists between having advantages during the negotiation and using them to reach the right deal. This also involves the personal motivation which leads to the successful completion of a deal.

Negotiation is difficult because salespeople and customers must work together to solve problems and make decisions, yet they do not start out with the same goals, wishes, and preferences. In summary, at the outset of any negotiation the strengths and weaknesses on both sides must be gauged. Salespeople must learn their customer's stated goals and gather information on their needs. The following prepatory questions should be used.

- What do I want?
- What is a reasonable expectation?
- Where, in terms of justifiable numbers, do I start?

- How many people will be present?
- If possible, can this negotiation take place in my office or a location of my choice?

With successful negotiation both sides experience a sense of accomplishment, each side also believes the other was fair, will keep the agreement, and would deal with the other again. To be a good negotiator, sales managers should make the sales force realize that negotiation is a two-way affair and pressure exists on both sides.

PROFILE: Dudley Coker, President and General Manager, Paging Products, Motorola

"Effective selling is a relationship-driven event. Today in sales, product and service quality is a given, not an order of magnitude. The difference is relationships that tell customers that they can believe in a salesperson who is there to solve their problems. Customers want different things, but by meeting their demands in a consistent, quality manner, business will be there.

Customer-driven negotiation is not an event, but a process where people deal jointly to establish agreement that they can live with. Even with the goal of seeking agreement with customers in negotiation, salespeople should not be afraid to say no, because they have different preferences from their clients. In fact in negotiation, saying no just establishes a starting point to begin to work things out and reach agreement."

Source: Dudley Coker (February 28, 1997). Personal Interview. Motorola, Boynton Beach, Florida.

SUMMARY

Selling involves direct customer contact to develop and actually transact business from clients. There is a level of selling skill that is needed to do this effectively, but understanding the basic selling mechanics can help any person in sales or business deal well with customers. Consultative and team selling are newer ways that companies are using to generate business when dealing with clients. Negotiation is also an important, complex process that warrants a level of skill to help customers solve problems and make decisions so that both sides experience benefits.

Questions

1. What is consultative selling?
2. How can the use of a team selling approach help sales organizations improve their results?
3. In the "Livingston Carpet" case, use selling teams representing the various "fast food" firms to prepare information and conduct a sales call on Walter Roberts with the goal of getting his business.
4. What are some various ways to overcome obstacles when dealing with customers?
5. How is "listening" important to the mechanics of selling?

CASE STUDY: RICHMOND CORPORATION

Objective

To implement the principles and practice of effective call planning, prospecting, and call preparation skills to improve the average per salesperson productivity to the level needed to deliver the sales plan.

Richmond Corporation is a privately held $520 million company. The core business of Richmond is the delivery of data products that have evolved from the credit report as it is known today. Teams of seven to nine sales representatives work with a Field Sales Manager who coordinates activity and offers advice and guidance. Under the leadership of a Branch Manager (BM) there is a branch support team whose primary role is to support the sales teams.

Jason Barnes is currently the manager of Field Sales. The vision for the sales force is to deliver best practices in both process and management skills. Their purpose is to ensure that their deliveries influence both branch and individuals to improve their attitudes, knowledge, and skills and subsequently their effectiveness. Jason Barnes is responsible for the sales of a division of Richmond called Insurance. This area markets data products, models, and delivery systems to the insurance industry. The division has grown aggressively since its beginnings in 1979. In order to meet customers' needs they have acquired other companies and structured several large joint partnership arrangements. As they acquire other business, Jason faces the challenge of managing their sales force and incorporating existing products with new ones. Joint partnership represents an even greater challenge in the structure of how to bring the new products to market.

Acquisitions require restructuring of the existing sales staff with that of the new company. Territories change and positions take on different levels of responsibility. The customer ultimately has the picture of one sales force bringing new products to market. Joint partnerships represent a new sales force selling new products that are hybrids of existing Richmond products. The challenge is to coordinate the sales forces.

Depending on the details of the partnership arrangement, several solutions have been attempted concerning to the coordination of sales teams. Training and communication to the teams is of paramount importance. Meetings are difficult because of travel and the number of people involved. Generally, after one large meeting many questions still exist and end up never being answered. Jason's sales force usually requires an alternative commission structure based on the new products and distribution channels. Customer perception is the largest challenge that Jason faces and can lead to confusion in the marketplace. Again, communication is the key, both written through press releases and virtually through the sales force.

Problem

During this same period the sales force has failed to achieve sales plans.

A major concern to Jason is the lack of knowledge and skills within his sales force to:

- plan sales calls and agree to targets based on potential;
- focus on structured prospecting, thereby seeing the right customer at the right time. Very often the same group of customers are called on to a point where the potential has been exhausted;
- preparing for the call so that both the salesperson and the company get value for money.

Question

Jason Barnes has contacted you as a senior level marketing executive in Richmond Corporation for advice on how to handle this situation. He greatly respects you for your thirty years sales and marketing experience in the industry and your tenure with Richmond since 1979. How would you advise Jason to proceed?

CASE STUDY (ROLE-PLAY): LIVINGSTON CARPET

Livingston is a large carpet company that manufactures and sells carpets throughout the United States. They have been in business for twenty years with assets of $750 million and with sixty offices and outlets in different parts of the country. The company is well regarded in the carpet industry and is expected to continue to grow in locations, staff, and profits in the future.

Once each year Livingston holds a four-day conference for its 125 managers. At last year's conference there had been so many complaints about the food from the attendees that the CEO, Walter Roberts, decided to ask the employees themselves what they wanted. The results from the survey showed that about 67 percent of those responding wanted "fast food" selection for meals throughout the four-day manager's conference. In fact, it was rumored that Walter Roberts was overheard saying to a colleague after the results of the survey were available, "If we could find one of the big franchises to do this successfully, I'd not only be willing to use them at the manager's conference every year, but any other events we have throughout the year."

Question

Livingston's upcoming manager's conference for this year will be taking place in the next few months. How should you respond to their dilemma?

Job Description: Marketing/Sales Vice Presidents

The vice presidents of marketing/sales report to the presidents of their divisions and are responsible for sales and marketing activities to support all food products by:

- developing marketing plans for current and new products
- assessing market conditions regarding food product/customer/ application trends and developments; monitoring competitive and customer trends and developing responses to advance the business' position
- monitoring and reporting progress of marketing programs
- managing sales force performance
- managing the customer service function
- directing export and overseas sales activities
- developing a marketing/sales budget
- recommending pricing strategies to food product line VPs
- developing and recommending advertising and merchandising support
- selecting outside resources (such as ad agencies) when needed
- determining staffing needs for the marketing/sales group
- recommending promotions and staffing changes for the marketing/sales group

Chapter 10

Customer Relationship Building

WHAT IS CUSTOMER RELATIONSHIP BUILDING?

Customer Relationship Building is a commitment to build a rapport with customers and provide a product or service through that relationship. It is being friendly, professional, and service oriented so that follow-up is prioritized. The highly competitive nature of business has dictated the need to go beyond good product or service quality at an affordable price and reach customers at a human level in a relationship-building manner. Consulting firm McKinsey & Company reports that its customer service work has tripled, a reflection of the significance of customer relationship building to many companies.

RELATIONSHIP SELLING

An important element of customer relationship building is relationship selling. Traditional selling is usually seen as a contest with a winner and a loser and the sale is the end of the transaction. However, relationship selling is getting customers to deal with a relationship-oriented person to neutralize their expectation of being exploited.[1]

Relationship selling combines elements of general advertising, sales promotion, public relations, and direct marketing to create more effective and more efficient ways of reaching consumers. It centers on developing a continuous relationship with customers by combining elements of general advertising, sales promotion, public relations, direct marketing, and related products or services. The importance of relationship selling to customer relationship building is that it creates more effective and efficient ways to reach customers.

The relationship selling process incorporates three key elements:

1. Identifying and building a computerized database of current and potential consumers that records and cross-references a wide

variety range of demographic, lifestyle, and purchase information;

2. Delivering differentiated messages to these through established and new media channels based on the consumer's characteristics and preferences; and

3. Tracking each relationship to monitor the cost of acquiring the consumer and the lifetime value of their purchases.

WHAT SHOULD BE DONE TO BUILD?

Customers want to trust the salesperson, so listening and good communication are important and the sale is considered to be the beginning of building a loyal relationship. Customer relationship building should be defined by a customer satisfaction program that does the following:

1. Establishes a procedure to accept customer communication.
2. Identifies what customers desire.
3. Identifies satisfaction customers derive from you.
4. Acts on customer communication.

To build this process it is necessary to consult customers for preferences, build familiarity and knowledge to build a relationship and conduct business in a customized fashion. The process takes every opportunity to build customer satisfaction with each contact.

The various methods available to build such a program can be memberships in professional organizations, the use of mailing and phone campaigns, and customer surveys.

Other tools to use can be employee suggestions, internal company newsletters, and corporate videos. Both newspapers and videos can be used to keep the customer informed. The information processed in a product warranty or financing application for clients could also be part of the program. A customer complaint system and exit interview system for dissatisfied customers can help track problems along with the use of focus groups or customer advisory boards. A focus group is a sales tool that gathers a group of representative clients, usually ten to twenty, for a one-time meeting to ask their questions about product and service preferences. It also determines why they select certain companies to do business with.

Sample Market Survey

	*HOW IMPORTANT THIS ATTRIBUTE IS TO YOU, THE CUSTOMER	*HOW WE PROVIDE THIS ATTRIBUTE COMPARED TO OTHERS IN THE INDUSTRY
EXPERTISE	————	————
ERROR FREE	————	————
CUSTOMIZED SERVICE	————	————
FINANCIAL STRENGTH	————	————
DEPTH OF STAFF	————	————
PERSONAL RELATIONSHIPS	————	————
QUALITY DIRECT SALES		
EFFORT	————	————
EDUCATIONAL SEMINARS	————	————
QUICK AND PROPER SOLUTIONS TO PROBLEMS	————	————
DEAL WITH FRIENDLY STAFF	————	————
PRICE	————	————
NATIONAL LEADER	————	————
LEADER IN THE LOCAL MARKET	————	————

*On a scale from 1 to 10, with 1 as extremely important, how important do you think these attributes are for you as a customer in selecting and maintaining a business relationship with a company?

The goal of any customer relationship-building program is to monitor the service that customers actually experience and then act on what provides customer satisfaction levels. The key is to pursue customer satisfaction as the main goal.

Customer relationship building does not seek a temporary increase in sales, or to sell products through the mail, but to create involvement and product or service loyalty by forming a lasting bond with the customer. Although it may be used to facilitate product repositioning, gain competitors' customers, or help launch new products, the ultimate goal is increased usage over time. With this clear objective, customer relationship building becomes a personalized form of communication.[2]

Companies that find a way to make life easier for their customers can have an advantage over their competition. Customer relationship building deals with convincing customers that you can give them the best value, and perhaps more value, for the least money. It is a sales strategy that requires a genuine focus on the customer.[3]

Customers can then become "advocates" for the company by encouraging their colleagues, friends, and acquaintances to also buy from the company. Looking after current customers makes sense for other reasons as well. Everyone has experienced a post-purchase moment of doubt by questioning the wisdom of the purchase they have just made. The more significant and costly the purchase, the greater the buyer's need to find reassuring information. If salespeople communicate with customers after they have purchased, they can help to reinforce the buyer's selection by providing cues and information about the quality of the purchased product or service.[4]

Loyalty will be more likely to occur if a customer feels rewarded for having purchased a particular product or brand. To promote relationship building, it is necessary for sales managers to have the sales force define their loyal customers and determine what drives their buying decision making. To retain customers, salespeople should establish a relationship with them. For most companies, a sale of its products or services is considered as the culmination of its contact with the customer.

To determine distinctions in loyal customer behavior, sales organizations should uncover exactly what loyal, heavy-consumption customers want. Since it is these customers who are the bedrock of sales activity business, it is important to understand what they want and how their needs are evolving. A useful approach to figuring out what they want is to analyze what they buy when they purchase from competitors and to determine whether these are permanent shifts in behavior or temporary lapses.

Research shows that it can cost a company anywhere from four to five times more to develop new business compared to maintaining existing business. However, it is still necessary to develop new business. Companies need to cultivate new customers because over time their existing ones may leave or become easier to maintain. This releases time to pursue new customers. Companies replenish their customer base by focusing on customers who exhibit the same behaviors as the current loyal ones.

Targeting loyal customers means making better business decisions, based on understanding the trade-offs among various customer segments. This effort to build customer loyalty by the sales force, is accomplished by giving customers intrinsic value with added features, enhanced service, and improved products all at an affordable price.

Developing and maintaining customer satisfaction should be important objectives of sales organizations. For example, 40 percent of the incentives of IBM's sales force is based on customer satisfaction ratings. Research demonstrates that salespeople who are compensated on customer satisfaction ratings demonstrated a higher level of customer service activity than salespeople who were compensated on sales volume. Training is also an important determinant of this relationship. The research also shows that training increases the customer service response of salespeople.[5]

TEAM BUILDING

Team building has emerged as a requirement for success. As industry faces this paradigm shift, a formal team structure is emerging that goes beyond that proposed by previous selling/buying center researchers.

Team building may be defined as a tendency to behave, contribute, and interrelate with others at work in certain distinctive ways. The salesperson represents those members of the core team who serve as primary contacts for customers. The salesperson is the individual who first recognizes a sales opportunity and conveys that information to the rest of the team. The salesperson is also the primary source of external information coming into the team. This information can be useful in determining sales strategies, making team decisions, and providing product development decisions. For example, the salesperson, after reviewing customer needs, may determine that an additional member is needed on the team.

Customer service representatives are those members of the core team who provide installation, maintenance, and other services to the customer. The customer service person can serve as a customer contact at the home office when the salesperson is unavailable, or when information is needed that does not require the salesperson's input. Through dealings with the team, the customer service person will have information on customer requirements, needs, and customer problems and complaints.

Besides playing an important role in keeping conflict constructive, open communication has been shown to be positively related to team building and performance. Because selling teams require information from internal and external sources to achieve their goals, teams need good communication channels to establish relationships and perform effectively.

REPEAT SALES

Today's sales force must deal with how to generate repeat business. Even though much of the time devoted to a sales effort is focused on cultivating new business, existing customers can be a lucrative source of business. Repeat sales occur when customers are satisfied and have had good buying experiences. Customers may continue to purchase again from a company because of the service levels and convenience provided by the salesperson. Repeat sales are important to the long-term success of the sales force because they not only represent a stable source of revenue, but may lead to referral business from other customers.[6]

It is easier to convince a current customer to buy from a company than a prospective customer. After the sale, customer dealings reinforce the importance of building a lasting relationship with customers. By doing this the sales force eliminates postpurchase doubt, especially with a significant purchase, and provides interest and support.[7]

CUSTOMER ADVISORY BOARDS AS A SALES TOOL FOR THE CUSTOMER RELATIONSHIP-BUILDING PROCESS

A Way to Reach Customers

A dynamic, practical sales tool that can greatly enhance the customer development and retention process and give firms a distinct competitive advantage is the Customer Advisory Board (see Figure 10.1). A board can help a sales force broaden its decision-making expertise and generate more business. Sales involves more than an upbeat personality and hard work. It involves product or service knowledge, a proficiency in selling, an awareness of market conditions, and adding value to what the customer is doing. Industries and markets that are changing so rapidly, due to globalization and advancing technology, pose a more complex business environment today. So some firms have a Customer Advisory Board, or its equivalent, to act as an advisory and management auxiliary resource in the face of these conditions.[8]

FIGURE 10.1. Customer Advisory Board Structure and Potential Benefits

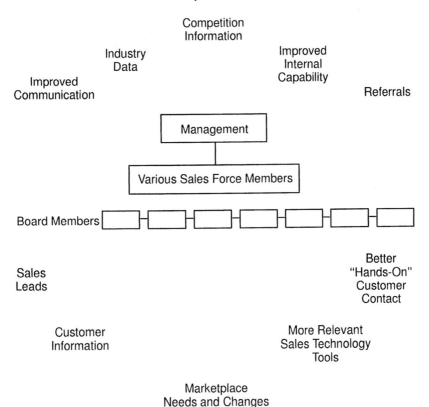

Customer retention is more complex than ever before and there has been a dramatic change in how selling takes place. Customer relationship building is a driving force in the selling process. In order to assess what entails an effective sales effort, companies must first identify why their customers chose them. It is essential to have a clear understanding of what customers want and concentrate on providing it. In a study conducted by Learning International, 29 percent of 210 corporate customers with vendors in the technology, financial services, and pharmaceutical industries reported interesting findings. The study found that business expertise and image ranked highest among various attributes that lead to satisfaction levels with a supplier.[9]

Instead of selecting what a company has to offer, today's customer tells the company what he or she wants. It is then up to the company to figure out how to supply it. These customers ask the following important questions. How can a product or service be differentiated when rising quality is forcing industries toward the same standard? How do you distinguish between what customers are saying and what they really mean? Where can you find your best customers? What service levels please customers most? How do you retain current customers? So, identifying relevant customer information is the essence of having the competitive advantage. A Customer Advisory Board can provide this edge and strengthen a company's presence in the marketplace.

An Effective Sales Tool

A board is far more effective than advisers because the board members are empowered to offer advice that can affect the company.[10] Allowing outsiders to look inside the workings of your company can cause a feeling of vulnerability. Only 5 percent of closely held companies actually do allow their boards to be dominated by outsiders.[11] Customer Advisory Boards, which essentially target actual and prospective customers as members, are a cost-effective way to find out from the marketplace how to become a firm they would do or continue to do business with. Their feedback also provides a fresh perspective to approach business opportunities.

The advisory board is more informal than the board of directors and counsels without the voting power and legal liability to protect shareholder interest. To be manageable, a board should have between five to ten members or a maximum of twelve to fifteen members who are prominent members of the business community. A revolving board that changes membership every one to two years can broaden the pool of participants.

The length of tenure for board members can be one to two years or longer depending on the needs and circumstances of the company and the board members. Newer members bring different perspectives, and a membership period of one to two years allows them to participate more frequently. Longer-term memberships provide a more stable, familiar board presence. The board can meet quarterly or more frequently if circumstances dictate urgency. In a crisis or emergency situation, the board may actually help a company identify a fuller range of perspectives that can help overcome the dilemma.[12] At a minimum, a board should meet at least twice a year; it does not have to be a totally time-consuming endeavor in order to provide some clear benefit.

The Customer Advisory Board can be comprised of CEOs and presidents or the functional executives who decide where they will direct their business. Members could be selected for their particular expertise. For example, a strategic planner with a good long-range perspective, or a technical expert who understands the features of a product or service might be good choices.[13]

Members could also be selected for their demographic segment, geographical location, revenue potential, reputation, and prestige in the marketplace. The board membership can serve as a perk for current customers to reward them for their loyalty or reach prospective customers that do not currently use a company. Customers want to believe that a company they do business with cares. The formation of a Customer Advisory Board shows this and helps to develop rapport. It is also possible for board members to network with each other. Availability and interest may be an issue for those who are approached for membership. It can be a stamp of success for candidates who accept invitations to serve as board members because prominence and knowledge are selection criteria; the members will expect their advice to be taken seriously.

In 1992, companies spent $3.5 billion with the fifty biggest research firms to learn about their customers. Market research can be extremely valuable, but it is expensive and can be conducted fraudulently. Companies can wield the information that comes out of board meetings as one source of market research and as a way to study the psychology of buyer behavior in order to enhance sales.[14] In many cases a Customer Advisory Board can be operated without any fee. Besides being cost effective, the rationale for this is to avoid any appearance of impropriety and buying business, while relying on the members' expertise in an advisory capacity.

An important part of an effective board is the participation of the sales force and management personnel. Their suggestions will help target desired board members and frame the relevant issues to be discussed when the board meets. In addition, if salespeople and managers are involved with the board, they are also in the position to build relationships.

A critical role for the board is to help identify and resolve strategy and performance issues. Thus, board members must have a solid understanding of both the industry and the individual functions as well as what creates value in the business. The board members should be routinely informed about relevant company, industry, and economic events. They should receive the appropriate press clippings, subscriptions to selected industry journals, and any other pertinent information that will keep them informed. Board members should know the concerns and thoughts of the people working in the company and should be knowledgable about the activities of the competition. Sales management should also be involved in the process of communication to and from the board so as to signal a serious commitment on the part of the corporation to provide high-level feedback that can impact company policy. Other favored board candidates are women and minorities. They can reflect a diversity of views and insights that can be of great benefit to a firm.

To maximize the effectiveness of the Advisory Board, a company should raise certain questions early in its operation to allow for necessary adjustments later on such as:

1. Do you want board members who act as thought partners over the major issues facing the business?
2. Can you count on the board to give you a fully informed and objective opinion?

3. Is the company getting full value from the board?
4. Is the board's perception of your performance in tune with your own?
5. If not, are you concerned about where that perception might lead if the company's performance took a turn for the worse?

Many firms, such as IBM, Merck & Company, and The Equitable, have a Customer Advisory Board or its equivalent. These companies have found the boards to be extremely helpful in their customer relationship-building process.

Customer Relationship-Building Process

Customers today are more demanding, sophisticated, educated, and comfortable speaking to the company as an equal. Customers have more customized expectations; they want to be reached as individuals. They know their businesses best, so the opportunity to listen to them through the dialogue from the advisory board will help uncover how to meet their needs.

Also, a disproportionate search for new business is costly with two-thirds of all revenue coming from current customers. A customer relationship-building process is necessary because 91 percent of unhappy customers will never again buy from a company that dissatisfied them and they will communicate this displeasure to other people. These dissatisfied customers may not even convey their displeasure. Without saying anything, they just stop doing business with that company, which may keep the company unaware of the problem for some time. Various reasons that customers become dissatisfied with a company include lack of product or service quality, price, lack of attentiveness, complacency, poor location, no customer complaint system, or a weak public image. Approximately one-third of all dissatisfied customers actually leave because they were unappreciated and some dissatisfied customers will never complain to the company. Thus, a process is needed to monitor customer satisfaction.

Research suggests that many firms do not have a specific Customer Satisfaction Program that impacts the Customer Relationship-Building Process and the resulting outcomes. Also, most firms do not have a Customer Advisory Board or its equivalent to help

track customer satisfaction levels and promote customer relationship building (see Table 10.1).

Customer Advisory Boards

The analysis revealed that although most of the companies did not have
a Customer Advisory Board, 91 percent of those that did felt it was
helpful to their Customer Relationship-Building Process. The analysis
further showed that 55 percent of these companies had a Customer
Satisfaction Program of some type that existed in their company. Two
clear messages emerged:

- Customer Advisory Boards, while predominantly underutilized, are
  found to be helpful and to have incredible merit when they are used.

- Given the risk of what is at stake when dissatisfied customers leave
  to do business elsewhere, more companies should develop a process to monitor customer satisfaction. A Customer Advisory Board
  could be one such method.

Source: *Carter Sales Force Survey* (1996).

The ability to maintain dynamic relationships effectively is affected by communicative competence, which is the ability to perceive interpersonal relationships and adapt one's interaction goals
and behaviors accordingly. Maintaining relationships involves the
use of five strategies: positivity, openness, assurances, sharing tasks,
and social networks. Positivity, assurances, and sharing tasks predict
relational commitment, satisfaction, and mutuality of control. A
recent study by Marshall Prisbell at the University of Nebraska
showed that individuals using strategies reflecting cooperation,
cheerfulness, patience, and time to interface with another person
rated themselves as showing warmth, empathy, composure, and
social confirmation.[15]

Relationship selling, which is the process of getting companies
and their customers closer together, is a growing trend that helps to
develop a friendly bond with customers. A Customer Advisory
Board can assist with the relationship-building process and meeting
customer satisfaction levels. Since the dynamics of a board actively
improve the contact and dialogue that a company has with the board

TABLE 10.1. Customer Advisory Board and Customer Satisfaction Program Statistics

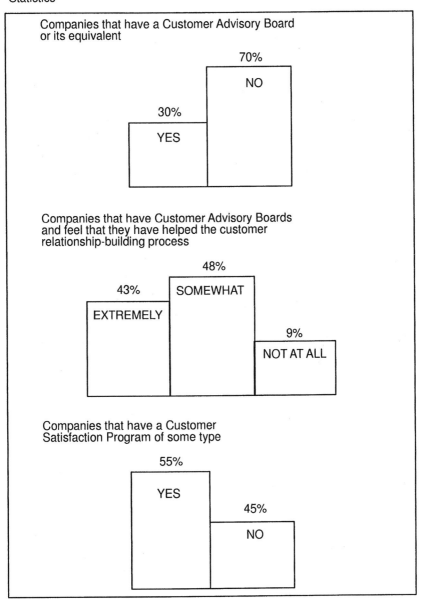

Source: *Carter Sales Force Survey* (1996).

members, who represent actual or prospective customers, they get an inside view on how to best deal with customers.

TRUST BUILDING

To most effectively reach customers it is important to gain their trust. In selling, it is difficult to get customers to do business without trust. Client trust promotes better communication that can be used to help customers make buying decisions. Customers want to be valued and this is done by listening to them and providing personal attention. Having customers involved as partners allows them to play a participatory role. This role, which can be performed by a Customer Advisory Board, enables the company to see things from the customer's standpoint. This is an invaluable insight. Trust is not only a function of understanding, but is fostered when people respect similar values. When trust is established, a customer will listen to the salesperson's suggestions and analysis more carefully. Genuinely listening to understand a customer can help identify the needs that can be filled with the particular product or service. Building customer loyalty is everyone's responsibility in the organization.

Interpersonal trust is an essential aspect of healthy relationships. People must act in a trustworthy manner for the trust to grow; just as trusting behavior should increase trust, nontrusting actions should lead to its deterioration.[16]

Building trust with customers entails the following:

1. Understanding, learning, and listening before selling
2. Asking focused, relevant questions
3. Being honorable and keeping commitments
4. Demonstrating to customers that you care about them
5. Being able to relate to customers on their terms and language and respecting their value system

Selling is actually happening when people in the customer development effort are building trust and focusing on the customer's needs. This element of trust may even cause customers to buy before they fully understand the product or service, based on their belief that a company understands them and their problems.[17] However, the choice of sales tools determines how effectively trust and loyalty can be built. Once clients become loyal they can also become advocates for the business by spreading positive "word-of-mouth messages" and by referring their friends and business associates as a source of business.

The power of customer loyalty comes from repeat sales and increased market share. It is the actual "face-to-face" contact with customers and feedback they provide that can have great impact on measuring those attributes most desired. Effective salespeople must be a valuable source of information and advice for clients in order to promote customer retention. Customer Advisory Boards are an effective way to build trust with customers by allowing a company to listen and keep in touch with their customers. The board should not be thought of or used to replace sales calls. It is instead a more formal customer interface sales tool that complements sales calls and provides industry and business information to keep both customers and the firm out in front of their respective competition.

EVALUATING BOARD MEMBERS

The characteristics of a good board member are intelligence combined with business savvy and relevant industry experience. A good board member asks many focused questions, and posesses the ability to provide informed feedback on a company's positive and negative aspects. Board members should be retained if they have demonstrated the ability to learn and interact with fellow board members and company employees in a stimulating environment. The advisory board members should be composed of people who are not only business advisers, but who are highly respected and who a firm would not want to disappoint. A company can turn to this group for guidance and advice in making difficult decisions. These are the people who should embody the core values and in making standards of the company.

The successful companies of the twenty-first century will be those that tailor their products and services to individual customer preferences. To do that effectively, companies will have to learn more about their customers. This will allow companies to actually get close enough to their customers to form friendships. To get that close, companies and customers must reach a level of mutual trust where their destinies are almost interrelated.

Today's consumer's know what they want and how much they are willing to pay. The sales force will not know what is important to a customer without asking; it could be durability, faster service, price, warranties, easier financing, or any number of features. The delivery of value to the customer calls for a clear understanding of customer needs, superior product design, intelligent application of technology, focus on quality, cost control, productivity, and always finding the competitive edge. A Customer Advisory Board would seem to facilitate this purpose because the dialogue with the board members permits better communication with the marketplace and a way to build and strengthen relationships with customers. Most important, Customer Advisory Boards can enhance a firm's awareness of the needs of the marketplace, thus providing opportunity for the company to improve itself.

PROFILE

"Customer relationship building, customer loyalty, and trust levels are important issues for today's sales force. The need to develop a strong connection with customers, at a human level, and go beyond the quality, price and delivery capability may present a new development in sales. The period leading up to the October 1987 stock market crash represented a time where it was much easier for a salesperson to initiate a sales transaction with customers based on blind faith. Of any recent single event in business, the aftermath of the October 1987 stock market crash confronted the marketplace with their need for salespeople to establish a rapport and instill them with trust. Customer relationship building gives the sales organization customer loyalty, which provides an additional dimension to keep customers with besides product or service capability."[18]

SUMMARY

The more the sales force knows about their customers and their businesses, the more prepared they will be to sell to them and provide terrific service afterward. Customers have different businesses, problems, needs, and goals. By understanding those differences it will be easier to customize products and services to meet their individual needs. Customer Advisory Boards, as a sales tool, can help the customer relationship-building process and help the sales force identify customer needs.

Salespeople should regularly ask customers for feedback on performance and for suggestions on how to meet their needs more effectively. Tell them how much their business is appreciated and how important it is that they are completely satisfied with the product or service. Take good care of customers. It often takes a lot more time, money, and effort to win a new customer than it does to maintain an existing one.

Questions

1. What is customer relationship building and why is it important in sales at this time?
2. How should sales organizations develop a customer relationship-building program?
3. What is relationship selling?
4. How can companies position themselves to benefit from "repeat sales?"
5. What are Customer Advisory Boards and how can they be used as a sales tool for the customer relationship-building process?

CASE STUDY: THAMES INTERNATIONAL, INC.

How to Target and Work with a Key Account

Description

Calvin and Walter Information Services was formed six years ago and is based in midtown Manhattan. Calvin and Walter provides financial information reports that can be used for credit or investment analysis that can provide a reliable measure of a company's financial stability. The founders of Calvin and Walter felt that financial information on businesses provided inexpensively and quickly, with the use of an extensive database, would be popular. Calvin and Walter is a small but growing company, due to the quality and price of their information services.

The industry itself is comprised of a high proportion of large-sized bureaucratic companies numbering between 250 to 1,000 employees.

In addition to their high staff levels these companies are also characterized by high costs. Calvin and Walter is streamlined, cost effective, and with its superior technology has one of the best information systems available in the industry. However, being relatively new, Calvin and Walter lacks the exposure, reputation for quality, and accordingly key accounts from the Fortune 500. The larger, more established, financial information firms that tend to work with these accounts.

One such key account that Calvin and Walter would love to get is Thames International, Inc., one of the largest investment companies in the United States. Thames handles pension funds, real estate investments, and loans, and has over $2 billion in assets. Calvin and Walter is annoyed that they have been unable to get anywhere with Thames. What makes matters worse is that they are located right across the street from the building Thames occupies in midtown Manhattan. Calvin and Walter founders have made doing business with Thames their number one priority for this year.

Question

You have been approached by Calvin and Walter as a sales consultant with your own firm. How would you advise them to develop business with Thames International, Inc.?

CASE STUDY: GLOBAL OPTICS

Battle Over Sales Strategy

Calvin Harris, the New York Division Manager for Global Optics (GO), now knows that he will have to take dramatic action if his office is to have any chance of making money or even surviving.

Description

Calvin has given thought to trying something that may be a "long shot" but if successfully developed could have a powerful impact on GO's revenue capabilities. Prior to being recruited by GO, Calvin had used Customer Advisory Boards as a sales management strategy. His experience had been that by asking ten to twelve prominent members of the business community to meet with him once or twice a year acting in an advisory capacity had led to successful results. In fact, Calvin had already contacted twenty-seven prospective board members from which twenty-four responded favorably. With so many people interested, Calvin is even considering having a main advisory board and an additional one representing a particular customer segment. Another variation could involve just having a single advisory board with a rotating membership from the pool of twenty-four people. Also, to make the board as cost effective as possible, Calvin wants to avoid paying an honorarium to the board members. The twenty-four prospective members have indicated no problem with this.

Since things have proceeded so well, Calvin has set up the first meeting of the board one month from today. He will use the fifteen highest ranking businesspeople as the members of a "general board." He will also still consider using the remaining nine as rotating members in the future or as members of a "financial services segment board" since most of them represent that industry. The meeting will take place in the late afternoon at the 101 Club in midtown Manhattan, where dinner will be available afterward. In addition to his boss, Senior Vice President Bill Dunn, Calvin wants others from his corporate headquarters in Baltimore, Maryland, to attend. Accordingly, Calvin made phone calls to invite Chief Executive Officer Gary Parks, Chief Operating Officer Jerry Smith, and Executive Vice President Joan Andrews.

Prior to their responding to Calvin, Greg Beck, the president of GO's affiliate, Global Telecommunications Optics (GTO) got word from a prospective board member of Calvin's efforts to form a board. Greg, who is notorious for his miserable temper, competitive nature, and attitude that the significant revenue-producing accounts in New York are his, is not happy about Calvin's board. Coincidentally, GO happens to be holding a New York managers' meeting at Hilton Head, South Carolina, two weeks before Calvin's first board meeting. Attending this meeting will be Calvin, Greg Beck, Gary Parks, Jerry Smith, and Joan Andrews. Also in attendance will be David Morris, GO's New York state manager, and Jack Garrison, GO's New York state legal counsel. These two have also had problems with Greg Beck.

Greg Beck telephoned Gary Parks in Charlotte. He usually screams at Gary Parks when he is mad at Calvin's office. This time he said, "I don't know if this board is Calvin's idea or yours, but I want this as the first item for discussion on the agenda when we meet in Hilton Head." Gary consoled Greg, as he usually did with these calls and replied, "Of course, Greg, and I'm sure we'll be able to sort all of this out at the meeting." During the managers' meeting, Greg began by yelling and lashing out at Calvin: "There are people on this board that work with my office. Why wasn't I informed that this board was being formed? I resent this!" Jerry Smith, the Chief Operating Officer and number two person in GO, responded, "I agree."

At that moment, Calvin really wished that he was back in New York. However, he calmly replied, "The people that responded favorably to the board invitation are high-level businesspeople that either work with my office or have indicated to my salespeople that they will work with my office." Greg just continued to loudly protest the board and added, "I make a lot of money for you. If GO is going to allow this, then I will have to seriously reconsider renewing GTO's contract with you." Everyone was astonished to hear this. Gary Parks then said, "Greg, I want you to know that we've valued our relationship with you." Bill Dunn offered a suggestion: "Maybe Calvin and Greg should jointly form a board." Calvin thought to himself, "This is really not what I want to hear." GO's management used tolerating Greg as their coping mechanism. Calvin knew that everyone at the meeting from GO had at one time criticized Greg's manner of handling things, but other than Gary and Bill's brief comments no one else said anything during the meeting. Calvin stood alone at the meeting.

As the meeting finally came to an end, Greg seemed pleased with himself. He said, "Why don't we hit the golf course for a round of golf?" Most of the attendees said they would join him. Calvin, who passed on the invitation, smiled when a thunderstorm began and rained them out.

Question

How should Calvin pursue the board? What's your assessment of how GO's senior level management handled the meeting and what should they do?

CASE STUDY: HENDRICKS INSURANCE COMPANY

Need to Improve Relationships with Independent Agents

The Hendricks Insurance Company services are sold in the marketplace by independent insurance agents. These agents are local entrepreneurs and respected members of their community. As agents, they represent an adequate number of insurance companies to serve their customers' needs.

These agents are considered by Hendricks Insurance to be their primary customers. Without them their product will not get sold. It has been generally accepted that an agent will only do business with a company that provides a quality product, reasonably priced, with timely and accurate service.

However, in recent years, changes in the marketplace have generated the need for agents to establish closer ties with their companies. Agents are now committing more business to fewer companies in hopes of establishing closer, long-term relationships. The adversarial relationship between agents and companies no longer exists. It has become a more personalized business with both parties searching for ways to strengthen relationships.

Hendricks Insurance has not been successful in developing these relationships. Their agents tell them the missing ingredient is trust. Over the past five years Hendricks Insurance has been struggling with improving its profitability. Their financial picture has been dismal in recent years. As a result they structured a more detailed underwriting process and a greater variety of financial services. This process, while creating an improved financial condition, is being perceived by their agents as a lack of trust. Although their competition is cultivating relationships with the agents, Hendricks Insurance is not.

This problem was described by their agents in the annual agents' advisory board meetings as well as through a customer survey and one-on-one discussions with various Hendricks Insurance executives.

The Underwriting department is separate from sales and marketing and they have difficulty in recognizing the fine line between trust and in-depth underwriting. The profit picture has improved and there is a well-disciplined underwriting process. The sales and marketing unit has supported the efforts by underwriting to accomplish the improvement in profitability.

Joan Meyers is the Director of Agency Relations at Hendricks Insurance Company. She believes the issue is not what is being done, but the manner in which the companay is doing it. However, she feels that it is imperative that Hendricks Insurance now change their agents' perception, not with rhetoric but action. Without a firm base of trust, strong relationships with their agents will never be achieved and their success will be limited.

Question

Joan has an upcoming annual agents' Advisory Board meeting. What should she tell the agents and what should she be doing?

Chapter 11

Total Quality Management

INTRODUCTION

Sales managers are involved with providing quality products and services for customers. *Total quality management* (TQM) is a philosophy that commits the organization to continuous quality improvements in all of its activities. TQM is a management concept usually applied to the production and operations area because it entails the measurement of quality levels. TQM tools involve focused processed improvement teams, directed measurement, and reward for effective performance systems. TQM focuses the efforts of the sales force on customer satisfaction because they are expected to build strong customer relationships and understand the customers criteria for quality.[1] TQM in sales means a commitment by the sales organization to performance excellence through continual improvement in the sales process.[2] One reason that TQM has particular relevance to the sales force is that customers define the quality levels that they desire. Salespeople are in the best position to identify customer-oriented definitions of TQM by asking customers to define quality. Another reason that TQM is relevant to salespeople is that, in part, sales force effectiveness with customers is based on the technical knowledge of the products and services that they sell. This technical knowledge allows salespeople to serve and solve problems for their customers. According to Table 11.1, not only do many salespeople and sales managers have a solid technical knowledge of their company's products or services, it seems to be a necessary selling skill.

TQM is a management concept that has far-reaching applicability for every aspect of a business. When first used in a particular business, it is most often applied to manufacturing processes. This makes sense, because the inputs, outputs, and timing of tangible manufacturing

TABLE 11.1. Technical Knowledge Level of Salespeople

Source: *Carter Sales Force Survey* (1996).

processes are generally easy to measure and understand. Business functions that are more difficult to measure, such as customer development or the effectiveness of advertising, have been far more problematic to cover using TQM methods.[3] This is why TQM is not frequently applied to the selling function. As firms gain experience with TQM, its application should spread to other customer-related functions, such as delivery, field service, the handling of complaints and billing. The role of the sales force in a company's TQM effort is important, because it is through the customer dealings that most of the information about customer needs and wants are collected.[4] Customer information is the very essence of the notion of Quality in the TQM concept. Companies that do not apply the TQM concepts to the sales function may be missing a significant opportunity to improve company performance.[5]

APPLYING TQM TO SALES

What Is TQM?

At its simplest, TQM represents a commitment on the part of a company to control its own processes and the endeavor to make continuing improvements to those processes to please customers. Companies that adopt TQM normally have to add mechanisms for monitoring, controlling, and improving their processes. Most companies start using TQM in production processes, then expand the system to encompass purchasing, delivery, customer service, and other functions.

How Does TQM Apply to Sales?

Understanding how TQM applies to the sales function means beginning with a broad description of "quality." In fact, quality cannot be meaningfully discussed without tying it directly to customer needs and expectations. Note, however, that the definition of "customer" is important. For salespeople, there are at least two kinds of customers: external customers, who are buying the products or services being offered, and internal customers, including management and peers. TQM activities can be applied to activities in service of either, or both, kinds of customers.

Quality is itself a rather all-encompassing word that applies in so many different ways that it can be difficult to discuss. One useful recent article proposed breaking quality down into various critical dimensions that can be more easily identified, monitored, measured, and acted upon.[6]

These dimensions are indeed critical dimensions of quality for sales activities. The application of TQM involves setting up measuring and monitoring mechanisms for the important quality dimensions and endeavoring to improve the performance of the sales process with respect to these dimensions. What is needed, then, is to determine if it is possible to develop processes for major sales activities that support the measurement, control, and improvement of TQM. These dimensions are:

- *Performance* - meeting sales targets
- *Features* - stable of appropriate sales skills
- *Reliability* - keeping customer commitments
- *Conformance* - obeying company policies
- *Durability* - tenacity in meeting customer needs
- *Serviceability* - being manageable and trainable
- *Aesthetics* - maintaining positive company image
- *Perceived Quality* - meeting customer satisfaction levels
- *Speed* - fast turnaround time in getting the product or service to the customer
- *Company Objectives* - reaching the "macro" organizational goals

- *Customer Responsiveness* - listening to customers and acting on that communication
- *Value* - giving customers their money's worth

SALES AS A PROCESS

The Sales Function Is a Process

A very useful definition of a process is "a system of interrelated activities that can, or must be understood and managed as a single entity."[7]

There are advantages to looking at sales as a process. As an interrelated system, the sales process can be thought of as having a set of attributes that are independent of the particular product or service that is being sold. Attributes of interest might include efficiency, speed, flexibility, and consistency. To ensure that the objectives of the business are met, it is necessary to design, implement, and continue to improve the sales process until its characteristics support those goals.

Another advantage to the process view of sales is that it is a reminder that the activities undertaken by salespeople and various employees are part of a sequence of events that depend on each other. Focused attention might be required on one or more steps while making process improvements or correcting problems. The application of quality principles applies to all company endeavors, including satisfying internal "customers." Manufacturing engineers, for instance, are customers of the design staff. Another signpost of quality is called *benchmarking*. This involves rating a company's major business practices against the world's best, not just the best in the same industry or the same country, and then emulating those practices. Probably the best first step toward customer satisfaction is to get employees to focus inward and please internal customers, the people just down the assembly line, or in the next office. Empowering workers may eventually give U.S. companies a shot at leapfrogging Japan in quality by unleashing a flood of creative talent; it is the employees themselves who generally find the best solution. Product and service quality is one of the most demanding challenges confronting corporate America. TQM embraces a strong customer orientation, a team-oriented corporate culture, and the use of statistical methods to analyze and improve all business processes including sales management.

TQM principles are directed at achieving internal efficiencies within a firm, in marketing, and in the external perception of the firm as representing a quality organization. The efforts to market a quality product and enhance the quality perception of the firm can be categorized in economics as methods of nonprice competition. Other non-TQM methods of nonprice competition that firms frequently engage in include extended warranties, free services, advertising, and so forth. TQM decisions often require a significant allocation of resources, whether a firm engages in the variety of quality activities in marketing their product, in enhancing their quality corporate image, product changes, or introducing new products with a quality strategy. The resource allocation issue asks what resources should be optimally allocated to TQM projects. In terms of efficiency, TQM projects should be undertaken as long as they are positive net present value projects. Accepting such projects increases the wealth of the shareholder, which is reflected in the price per share of common stock.

The Sales Process

Regardless of the exact style of selling that is used by the sales force, there are six basic steps used in the sales process.[8] These steps are:

1. *Planning.* Includes market research, organization, and other preparations.
2. *Meeting.* Includes making contact with client and building relationship.
3. *Studying.* Includes studying client needs.
4. *Proposing.* Includes proposing solutions to client's needs or concerns.
5. *Confirming.* Making the sale official and receiving confirmation.
6. *Assuring.* Following up with client satisfaction.

Although this process is sequential, and a closed loop, each sales cycle leads to a new round of planning, meeting, and potential additional sales. This view is shown in Figure 11.1. Note that the normal path from task to task leads clockwise, but that some circumstances lead back to previous tasks for rework or new opportunities.

FIGURE 11.1. The Handerson "Closed-Loop" Sales Process

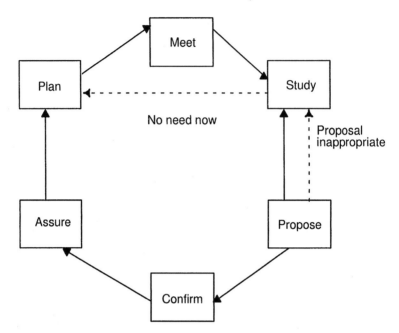

What Kind of Process?

Although every process is unique when viewed in the particular, experts on process theory can generally classify processes into one of a few major types. These types include the following:[9]

1. *Projects* generally consist of a series of discrete steps to produce one-of-a-kind items. An example is the production of a piece of customized machinery.
2. *Job Shops* generally produce a greater variety of products but in small batches. An example is a hospital emergency room.
3. *Batch Processes* are similar to job shops but produce more standardized products in larger lot sizes. An example is bookbinding.
4. *Line Flows* use narrowly defined tasks and specialized assembly lines to produce even larger volumes of standard products. An example is an auto assembly plant.

5. *Continuous Processes* are usually highly automated and produce the largest volumes of product. Examples are chemical or paper plants.

After studying these process types and their relationship with the sales process, it becomes apparent that different kinds of selling can be described as different kinds of processes. For example, selling a countrywide cellular system to Argentina seems to be best described as a project. For this sale, there might be a particular sequence of tasks required to understand the customer need, plan a response, produce the proposal, confirm the sale, deliver the product, and assure customer satisfaction. This particular sale could occupy salespeople for months or even years. An alternative example might be a personal selling approach to medical instrumentation sales. In this case, the process seems to be better described as a job shop process, using fewer, more predictable steps to sell from a family of products. There might even be an arguable case for a line flow or continuous sales process in, say, long-distance telephone service where the process is highly automated and there is a high volume of sales. Thus, the sales process can be a different kind of process depending on the situation.

TQM Measurement, Control, and Improvement

Previous studies have investigated aspects of sales performance. Many works have attempted to develop models that would allow sales managers to better predict territory sales response and/or salesperson performance within those territories.[10] These studies had very important results and the research shows that models of territory response can actually be developed and that results can successfully be replicated in other settings. What is more, a later study that followed up the territory response modeling effort showed that the results were stable over time, at least through the duration of the follow-up.[11] Thus, there is a basis in research for developing a process for predicting territory sales response.

Studies have also been conducted that predict the performance of individual salespeople. Most of this research is concerned with a single aspect of individual performance. As an example, one study examined communication style and its effect on sales performance.[12] The study concluded that communication style was a determinant of sales performance, but because the explained variance was low, not much else could be said. A more useful, and a more convincing, result was obtained by performing a meta-analysis on a large body of previous studies.[13] This technique treats individual study findings as dependent variables and seeks to find larger patterns in the results of many studies. This work concluded that the key determinants of sales performance in individuals are, in order of importance: personal factors, skill, role variables, aptitude, motivation, and organizational/environmental factors. Another conclusion was that none of these predictors by themselves account for much of the variation in performance less than 10 percent on average, and that the correlation between determinants and performance is affected by the type of products that are being sold. There is a basis in research for developing a process for selecting sales staff and for predicting future sales performance.

In a similar vein, another academically rigorous study has examined other aspects of sales-related activities. Several topics of interest covered by this work include comparisons of behavior-based versus outcome-based sales force control systems, the importance of including effort and task difficulty information in salespeople performance evaluations, understanding, developing, and influencing sales force culture, and processes for salesperson performance evaluation.[14]

TQM TERMS

The following terms are used to describe TQM-related issues:

- *Continuous-Improvement Process (CIP):* Searching for higher levels of quality by isolating sources of defects with a goal of zero defects. The Japanese call it *Kaizen.*
- *Just-in-Time (JIT):* The delivery of materials and parts just at the moment a factory needs them, which eliminates costly inventories.
- *Quality Function Deployment (QFD):* A system that pays special attention to customer wants in which activities that do not contribute are considered wasteful.
- *Six-Sigma Quality:* A statistical measure of how close a product comes to its quality goal. One-sigma means 68 percent of products are acceptable; three-sigma means 99.7 percent. Six-sigma is 99.999997 percent perfect: 3.4 defects per million parts.

There is a basis in research for developing a full range of subprocesses for the overall sales process, including salesperson selection and control, evaluation of salesperson performance, predicting and evaluating territory response, and other activities. These processes can be defined and developed in a way that allows measurement and improvement to take place, which allows a TQM approach to be adopted to cover these processes. Adopting such an approach will allow an improved focus on customer satisfaction and continuing process improvements to the betterment of the firm.

IMPLEMENTATION ISSUES

Malcolm Baldridge National Quality Award

The Malcolm Baldridge National Quality Award defines the principles of quality management in clear language and provides companies with a comprehensive framework for achieving customer satisfaction and increased employee involvement. The award was created when the Malcolm Baldridge National Quality Improvement Act was signed by President Ronald Reagan on August 20, 1987. The purpose of the award is to provide guidelines and criteria that organizations could use to evaluate their quality improvement efforts. By submitting an application describing their quality practices and performance, managers and organizations are selected by teams of judges for awards in manufacturing service and small business. The Baldridge judges are teams of trained quality expert examiners who come from industry, academia, and consulting firms who visit each company for several days in order to review the top applicants and choose award winners.[15]

Although we have seen that firms can define sales processes and apply TQM methodologies to support customer focus and continuing improvements, there are pitfalls and opportunities in doing so. In this section, some of the more significant considerations are reviewed, with references to company experiences or research indications as appropriate.

Sales Manager's Role

Changes that are significant to the business, and especially those that involve fundamental changes in thinking and approach such as

TQM, should be viewed as reengineering efforts. Changes of this type take time and effort to be successful, and cannot be expected to have positive short-term effects in every case. Time after time, companies have found that high-level involvement and patience are critical to ensure success.[16] Without this level and duration of commitment, efforts to implement TQM will be disappointing at best, and may even result in significant employee and management dissatisfaction.[17]

Sales Force Role

Companies that report some of the most successful efforts emphasize the role that employee involvement played in their efforts. The key idea seems to be that employees themselves are in the best position to understand the realities of their assignments and can make meaningful contributions.[18] By allowing salespeople to take an active role in the definition of process changes for implementation or performance, the process will have a greater chance of being successful.

Training is another form of employee involvement that will help involve salespeople in process definitions. The importance and impact of sales force training programs have been reported by many companies in aiding process definitions.[19]

Fact Finding

Research results are available to provide guidance for many aspects of the sales process. Given that this information is available, it makes sense to use applicable results when setting up or modifying sales process definitions.

For example, specific guidance is available for the process of setting up sales territories and forecasts. This research indicates that sales territories should not be described using potential and the number of accounts, but instead using potential, concentration, and geographic dispersion results in a far higher correlation with actual response.

Another example is the choice between behavior-based and outcome-based sales force control systems.[20] Here there was an extremely useful result that used attributes of the firm's structure and expected sales transactions to provide guidance on the choice of control system to obtain the best fit between the process and the needs of the customers and the business.

Without using the available theory to make important decisions on sales force management, firms might leave such decisions to the subjective judgment of sales managers, whether or not those experiences were applicable to the new situation or even valid at all. Another approach could be to begin with available research information, then adjust it in a controlled way using employee input, customer input, and actual measurable results. There remain a large number of managerial decisions where sales managers will make a personal impact on the company style and effectiveness.

Ongoing Assessment

It is important to maintain flexibility during the improvement process to continue to incorporate improvements without getting "locked in" to particular task definitions. This requires careful judgment on the part of sales managers, however, to differentiate between an idea that has not yet been given time to prove itself and an idea that is not working and should be abandoned. The one area that must remain constant is the commitment of sales managers to continue quality improvements. The idea of continuous improvement is central to TQM and several companies have emphasized specific benefits that have been obtained from this approach (see Figure 11.2).[21]

SUMMARY

The TQM "revolution" has been applied to many kinds of systems, but has not yet been widely used in the sales process or in managing sales activity. Based on the available research, literature, and company testimonials, there is no valid reason why this situation has persisted. One primary reason could be due to a belief that the sales function is more an art and soft skill than a process, and therefore the measurement and process improvement.

TQM techniques that have been successfully used in other functional areas of business, such as production, cannot be used in sales. The available evidence does not support this view.

Although some aspects of the sales function are more difficult to measure than the production processes, there are many subprocesses that have been carefully studied and basic models exist that can be used as a basis for new process definitions.

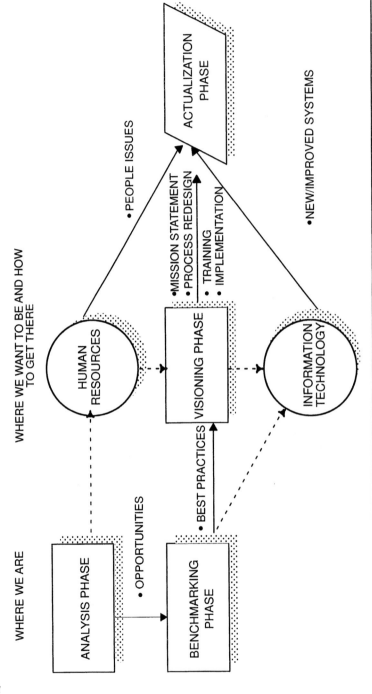

FIGURE 11.2. Chatham Consulting Group: Quality Process Flow

WHERE WE WANT TO BE AND HOW
TO GET THERE

WHERE WE ARE

ACTUALIZATION
PHASE

•PEOPLE ISSUES

•MISSION STATEMENT
•PROCESS REDESIGN
• TRAINING
• IMPLEMENTATION

•NEW/IMPROVED SYSTEMS

HUMAN
RESOURCES

VISIONING PHASE

INFORMATION
TECHNOLOGY

• OPPORTUNITIES

• BEST PRACTICES

ANALYSIS PHASE

BENCHMARKING
PHASE

Quality can be as simple as a four-phase process. It is the preparation and dedication that propels it to success.

PROFILE: Dr. Kenneth Preiss, Author of *Agile Competition and Virtual Organizations: Strategies for Enriching the Customer* and *Cooperate to Compete,* The Sir Leon Bagrit Chair and Professor, Ben Gurion, Tel Aviv, Israel.

> "The word sales conjures up the image of selling a product or service at a single instant, or for a limited period of time. I believe that the basics of competition in the high value-added economies has changed. For a long period, competitiveness was based on price. Then, competitiveness was based on the price and quality of the product or service. Then, competitiveness was based on price, quality, and the timeliness of the product or service. Then as price, quality, and timeliness became widely available, and therefore taken for granted, another competitive parameter entered the equation. Competitiveness now requires price, quality, and timeliness of the product or service, but in the context of an interactive relationship between supplier and customer, where the supplier supports the commercial competitiveness of the commercial supplier, or the lifestyle of the consumer customer. Quality therefore now needs to be perceived not only as quality of the product or service, but as an attribute permeating all the components of a company reflected in all the company does. If a company produces a good product, but lacks quality as a characteristic permeating its entire structure and culture, it will be a poor interactor and will not manage to nurture the relationships needed for today's success."

Source: Dr. Kenneth Preiss (February 25,1997). Personal Interview. Agility Forum, Bethlehem, Pennsylvania.

Once a company has decided to implement a TQM approach to the sales function, there are some practical challenges for implementing improvements to sales systems.

If a sales organization commits to making the effort to implement a TQM approach and successfully implements the TQM system, it can expect significant benefits for the long term. Companies such as Teladyne, Hewlett-Packard, and others have proved that using this approach is not a fad and can successfully transform firms into market leaders with a competitive edge.[22]

Questions

1. What is TQM and why is it relevant to the sales force?
2. Describe how sales is a process.
3. What is the Malcolm Baldridge National Quality Award and why was it created?
4. As sales manager for a corporation in the computer industry, you have just reviewed your end-of-the-year sales results.

Although the results show slight profitability, you are concerned with what you perceive as a certain sense of complacency in the sales force. They have conveyed to you in sales meetings and informal conversations that they do not feel that they need to perform better and have, in fact, generated profitable results. How can you as sales manager use "benchmarking" to improve their performance levels and change the attitude of the sales force?

5. Please describe the purpose of each of the various Critical Quality Dimensions.

CASE STUDY: SEBCO, INC.

Synopsis

Develop a plan to establish both routine and strategic sales goals, accurately measure a salesperson's performance relative to those goals and measure sales force quality levels.

Background

Sebco, Inc. is a regional manufacturer of setting and maintenance products for the ceramic/vinyl tile, marble, granite, and masonry industries. The company was formed in 1979. It employs approximately seveny-four people and its office and plant is located in Pittsburgh, Pennsylvania. The products manufactured include cement mortars and grouts, adhesives, additives, cleaners, and sealers. Primarily, the markets sold to are tile/marble distributors, flooring dealers, lumber and masonry yards, and hardware stores. The sales force consists of ten company representatives and eight independent representatives. One of the independent sales reps sells a specific product to the plastics industry both nationally and internationally. The remaining reps sell the entire product line to specific regional territories from Maine to Florida. The company is in the process of hiring an additional company representative. Mary Lawrence is the Sales Manager of the company. As a result, she has responsibilities in addition to sales management, for supervising customer service, overseeing collections, delivery scheduling and hiring of personnel.

Problem/Issue

Until recently, Sebco, Inc. employed only independent representatives to sell its products. The sales reps were assigned territories and given existing accounts to service. In addition, they were responsible for developing new accounts. Their activities and performance were very loosely monitored. The sales reps were not given any specific quotas or goals to meet. Rather, monthly sales totals were monitored for significant positive or negative effects and the sales rep was held accountable in a very informal manner.

During the past year Sebco, Inc. has changed its strategy with respect to salespeople. It is in the process of eliminating independent representatives and hiring company-employed salespeople. This is in an effort to maintain better control and maximize both performance and customer service. Additionally, during the past year, Sebco, Inc. changed its strategy with respect to account management. At the beginning of the year, the sales reps were given accounts based on business size, e.g., large or small, as opposed to by territory. Recently, they were reorganized into specific territories, regardless of account size within that territory. Currently, they service all accounts within their territory and are responsible for developing new accounts.

Due to these strategic changes, assigning sales quotas, measuring performance, and determining compensation have been difficult, if not impossible, to manage. Additionally, there was no prior plan in effect for managing the above. The company is therefore looking to establish a plan for setting routine sales quotas and goals and developing strategic goals. Along with this, a system is needed to fairly and accurately measure the salesperson's achievement of those goals and compensate for performance. As additional staff is hired, there is a growing concern that each individual is being compensated fairly with respect to one another and that individual achievements and performance are being recognized.

Questions

Currently, Sebco, Inc. does not have a system in place for determining sales performance goals. They do, however, have tools available to monitor sales activity by salesperson and by territory.

Their accounting system is computerized and they have additional software packages that can be utilized to track sales figures. More specifically, though, assistance in addressing the following issues/ questions would be helpful to the implementation of a system for establishing and measuring sales goals and compensating performance:

1. Who should set goals: the salesperson, manager, or both?
2. How can a fair performance goal be set for the chosen time frame when business has seasonal swings?
3. How do you measure sales force quality levels (e.g., providing exceptional customer service)?

Chapter 12

Mentorships and Time Management

MENTORSHIPS

Many of today's salespeople start their work with a genuine interest in discovering what it may be really like out there in the work environment. Others come to corporations unsure of what they want to do and may even perform without any better idea. One way to help both types learn about and then learn how to handle the uncertainties and harsh realities of the job market is to align them with mentors.

A *mentor* is a professional person, usually one at an executive level in an organization, who acts as a counselor, adviser, and professional guide to a less-experienced person often in the same organization. It is helpful to the growth of any sales professional to have access to this kind of guidance, but in fact, this process can begin early in the sales career. Mentoring can be an extremely valuable tool for the sales force manager dedicated to helping salespeople plan the direction of their careers. The cultivation of mentor programs allows sales organizations to provide salespeople with some "real world" preparation, thus enhancing the quality of their sales development experience.

THE MENTOR PROGRAM

When offered at work, a mentor program provides salespeople the opportunity to meet and talk with various sales professionals. This interaction allows salespeople to benefit from the mentors' insights and experiences and to use them in developing their own career directions. Positive mentor relationships are therefore extremely important to the success of the program. Moreover, a well-structured program will give salespeople a good idea of how to select and develop mentors on their own in the more threatening environment of the workplace.

Making the Match

Having located the salespeople with their expressed desire to listen and learn, and having found the mentors with their commitment to help, then it is appropriate to set about the task of assigning the salespeople to the mentors. The match between these individuals needs to be based upon their having similar career interests and even similar backgrounds when possible. By reviewing the career profiles of the mentors along with the salesperson's particular fields of interest, sales managers can select the matches that seem most appropriate.

Ideally, each mentor should be assigned to one salesperson, and generally this is the case. However, there may be instances where three or four salespeople work with a single mentor. This is the kind of adjustment that can be made, depending on the given circumstances.

Mentors and salespeople should be given feedback in order to facilitate their relationships. The sales manager is responsible for providing this feedback on how well things are going and if any adjustments should be made. The feedback is transmitted by phone, mailings, reminder notes, or by meeting salespeople and mentors. While the point is not to overburden mentors who have their own professional and personal obligations, it should be made clear that after the initial meeting there should be an opportunity to "shadow" the mentor either in his or her office or in the field.

The objective of a mentor program is not to force salespeople into particular viewpoints, but instead to give them valuable information about specific job positions as well as on a variety of career opportunities. Salespeople can stay with their designated mentor until the end of the year. At that point they can continue with that same mentor or be reassigned to another. The dynamics that take place in a mentor relationship provide not only an added dimension to the learning experience with "real world" perspectives, but also a starting point for salespeople to identify their professional and sales directions. As a result of clarified sales direction, they can also improve their customer preparation.

Questions for Mentors

Prior to the first mentor meeting, give an orientation for the salespeople. The sales manager should explain the purpose and format of the program, how to deal with a mentor in a businesslike manner, and how to ask effective questions. Salespeople should not only ask but *bombard* their mentors with questions as they focus on their own professional direction. Here are some of the questions that salespeople should be encouraged to ask:

Job Description

- What is a typical day on the job like for you?
- What percent of your time do you spend each day in various activities of your work?
- How free are you to do your work as you want to?
- Where are you located in a normal working day?
- What types of problems are you likely to face in a day's time?
- What are the most satisfying and the most frustrating parts of your work?

Advancement

- How did you get to your current position?
- What are the trends and developments in the field that you see affecting careers in the future?

Preparation

- How did you prepare for this occupation? What do you recommend for a person entering this occupation from (your current position)?
- What education/degrees/training/licenses are required? If not required, which are recommended?
- What are the best places to go for additional education or training for a position like yours?
- If you could start all over again in launching your career, what steps would you take?
- What courses do you recommend should be taken for this occupation?

Lifestyle

- What hours do you normally work?
- In what ways is travel a factor in this job?

- What are the professional organizations in this field?
- How do these organizations serve their members?
- What are the pressures that you contend with?
- How does this occupation affect your private life?
- What other things are expected of you outside of working hours?

The value of mentor programs is recognized very early by its participants. For example, mentor John Birstler, a vice president for Merrill Lynch, noted that "this gives me the chance to advise my protégée regarding career opportunities and how I made it. I'll do all I can to help him or her succeed."[1] Many salespeople in mentor programs have remarked that they now feel more focused on their future goals. There is little doubt that without mentors they would have had to wait until much later to discover some major details on their particular professions.

Importance in the Workplace

A mentor program in the sales force not only helps salespeople determine career goals, but also acts as a lead-in for them to seek "on-the-job" mentors once they have joined the work force. It is essential to career advancement and job security to align with someone who is successful and knows what to do next. A seasoned "guru" can help an employee deal with situations that may otherwise take years of experience to know how to handle. It is an advantage to have access to someone who has done it all before and has his or her own network of professional contacts that may be of use to a protégée. Many organizations so strongly believe in mentorships that while this is usually an informal, unofficial process, they officially nurture mentor/protégée relationships in their firms.[2]

"On-the-job" mentors also fulfill a very important career enhancement and psychosocial function. This means the mentor takes an active role in the protégé's career growth and the protégé even feels more a part of the organization.[3] Organizations that seek to develop their own leaders may even find that having mentors who can urge, direct, and provide feedback can help produce effective leaders.

Some organizations use mentorships to address specific problems. Some, for example, have developed mentor programs to foster diversity in the workplace. Such programs encourage women and minorities to establish a network of professionals—and mentors in particular—to listen to their experiences on coping in the work environment and to lend psychological support.[4] Some organizations encourage women and minorities to go beyond their own groups to seek out mentors who will share information, advise on organizational norms, and assist in career development with their insights, authority, and expertise.

More organizations are forming formal mentor programs that benefit sales managers, salespeople, and entrepreneurs. These programs can help the sales force find new and creative ways to help themselves and each other. An organization designed to offer members, at the executive level, to get new perspectives from outsiders in a confidential atmosphere is in the Executive committee. The Executive Committee is based in San Diego, California, and is comprised of executives of noncompeting companies in the United States, Canada, Australia, England, and Japan. Another similar organization that gives advice on business problems is the Crossroads Group in Los Angeles, California.[5]

Under the direction and support of sales managers, salespeople should be allowed and encouraged to help manage and train each other. Veteran salespeople helping newcomers can promote teamwork, camaraderie, ideas, and selling techniques. It also provides sales managers with a means to maximize limited training resources that the sales organization may lack and let salespeople learn from one another. This sales force level mentoring and coaching also allows the salespeople to share some of the responsibility for the development of the sales force and have a chance to polish their management skills as well as keep their knowledge level current.[6]

Coaching

As with coaching, mentoring is a practice that can help sales managers maximize the performance levels of their sales force. In effect, coaching is teaching, and sales managers must present relevant information and materials so that salespeople can absorb it easily.[7] In order to do this, sales managers must be knowledgeable and stay informed themselves, avoid competition with the sales force, encourage communication, and keep their word.[8] Equally important is to make the sales force feel responsible for their own professional development.

Teaming

Teaming, a related concept to mentoring and coaching, uses self-managed sales teams and cross-functional subgroups, which may comprise some people from the sales force, marketing, information technology, and production to work together on specific projects or customers. For teaming to be successful, several things should occur. First, salespeople should be cross-trained on how the company works in different functional areas to gain a companywide perspective. This training will increase the capability of the team and the individual salespeople. Next, a climate that shares information concerning company goals, strategies, and customers with sales teams is necessary. This helps to establish a more informed group that is better prepared and can act more effectively.[9] Despite the competitive nature of sales and salespeople, discussing success stories and problems dealing with customers in the sales process at annual or periodic sales meetings is a good way to share constructive information between salespeople. This process is known as the concept of *Shared Intelligence.*

TIME MANAGEMENT

Time management is a valued asset and a dilemma for sales managers because time itself is a scarce and valuable resource. Time cerainly poses productivity and performance problems for the sales force.[10]

On average, salespeople spend about forty-seven hours a week at work of which 55 percent is spent on selling activities and 45 percent on nonselling activities. Out of the total forty-seven hours, on average, only fourteen hours per week are spent by salespeople in direct contact with customers.[11]

Keys for time management are:

• Corporate restructuring and reengineering have dictated the need for the sales force to accomplish more tasks in the same amount of time.

- Sales managers need to focus on being results-oriented and generating effective performance in the sales force.
- The sales force must have the ability to neutralize the trauma of time despite having to perform discretionary tasks in blocks of unstructured time.
- A sales manager's true value to an organization lies in the ability to create a sales organization that practices efficient, productive time management.

Sales managers cannot ignore long-term sales issues for the pressures of the moment. It is difficult for sales managers to do all of the routine things and resolve the problems that come with the job, so the return on invested time is as important as the return on invested money. The flexible work hours and lack of a typical nine to five workday for salespeople makes their use of time management skills essential. An effective time management device is for sales managers to avoid being surprised and use anticipatory action. This forces the use of effective planning which results in deliberate objective and priority setting to show sales managers a sequential order of action steps to follow. The following is a recommended "Time Management Self-Analysis" that sales managers can apply for themselves and the sales force.

- How much time will be allotted to each management or sales task?
- How is time allocated to do important tasks?
- How do I force myself to make decisions systematically and as quickly as possible?
- Are my short-term and long-term goals clearly defined?
- Has a detailed schedule been made for each day?
- Has a checklist been made for major daily, weekly, and monthly activities?
- Has a daily progress review been made to measure effectiveness?
- Are ideas and results recorded in a journal, software program, or some other manner?
- Are my actions and those of the sales force wasting time by being more activity-oriented instead of results-oriented?

Comparative Advantage and Time Management

The concept of comparative advantage can also help sales managers with time management. Comparative advantage states that each person should do the work for which they are best qualified. So, to avoid wasting time, salespeople should be assigned those customers and responsibilities that are commensurate with their expertise.

Time is a critical source of competitive advantage and is a strategic tool with value comparable to many business resources such as revenue, speed, efficiency, and quality. Examples of improvements from time-based customer-oriented strategies can be customized products services bringing sales organizations closer to their customers, quick turnaround, expanded variety, and greater innovation. In the late 1970s, Toyota, the Japanese auto manufacturer, experienced the impact of poor sales cycle time coordination between the sales and manufacturing areas. Toyota Manufacturing and Toyota Sales were separate divisions. Although Toyota Manufacturing could make a car in two days, it took Toyota Sales anywhere from two weeks to three and one-half weeks to close the sale and deliver the car to the customer. Another significant problem was that Toyota Sales was responsible for 20 to 30 percent of the overall car costs, which was greater than the manufacturing costs. In the early 1980s these two divisions merged and made improving customer service and eliminating sales time delays priorities. By 1987, Toyota reduced their sales cycle to eight days which resulted in lower expenses and more satisfied customers. Reducing and eliminating delays and using faster response time for customers has the advantage of attracting more profitable customers.[12]

Delegation and Time Management

Delegation, as a management skill, is an additional tool available to sales managers that can help with time management. Delegation is the actual managerial aspect of having subordinates do their jobs and assigning them work that would otherwise be time consuming for the sales maanger to perform. When delegating, sales managers should ask:

- Can someone else perform this task better than I can?
- Can this be performed at a lower cost by someone other than myself?

- Is work being delegated in a manner that takes full advantage of the knowledge, background, and experience level of the sales force?

When sales managers delegate tasks to the sales force, the use of time management guidelines provides empowerment, enriches the job, creates better morale, reduces turnover, encourages initiative and develops the essential time management skills of the salespeople. The failure to delegate not only puts additional time burdens on a sales manager and denies the sales force the opportunity to maximize their performance capability, and to some extent, it excludes them from the decision making process.

Team Building and Time Management

Team building within the sales organization and between salespeople and other functional areas in the company can contribute to efficient, on-time production. By giving salespeople working in teams authority to speed up delivery, it can be easier to meet strict deadlines. Also, effective time-saving ideas developed out of the efforts of team players is a good way to generate many useful ideas. In fact, cross-functional teams representing employees from sales, finance, and production are being used by firms such as Johnson & Johnson and Procter & Gamble to successfully speed up the time frame to launch new products and services or reposition existing ones. Team players produce benefits such as greater production, better quality levels, lower costs, and on-time delivery of products and services.[13]

SUMMARY

Mentor programs run by sales force managers can have these same types of features. They can offer salespeople the opportunity to acquire a depth of information that cannot help but improve their career development and focus on the future. Beyond that, they can lead salespeople to develop an increased confidence in themselves. But maybe the greatest benefit of a mentor program in the sales force is that it shows salespeople the great value of the mentor process so that they will use the same system when on the job to

PROFILE: Dr. Walter Rohrs, Author of *Time Management*, Professor Emeritus, Wagner College, Staten Island, New York.

Mentorship

"In recent years the idea of mentorships has become popular and widespread. A mentor is usually a senior employee of a firm who establishes a special advisory relationship with someone who was newly hired. The mentor's role is to provide guidance and information for the purpose of furthering and aiding the new employee's career development within the organization. This may be accomplished by being helpful in providing background information about the organization as well as answering questions, making suggestions and clarifying specific policies and procedures concerning a current task or assignment.

A good analogy would be comparing a mentor to a person who coaches individuals who have professional careers in sports or in the world of entertainment.

If a mentor works with a number of people engaged in a team effort, such as a sales force, the results can be phenomenal.

Isn't having a teacher, advocate, advisor, and friend at and on your side an ideal situation? Everyone wins, including the firm.

Time Management

While most people will agree that in order to operate a business successfully, a firm requires adequate and accessible resources, the availability and proper use of time may be overlooked.

For people in the area of sales, time is particularly important for two reasons. First, sales personnel are not as closely monitored as employees in other activities. Second, the amount of time spent in the presence of a buyer may be severely restricted. Because of such a limitation, the use of the allotted amount of time must be carefully planned to achieve the desired objective—a profitable sale.

Calendars and clocks continuously indicate a seemingly never-ending supply of time, but they also make evident its fleeting nature. As each minute passes, it is gone forever, never to be recalled, renewed, or recycled.

When an opportunity presents itself in a particular time frame, the perishability of time requires that the time must be used wisely in order to maximize any possible benefits for the firm. What was accomplished today?

The reality is there may be no tomorrow."

Source: Dr. Walter Rohrs (March 11, 1997). Personal Interview. Wagner College, Staten Island, New York.

help and improve their careers. In fact, their relationship with a mentor may not only prepare them for the realities of the workplace, but might actually be responsible for getting them an effective process for dealing with their customers. Time management is a useful skill that can help sales managers and salespeople maximize their performance levels in the time frame alloted to them to achieve their revenue goals. Developing efficient time management skills should be an ongoing goal for the sales force (see Table 12.1).

CONCLUSION

Survey results that reflect future trends in customer development and sales, important attributes desired in effective salespeople and the number of sales-related positions in the next decade, show that sales will continue to be a dynamic and challenging process and profession.[14]

Sales managers will play the critical role in this competitive sales environment by helping organizations meet the needs of their lifeblood, "the customer." To do this, sales managers and their organizations must never forget that they must continue to develop a mosaic of proficient business skills to meet the challenges of the always evolving marketplace (see Table 12.2).

Questions

1. How does mentoring differ from coaching and teaming?
2. How can mentoring be used to address specific problems in the sales organization?
3. Why is time management an important skill for sales managers and salespeople?
4. What are comparative advantage, delegation, and team building and what is their relationship to time management?
5. Construct a chart covering a recent, typical two-week period of time and describe what your activities were. Then construct a chart covering the same period if you could have spent the time doing these tasks in a manner chosen by you. Compare the two. Would the time accomplish those tasks and perform those activities more effectively?

TABLE 12.1. Future Trends

The top future trends in customer development and sales according to sales organizations:

- Forming customer partnerships and alliances
- Fewer salespeople
- Electronic purchases and the emergence of teleconferencing and virtual offices
- More emphasis on increasing the percentage of business from existing customers
- Providing value-added services to customers
- Total quality service
- The greater role of the sales force technology and database marketing
- Selling via the Internet
- Increased importance of providing customer satisfaction levels
- Increased presence of "key accounts"
- Salespeople will need to become businesspeople
- Increased team selling
- More knowledgeable customer base
- More sales force mentoring and coaching
- Growing impact of the global marketplace as a source of new business opportunities

The most important attributes in hiring effective salespeople as defined by sales managers:

- Self-motivating
- Good communication, interpersonal, and listening skills
- Enthusiastic and energetic
- Intuition
- Tenacity and drive
- Intelligence
- Creative instincts and innovation
- Ability to handle rejection
- Values teamwork yet has a competitive spirit
- Common sense
- Honesty, integrity, and a strong work ethic
- Excellent sales skills
- Polished, professional conduct and appearance
- Values-building customer relationships
- Solid product knowledge
- Great attitude and personality
- Good analytical and problem-solving skills
- People who have a track record of success in anything—not just sales
- Adaptable and flexible
- Success and stability in past employment

TABLE 12.2. Potential Increase in Sales Positions

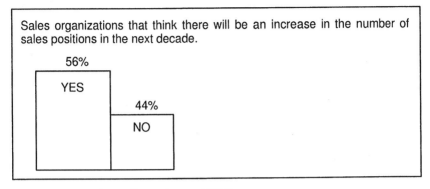

Source: *Carter Sales Force Survey* (1996).

CASE STUDY: JANSEN MANUFACTURING

Business Description

The Plastics Products Group of Jansen Manufacturing generated approximately $200 million in sales revenues last year.

Jansen's products are used to reinforce plastic composites for the manufacture of various end-use markets. They offer a variety of products in areas such as: Marine: boats, jet skis, and skis; Construction: bathtubs, showers and roofing shingles; Corrosion: pipe and storage tanks; Electrical: appliances, insulators, and utility poles; and Automotive: body panels, valve covers, and air-intake manifolds.

The manufacturing of plastic products is a capital-intensive business. Projected demand is expected to increase an estimated 5 percent annually through year 2000, barring unforseen recession.

Problem

The Business Unit which is responsible for sales and customer development decided to take advantage of the current strong economy to relocate salespeople who were static in previous assignments. Tom Brewer, manager of the Business Unit, currently has Art Cohen reporting to him. Art is a relocated salesperson with

272 CONTEMPORARY SALES FORCE MANAGEMENT

more seniority who may have a chip on his shoulder regarding Tom's promotion. Tom also has another salesperson in his territory with a similar chip. He recently had a salesperson resign over differences in opinions relative to business decisions made in corporate headquarters that were no reflection of his relationship with this particular salesperson. This position needed to be filled immediately. Tom also has a recent college graduate as a sales trainee reporting to him. Tom has never had any experience in subordinate management, mentoring, or coaching.

The first salesperson mentioned is Art, an older relocatee, who has been extremely slow to acclimate and who had a very bad incident with a major customer. Tom has had to have tough conversations with Art regarding performance to date. Tom documented Art's third-quarter performance, and used strong language to encourage improvement. This was only recently submitted so it is too early to determine its effectiveness.

Question

Tom is looking for tips on subordinate management, especially with poor performers and new trainees. Please advise him.

Notes

SECTION I: INTRODUCTION TO CONTEMPORARY SALES FORCE MANAGEMENT

Chapter 1

1. Walter Kiechel, "A Manager's Career in the Economy," *Fortune* (April 4, 1994), pp. 68-72.

2. John Graham, "Customers for Keeps," *Selling Power* (April 1996), pp. 50-51.

3. Frederick Langrehr, Scott Smith, Michael Swenson, and William Swinyard, "The Appeal of Personal Selling as a Career: A Decade Later," *Journal of Personal Selling and Sales Management 13*(1), Winter 1993, pp. 51-64.

4. Christen Heide, *Dartnell's 29th Sales Force Compensation Survey,* (Chicago: Dartnell, 1996-1997), pp. 13-14.

5. Timothy Schellhardt, "The Selling Game," *The Wall Street Journal* (March 24, 1994).

6. Ginger Trumfio, "Are You an Effective Motivator?" *Sales & Marketing Management Magazine* (May 1994), p. 136.

7. Lisa Bush-Hankin and Bill O'Connell, "If You Pay They Will Come," *Sales and Marketing Management Magazine* (September 1994), pp. 123-126.

8. Melissa Campanelli, "What Price Sales Force Satisfaction?", *Sales and Marketing Management Magazine* (July 1994), p. 37.

9. Alfie Kohn, "Why Incentive Plans Cannot Work," *Harvard Business Review,* (September-October 1993) pp. 54-63.

10. Alfie Kohn, "Breaking with Tradition," *Sales and Marketing Management Magazine,* (June, 1994), p. 94.

11. Ginger Trumfio, "What's Your Vision?", *Sales and Marketing Management Magazine,* (June 1994), p. 41.

12. Jeffrey Hanson and David Krackhardt, "Informal Networks: The Company Behind the Chart," *Harvard Business Review* (July-August 1993), pp. 104-111.

13. Joseph Pereira, "Bosses Will Do Almost Anything to Light Fires Under Salespeople" *The New York Times,* (April 26, 1993).

SECTION II:
AUTOMATION AND SALES FORCE MANAGEMENT

Chapter 2

1. J. DeJong, "Turbo-Charging Customer Service," *INC.,* (No. 2, 1995), pp. 35-39.

2. M. Boone, "Make Technology Your Ally," *Sales and Marketing Technology,* (June 1996), p. 13.

3. Jeffrey Young, "Can Computers Really Boost Sales?", *Forbes ASAP,* (August 28, 1995), pp. 85-98.

4. T. Dellecave Jr., "Chipping In," *Sales and Marketing Technology,* (June 1996), p. 35.

5. W. Pape, "Becoming a Virtual Company," *INC. Technology,* (No. 4, 1995), pp. 29-31.

6. M. Berger, "Making the Virtual Office A Reality," *Sales and Marketing Technology,* (June 1996), pp. 19-22.

7. Christen Heide, *Sales and Marketing Executive Report,* (April 17, 1996), p. 3.

8. Thayer Taylor, "Sales Automation Cuts the Cord," *Sales and Marketing Management Magazine,* (July 1995), p. 110.

9. A. Lucas, "What in the World Is Electronic Commerce?", *Sales and Marketing Technology,* (June 1996), pp. 24-29.

10. S. Ditlea, "Managing Sales with Software," *Nations Business,* (*84,* No. 3, March 1996), pp. 29-30.

11. T. Dellecave Jr., "Getting the Bugs Out," *Sales and Marketing Management Magazine,* (December 1995), pp. 23-27.

12. B. Jeffery, "Automate with Care," *Selling Power,* (April 1996), pp. 30-31.

13. Editions Choice, "Goldmine for Windows 95," *PC Magazine,* (April 23, 1996), p. 1.

14. Tom Dellecave Jr., "Now Showing" *Sales and Marketing Management Magazine,* (February 1996), pp. 68-72.

15. G.R. Garner, *Computerworld Electronic Commerce Journal,* (April 29 1996), pp. 28-30.

16. L. Klein and J. Quelch, "The Internet and International Marketing," *Sloan Management Review,* (Spring 1996), pp. 60-65.

17. Jared Sandberg, "Internet Access Doubled in Past Year," *The Wall Street Journal,* (October 21, 1996), pp. B11.

18. T. Dellecave Jr., "The Net Effect," *Sales and Marketing Technology,* (March 1996), pp. 17-20.

19. A. Cohen, "Feeling a Little Overwhelmed," *Sales and Marketing Management Magazine,* (December 1995), pp. 14-21.

SECTION III: GLOBALIZATION

Chapter 3

1. Richard Horlick, Personal interview. Fidelity Investments, London, England, (March 13, 1995).

2. S. Enfield, "South of the Border Blues," *Sales and Marketing Management Magazine,* (May 1995), pp. 79-84.

3. Nick Hodgson, Personal interview. Thornton's Inc., London, England, (March 15, 1995).

4. David Jones, Personal interview. The Securities Futures Authority, London, England, (March 14, 1995).

5. S. Brown, "Now It Can Be Told," *Sales and Marketing Management Magazine,* (November 1994).

6. L. Smith, "Time to Buy Mexico?" *Fortune,* (February 1995), pp. 122-126.

7. Christopher Bailey, Personal interview. Bank of England, London, England, (March 15, 1995).

8. C. Rapoport, "The New United States Push into Europe," *Fortune,* (January 1994), pp. 73-74.

9. H.D. Hennessey and J.P. Jeannet, (1995), "Global Marketing Strategies," (Boston: Houghton, 1995).

10. W. Bounds and B. Davis, "Kodak Charges Japan, Fuji Block Access," *The Wall Street Journal,* (May 19, 1995).

11. A. Cooper, "Kodak Case Against Japan Is Stronger Than That of Auto Firms," *The Wall Street Journal,* (June 9, 1995).

12. D. Hamilton, "Revisionists on Japan Get Their Chance," *The Wall Street Journal,* (June 8, 1995),

13. J. Friedland, "Potent Brew for Argentine Firm," *The Wall Street Journal,* (May 22, 1995).

14. P. Gumbel, "Daimler Is to Pay ABB $900 Million to Form Big Railroad Joint Venture," *The Wall Street Journal,* (April 7, 1995).

15. A. Choi, "GM Seeds Grow Nicely in Eastern Europe," *The Wall Street Journal,* (May 5, 1995).

16. A. Guinet, "Trading Technology for Market Access," *European Commission Innovation & Technology Transfer,* (March 1995), p. 15.

17. E. Lacttica, "Lawmakers Take Aim at Trade Agencies," *The Wall Street Journal,* (May 5, 1995).

18. Jennifer Coughlan, "A New Trade Watchdog," *Europa Times,* (March 1995), p. 14.

19. G. Steinmetz, "European Panel Widens Probe of Purchase Planned by Dow," *The Wall Street Journal,* (June 8, 1995).

20. Geoffrey Brewer, "New World Order," *Sales and Marketing Management Magazine,* (January 1994), pp. 59-63.

21. M. Monti, "Proportionality: A Quality Principle for the Internal Market," *European Commission Newsletter,* (September/October 1995).

22. D. Turcq, "India and China, Asia's Non-Identical Twins," *The McKinsey Quarterly,* (No. 2, 1995), pp. 4-19.

23. *United Nations World Investment Report,* (1995).

24. J. Jiewei, Personal interview. Shanghai Pudong New Area International Exchange Center, Shanghai, China, (June 3, 1996).

25. R. Hu, Personal interview. Motorola, Beijing, China, (May 29, 1996).

26. J. Meier, J. Perez and J. Woetzel, "Solving the Puzzle: MNCs in China," *The McKinsey Quarterly,* (No. 2, 1995), pp. 20-33.

27. *Carter Sales Force Survey,* (1996).

28. A. Pawlyna, "Packed to Perfection," *Asian Business,* (March 1996).

29. M. Forney, "Death of a Salesman," *Far Eastern Economic Review 159,* (No. 16, April 1996).

SECTION IV: EFFECTIVE SALES FORCE MANAGEMENT IN A VOLATILE BUSINESS ENVIRONMENT

Chapter 4

1. John Graham, "Customers for Keeps," *Selling Power,* (April, 1996), p. 50-51.

2. M. Campanelli, "Jim Champy on Reengineering Managers," *Sales and Marketing Management Magazine,* (April, 1995), p. 36.

3. A. Markets, "Restructuring Alters Middle Manager Role but Leaves It Robust," *The Wall Street Journal,* (September 25, 1995), p. A.1.

4. A. Lucas, "Down and Out," *Sales and Marketing Management Magazine,* (February, 1996), p. 11.

5. T. Stewart, "Reengineering: The Hot New Managing Tool," *Fortune,* (August 23, 1993), p. 41.

6. Mark Blessington and Bill O'Connell, *Sales Reengineering from the Outside In,* (New York: McGraw-Hill, 1995).

7. Gene Hall, Jim Rosenthal and Judy Wade, "How to Make Reengineering Really Work," *Harvard Business Review, 7,* No. 6, November/December, 1993) pp. 119-131.

8. F. Rose, "Times Mirror Seeks to Turn Page After Cutbacks," *The Wall Street Journal,* (January 12, 1996), p. B.4.

9. Mike Mazzarese, "Downsizing: Reengineering Managers," *Executive Directions,* (September/October, 1994), p. 36.

10. R. Gibson, "General Mills Gets in Shape for Turnaround," *The Wall Street Journal,* (October 26, 1995), p. B.3.

11. D. Dearlove, "The Perils of Getting Flatter," *The Times,* (March, 1996), p. 24.

12. C. Painter, "Reengineering: Road to Rebirth," *Chatham Lights,* (*1* Issue 1, December 1994), p. 1.

13. William Keenan, Jr., "Death of the Sales Manager," *Sales and Marketing Management Magazine,* (October 1994), p. 68.

14. J. Applegate, "Outsourcing Opening Doors for Entrepreneurs," *The Record,* (September 19, 1994), p. C.1.

15. F. Hilmer and J. Quinn, "Strategic Outsourcing," *The McKinsey Quarterly,* (No. 1, Spring, 1995) pp. 49-69.

16. Digital Equipment, Annual Report, 1996, pp. 2-5.

Chapter 5

1. Larry Barton, *Crisis in Organizations: Managing and Communicating in the Heat of Chaos,* (Cincinnati, OH: South Western, 1993).

2. M. Carter, "Risk Management," *Bank Management* (May/June 1995), p. 26.

3. J. Huey, "Managing in the Midst of Chaos," *Fortune* (April 5, 1993), p. 38.

4. Faye Rice, "Denny's Changes Its Spots," *Fortune* (May 13, 1996), pp. 137-142.

5. L. Lindsay and R. Raspberry, (1994), *Effective Managerial Communication,* (Belmont, CA: Wadsworth).

6. K. Labich, "Why Companies Fail," *Fortune* (November 14, 1994), p. 53.

7. G. Harrar, "Running the Risk," *Enterprise* (April 1994), pp. 36-40.

8. E. Furash, "Risk Challenges and Opportunities," *Bank Management* (May/June 1995), p. 34.

9. L. Paulson, "Customers for Life," *Executive Excellence* (September 1994), p. 12.

10. G. Eisenstadt, "Shakeup Artist," *Forbes* (June 19, 1995), pp. 46-49.

11. M. Everett, "Honda Hits Emergency Brake After Sales Scandal," *Sales and Marketing Management Magazine* (May 1994), p. 13.

12. J. Fireman, "Winning Ideas from a Maverick Manager," *Fortune* (February 6, 1995), pp. 66-80.

13. Nancy Arnot, "Xerox Doesn't Want the Force to Be with You," *Sales and Marketing Management Magazine,* (July 1994), p. 11.

Chapter 6

1. John Moran, *Practical Business Law,* Third Edition, (Englewood Cliffs, NJ: Prentice-Hall, 1995), pp. 206-208.

2. Lawrence Chonko, John Tanner, and William Weeks, "Ethics in Salesperson Decision Making," *Journal of Personal Selling & Sales Management, 16,* (No. 1, Winter, 1996), pp. 35-52.

3. *S.E.C. v Chenery,* 332 US 194 (1947).

4. *N.L.R.B. v Bell Aerospace Company,* 416 US 267 (1974).

5. Eric Calonius, "The FAA's Loose Grip on Air Safety," *Fortune,* (October 8, 1990), p. 94.

6. Louis S. Richman, "Bringing Reason to Regulation," *Fortune,* (October 19, 1992), p. 94.

7. Sean Armstrong, "The Good, The Bad, and The Industry," *Life/Health, 95,* No. 1, May 1994), pp. 28-35.

8. W. P. Madar, "Good Guys Need Not Finish Last," *Executive Speeches, 9*, No. 1, August/September 1994), pp. 22-27.

9. Nancy Hass, "Truths of Commission," *Financial World,* (January 19, 1993), pp. 28-29.

10. Dan Cordtz, "Always Do the Right Thing," *Financial World,* (August 16, 1994), pp. 42-43.

11. Lawrence Chonko, John Tanner, and William Weeks, " Ethics in Salesperson Decision Making," *Journal of Personal Selling and Sales Management, 16*, (No. 1, Winter 1996), pp. 35-52.

12. Arturo Z .Vasquez-Parraga, Ali Kara, "Ethical Decision Making in Turkish Sales Management," *Journal of Euromarketing, 14*, (No. 2, 1995), pp. 61-86.

13. Leslie M. Dawson, "Will Feminization Change the Ethics of the Sales Profession?" *Journal of Personal Selling & Sales Management, 12*, (No. 1, Winter 1992), pp. 21-32.

14. William N. Albus, "Producer Database," *Life Association News, 90*, (No. 7, July 1995), pp. 130-132.

15. Stephen Piontek, "Bad News," *National Underwriter, 98*, (No. 6, February 7, 1994), p. 39.

16. Virginia Matthews, "Our Alarm Bells Are Ringing," *Marketing Week, 16*, (No. 48, February 18, 1994), p. 22.

Chapter 7

1. S. Jackson, *"Diversity in the Workplace,"* (New York: Guilford Press, 1992).

2. U.S. Congress, (1991), *Civil Rights Act.*

3. D. Yates, "Managing Diversity in the Global Market: The Coming Revolution in Organizational Management," *The Journal of Global Competitiveness,* (October 1994), p. 503-509.

4. Catalyst Performance Report, "Knowing the Territory: Women in Sales," New York: Catalyst, (1995).

5. William Kenan Jr., "Compensation Survey in Search of Equity," *Sales and Marketing Management Magazine,* (November 1993), p. 82.

6. M. Markarian, "Cultural Evolution," *Sales and Marketing Management Magazine,* (May 1994), p. 128.

7. Tony Williams, Personal interview. Phillips Industrial, Mahwah, New Jersey, (June 19, 1994).

8. Arthur Brimmer, *"Economic Cost of Discrimination Against Black Americans,"* (Washington: Brimmer, January, 1993).

9. Christen Heide, *Dartnell 29th Sales Force Compensation Survey,* (1996-1997) (Chicago: Dartnell, 1996).

10. K. Judge, "A Matter of Prevention," *The Journal of Work Force Diversity,* (January 1995), p. 52.

11. S. Overman, "A Measure of Success," *Human Resources Magazine,* (December 1992), pp. 38-42.

12. M. Loden and Judith Rosener, *"Work Force America,"* (Homewood: Irwin, 1991).

13. S. Shellenbarger, "Sales Offers Women Fairer Pay, But Bias Lingers," *The Wall Street Journal,* (January 24, 1995), p. B1.

14. M. Yagos. Panel discussion (March 1993). "What Women Face in the Workplace." Conducted at Wagner College, New York.

15. Lucette Comer, Alan Dubinsky, Marvin Jolson, and Francis Yamarrino, "Women in Management: An Exploration into the Relationship Between Salespeople's Gender and Their Responses to Leadership Styles," *Journal of Personal Selling and Sales Management, 15,* (No. 4, 1995), pp. 17-32.

16. Joyce Miller, Personal interview. Department of Labor, Washington, DC, (April 10, 1994).

17. Ray Habib, Telephone interview. Everything Yogurt, Staten Island, New York, (June 1994).

SECTION V: CURRENT SELLING SKILLS AND TOOLS

Chapter 8

1. Patricia Sellers, "How Coke Is Kicking Pepsi's Can," *Fortune,* (October 28, 1996), p. 70-84.

2. Adrian Slywotsky, "Taking the Low Road," *Sales and Marketing Magazine,* (January 1996), pp. 53-61.

3. Sally Silberman, "Can You Think Strategically?" *Sales and Marketing Magazine,* (June 1996), pp. 36-49.

4. Michael Porter, "What Is Strategy?" *Harvard Business Review,* 74 (No. 6, November/December 1996), pp. 61-78.

5. John Whitney, "Strategic Renewal for Business Units," *Harvard Business Review, 74,* (No. 4, July/August 1996), pp. 84-98.

6. Robin Cooper and Robert Kaplan, "Profit Priorities from Activity-Based Costing," *Harvard Business Review, 69* No. 3, (May/June 1991), pp. 130-135.

7. Dale Achabal, Shelby McIntyre, and Stephen Smith, "A Two-Stage Sales Forecasting Procedure Using Discounted Least Squares," *Journal of Marketing Research,* (February 1994), pp. 44-56.

8. Marshall Fisher, "Making Supply Meet Demand in an Uncertain World," *Harvard Business Review, 72* (No. 3, May/June 1994), p. 83.

9. Melissa Campbell, "The Price to Pay," *Sales and Marketing Magazine,* (September 1994), pp. 96-102.

10. Michael Etzel, William Stanton, and Bruce Walker, (1994), "Fundamentals of Marketing," New York: McGraw Hill, p. 311.

11. Allan Magrath, "Ten Timeless Truths About Pricing," *Journal of Consumer Marketing,* (Winter 1991), pp. 161-169.

12. Michael Mondello, "Naming Your Price," *INC.,* (July 1992), pp. 157-160.

Chapter 9

1. Joshua Hyatt, "Hot Commodity," *INC.,* (February 1996), pp. 50-61.

2. Jan Owens and Daniel Smith, "Knowledge of Customers' Customers as a Basis of Sales Force Differentiation," *Journal of Personal Selling and Sales Management, 15* (No. 3, Summer 1995), p. 1.

3. Stephen Castleberry and C. Davis Shepherd, "Effective Interpersonal Listening and Personal Selling," *Journal of Personal Selling and Sales Management,* (Winter 1993), pp. 35-49.

4. Nancy Gibbs, "The EQ Factor," *Time,* (October 2, 1995), pp. 60-68.

5. Gary Armstrong and Mark Moon, "Selling Teams: A Conceptual Framework and Research Agenda," *Journal of Personal Selling and Sales Management, 14* (No. 1, Winter 1994), p. 18.

6. Rosemary Ramsey and Dawn Schmelz, "A Conceptualization of the Functions and Roles of Formalized Selling and Buying Teams," *Journal of Personal Selling and Sales Management, 15* (No. 2, Spring 1995), p. 57.

7. John Patrick Dolan, *"Negotiate Like the Pros,"* (New York: Berkley, 1992).

8. Anne Perkins, "Are Two Heads Better Than One?" *Harvard Business Review, 71* (No. 3, May/June 1993), pp. 13-14.

Chapter 10

1. C. Romano, "Death of a Salesman," *American Management Association,* (September 1994), pp. 10-16.

2. J. Graham, "Customers for Keeps," *Selling Power, 16* (No. 3, April 1996), pp. 50-51.

3. L. Paulson, "Customers for Life," *Executive Excellence,* (September 1994), p. 12.

4. R. Stillwell, "Five Secrets to Keeping Your Clients," *LAN,* (September 1994), p. 158.

5. Dan Sarel and Arun Sharma, "The Impact of Customer Satisfaction-Based Incentive Systems on Salespeople's Customer Service Response: An Empirical Study," *Journal of Personal Selling and Sales Management, 15* (No. 3, Summer, 1995), pp. 17-26.

6. Mary Raymond and John Tanner, "Maintaining Customer Relationships in Direct Sales: Stimulating Repeat Purchase Behavior," *Journal of Personal Selling and Sales Management, 14* (No. 3, Summer, 1994), p. 67.

7. Terry Varvra, "Selling After the Sale: The Advantages of Aftermarketing," *Supervision,* (October, 1994), pp. 9-11, 21.

8. Judith Ross, "Why Not a Customer Advisory Board?", *Harvard Business Review, 75* (No. 1, January/February, 1997), p. 12.

9. R. Jacob, "Why Some Customers Are More Equal Than Others," *Fortune,* (September 9, 1994), p. 215-224.

10. B. Ettore, "Changing the Rules of the Board Game," *Management Review, 85* (No. 4, April, 1996), pp. 13-17.

11. C. Friday, A. Miller, J. Solomon, K. Springen, A. Underwood, F. Washington, "Brave New Directors," *Newsweek,* (March 1, 1993) pp. 59-60.

12. D. Buss, "How Advisers Can Help You Grow," *Nation's Business, 84* (No. 3, March 1996), pp. 47-50.

13. J. Collins, "Looking Out for Number One," *INC.,* (June 1996), pp. 29-30.

14. Robert Felton, Alec Hudnut, Valda Witt, "Building a Stronger Board," *The McKinsey Quarterly, 2,* (1995), pp. 163-175.

15. M. Prisbell, "Strategies for Maintaining Relationships and Self-Related Competence in Ongoing Relationships," *Psychological Reports,* (February 1995), p. 63.

16. A. Zak, "Recollection of Trusting and Nontrusting Behaviors in Intimate Relationships," *Psychological Reports,* (June, 1995), p. 1194.

17. K. Johnson, "Mirror Your Prospects to Gain Their Trust," *Best's Review,* (September, 1994), pp. 76-81.

18. Harold Theurer, Personal interview. Paine Webber Incorporated, New York, NY. (October 22, 1996).

Chapter 11

1. Daniel Niven, "When Times Get Tough, What Happens to TQM?", *Harvard Business Review, 71* (No. 3, May/June, 1993), pp. 20-26.

2. Roy Clinton, Robert Stevens, and Stan Williamson, "Implementing a TQM Strategy," *Journal of Customer Service in Marketing and Management, 71* (No. 4, 1995), pp. 11-20.

3. Margaret Henderson Blair, "Measure for Measure, Advertising's Eluded Total Quality Management Model," *Brandweek, 36* (Issue 25, June 19, 1995), p. 17.

4. William J. Stanton, Richard H. Buskirk, Rosann L. Spiro, *"Management of a Sales Force, "* (Chicago: Richard D. Irwin, Inc., 1995).

5. Ronen Boaz, Shimeon Paas, "Focused Management: A Business-Oriented Approach to Total Quality Management," *Industrial Management, 36* (Issue 3, May/June, 1994), pp. 9-12.

6. David A. Garvin, "Competing on the Eight Dimensions of Quality," *Harvard Business Review, 65* (No. 6, November, 1987), pp. 101-109.

7. Garrett VanRyzin, *A Note on Production Processes and Process Flow Analysis,* (New York: Columbia University Press, 1994).

8. Jim Cathcart, *Relationship Selling,* (New York: Putnam Books, 1990).

9. David A. Garvin, *Types of Processes,* (Harvard Business School, Boston, 1981), Case Note 9-682-008.

10. Charles A. Beswick, David W. Cravens, "A Multistage Decision Model for Sales Force Management," *Journal of Marketing Research, 14* (May 1977), pp. 135-144.

11. Adrian B. Ryans, Charles B. Weinberg, "Territory Sales Response," *Journal of Marketing Research, 16* (November 1979), pp. 453-465.

12. Kaylene C. Williams, Rosann L. Spiro, "Communication Style in the Salesperson-Customer Dyad," *Journal of Marketing Research, 22* (November 1985), pp. 434-442.

13. Gilbert A. Churchill Jr., Neil A. Ford, Steven W. Hartley, Orville C. Walker Jr., "The Determinants of Salesperson Performance: A Meta-Analysis," *Journal of Marketing Research, 22* (May 1985), pp. 103-118.

14. Donald W. Jackson Jr., Stephen S. Tax, John W. Barnes, "Examining the Sales Force Culture: Managerial Applications and Research Propositions," *Journal of Personal Selling & Sales Management, 14* (Issue 4, Fall 1994), pp. 1-14.

15. David Garvin, "How the Baldridge Award Really Works," *Harvard Business Review, 69* (No. 6, November/December 1991), pp. 80-93.

16. Dawn Anfuso, "L.L. Bean's TQM Efforts Put People Before Processes," *Personnel Journal, 73* (Issue 7, July 1994), pp. 72-83.

17. William P. Cordeiro, Robert H. Turner, "20/30 Hindsight: Managers Must Commit to TQM," *Interfaces, 25* (Issue 3, May/June, 1995), pp. 104-112.

18. Ed Hanke, "Quality Circle," *Credit Union Management, 17* (Issue 1, January, 1994), pp. 44-46.

19. Nancy Lowther, "Total Quality Sales," *American Printer, 214* (Issue 3, December, 1994) pp. 57-59.

20. Erin Anderson, Richard L. Oliver, "Perspectives on Behavior-Based Versus Outcome-Based Sales Force Control Systems," *Journal of Marketing, 51* (October, 1987), pp. 76-88.

21. Clive E. Hoare, "Appreciative Management Systems," *TQM Magazine, 6* (Issue 1, 1994), pp. 35-37.

22. Lewis Rich, "The Proof is in the Marketplace," *America's Network,* Issue Quality Supplement, (1994), pp. 14-17.

Chapter 12

1. John Birstler, Personal interview. Merrill Lynch, New York, NY (April 24, 1995).

2. B. Rogers, "Mentoring Takes a New Twist," *HR Magazine, 37* (No. 8, August, 1992), p. 48.

3. K. Kram, "Phases of the Mentor Relationship," *Academy of Management Journal, 26* (No. 4, December, 1983), p. 614.

4. D. Dunbar, "Desperately Seeking Mentors," *Black Enterprise Magazine, 20* (No. 8, March, 1990), p. 56.

5. Jerry Kline, "Modern Mentoring Helps People Help Themselves—Inside and Outside the Workplace," *John Naisbitt's Trend Letter/The Global Network, 14* (No. 9, April 27, 1995), pp. 4-5.

6. Pete Radigan, "Lighten Your Load," *Selling Power,* (April, 1996), p. 48.

7. Ken Liebeskind, "Selling 101," *Selling Power,* (June, 1996), pp. 49-57.

8. Bill Cates, "A Coach for all Reasons," *Selling Power,* (June, 1996), pp. 64-65.

9. Ken Blanchard, "A New Chain of Command," *Selling Power,* (January/February, 1995), pp. 58-59.

10. Stephen Appelbaum and Walter Rohrs, *Time Management,* Rockville, Maryland: Aspen Systems Corporation, (1981).

11. Christen Heide, *Dartnell's 29th Sales Force Compensation Survey 1996-1997,* (Chicago: Dartnell 1996).

12. George Stalk, "Time—The Next Source of Competitive Advantage," *Harvard Business Review, 68* (No. 4, July/August, 1988), p. 34.

13. Glenn Parker, "Team Players and Teamwork: The New Competitive Business Strategy," San Francisco: Jossey-Bass, (1990).

14. *Carter Sales Force Survey,* (1996).

Bibliography

Chapter 3

Hill, G. C. (March 13, 1995). "Foreign Semiconductor Makers Took 22.4 percent of Japan Market Share Last Year." *The Wall Street Journal.*

Maryuma, W. and Yeutter, C. (May 19, 1995). "A NAFTA for Europe." *The Wall Street Journal.*

Wolif, J. (June 2, 1995). "EU Still Seeks to Take Part in Auto Talks." *The Wall Street Journal.*

Chapter 5

Donoho, R. (October 1994). "Managing Crisis at U.S. Air." *Sales and Marketing Management Magazine,* p. 13.

Jones, D., Personal interview. (March 14, 1995).

Chapter 6

Uniform Commercial Code,   Section 2-103
Section 2-105
Section 2-201
Section 2-204
Section 2-205
Section 2-207
Section 2-209
Section 2-302
Section 2-306
Section 2-308
Section 2-310
Section 2-311
Section 2-513

Chapter 7

Arnott, Nancy (March, 1995). "It's a Woman's World." *Sales and Marketing Management Magazine,* p. 59.

Carter, Tony (April 1994). *Report to the British Consulate on Initiatives Between the British Government and the African-American and Latino Communities.*

Chapter 11

Cortada, James. (1993). *TQM For Sales and Marketing Management.* New York: McGraw Hill.

Chapter 12

Moore, L., M. Naylor, and J. Taggart. (March, 1990). "You Know Someone Who Knows Someone." *National Business Employment Weekly*, pp. 9-10.

Index

Page numbers followed by the letter "f" indicate figures; those followed by the letter "t" indicate tables.

Order Your Own Copy of
This Important Book for Your Personal Library!

CONTEMPORARY SALES FORCE MANAGEMENT

_____ in hardbound at $49.95 (ISBN: 0-7890-0113-6)

_____ in softbound at $29.95 (ISBN: 0-7890-0423-2)

COST OF BOOKS _____

OUTSIDE USA/CANADA/
MEXICO: ADD 20% _____

POSTAGE & HANDLING _____
(US: $3.00 for first book & $1.25
for each additional book)
Outside US: $4.75 for first book
& $1.75 for each additional book)

SUBTOTAL _____

IN CANADA: ADD 7% GST _____

STATE TAX _____
(NY, OH & MN residents, please
add appropriate local sales tax)

FINAL TOTAL _____
(If paying in Canadian funds,
convert using the current
exchange rate. UNESCO
coupons welcome.)

☐ **BILL ME LATER:** ($5 service charge will be added)
(Bill-me option is good on US/Canada/Mexico orders only;
not good to jobbers, wholesalers, or subscription agencies.)

☐ Check here if billing address is different from
shipping address and attach purchase order and
billing address information.

Signature _____

☐ **PAYMENT ENCLOSED: $** _____

☐ **PLEASE CHARGE TO MY CREDIT CARD.**

☐ Visa ☐ MasterCard ☐ AmEx ☐ Discover
☐ Diners Club
Account # _____

Exp. Date _____

Signature _____

Prices in US dollars and subject to change without notice.

NAME _____

INSTITUTION _____

ADDRESS _____

CITY _____

STATE/ZIP _____

COUNTRY _____ COUNTY (NY residents only) _____

TEL _____ FAX _____

E-MAIL_____
May we use your e-mail address for confirmations and other types of information? ☐ Yes ☐ No

Order From Your Local Bookstore or Directly From
The Haworth Press, Inc.
10 Alice Street, Binghamton, New York 13904-1580 • USA
TELEPHONE: 1-800-HAWORTH (1-800-429-6784) / Outside US/Canada: (607) 722-5857
FAX: 1-800-895-0582 / Outside US/Canada: (607) 772-6362
E-mail: getinfo@haworth.com
PLEASE PHOTOCOPY THIS FORM FOR YOUR PERSONAL USE.

BOF96